THE VETERINARIANS' GUIDE TO
NATURAL REMEDIES FOR DOGS

ALSO BY MARTIN ZUCKER

The Veterinarian's Guide to Natural Remedies for Cats

THE VETERINARIANS' GUIDE TO
NATURAL REMEDIES
FOR
DOGS

Safe and Effective Alternative Treatments and Healing
Techniques from the Nation's Top Holistic Veterinarians

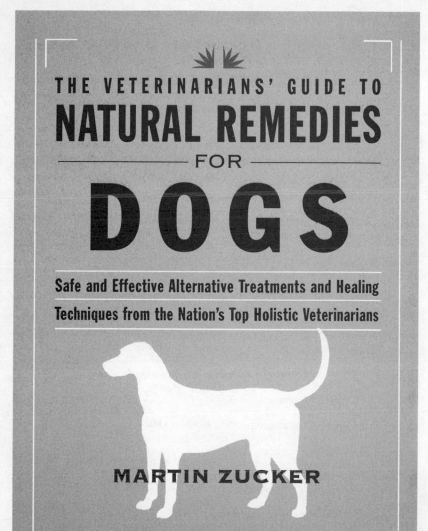

MARTIN ZUCKER

Foreword by Carvel Tiekert, DVM
Founder, American Holistic Veterinary Medical Association

THREE RIVERS PRESS • NEW YORK

Note to the Reader

This book about natural remedies is intended for educational purposes and is not meant to replace veterinary medical care or any therapeutic program recommended by a veterinarian.

The recommendations contained in this book involve methods and remedies based on the experiences of individual veterinarians. Such information is general in nature and may not apply to your animal's particular condition.

If your pet has a health problem, see a qualified veterinarian, preferably one who practices complementary medicine.

Neither the author nor the publisher can be held responsible for any adverse reactions to the recipes, recommendations, or ideas in this book.

Published by Three Rivers Press, New York, New York.
Member of the Crown Publishing Group.

Random House, Inc. New York, Toronto, London, Sydney, Auckland
www.randomhouse.com

THREE RIVERS PRESS is a registered trademark and the Three Rivers Press colophon is a trademark of Random House, Inc.

Printed in the United States of America

Design by Cynthia Dunne

Library of Congress Cataloging-in-Publication Data

Zucker, Martin.
    The veterinarians' guide to natural remedies for dogs: safe and effective alternative treatments and healing techniques from the nation's top holistic veterinarians / by Martin Zucker; foreword by Carvel Tiekert.—1st pbk. ed.
    Includes bibliographical references.
    1. Dogs—Diseases—Alternative treatment.   2. Dogs—Health.
3. Holistic veterinary medicine.   I. Title.
SF991.Z83 1999
636.7'089—dc21   99–23709
                                                                CIP

ISBN 0-609-80372-7

10   9   8   7

To Louis and Joyce, Mark and Rita, for sharing so much,
above all, Joshua, Max, Noah, Nathan, Aaron,
and Rachel...and "Bella."

Acknowledgments

I AM DEEPLY grateful to the many veterinarians who generously shared their unique clinical experience and ideas about health and healing. Among them are some of the true pioneers of veterinary medicine, whose visions and innovations are finding growing acceptance today as more and more practitioners realize that good medicine is not just treating symptoms with surgery and drugs. Thanks to Nino Aloro, DVM; Wendell O. Belfield, DVM; Jan Bellows, DVM; Karen Bentley, DVM; Carolyn S. Blakey, DVM; Ron Carsten, DVM; Christina Chambreau, DVM; Roger DeHaan, DVM; Joseph Demers, DVM; Edmund R. Dorosz, DVM; Lynne M. Friday, DVM; Maria Glinski, DVM; Robert Goldstein, VMD; Stan Gorlitsky, DVM; Clarence E. Hardin, DVM; Mark Haverkos, DVM; Shannon Hines, DVM; Jean Hofve, DVM; A. Greig Howie, DVM; Jody Kincaid, DVM; Charles Loops, DVM; Paul McCutcheon, DVM; Donna Starita Mehan, DVM; Alfred J. Plechner, DVM; William Pollak, DVM; Pedro Luis Rivera, DVM; Allen Schoen, DVM; Nancy Scanlan, DVM; Tejinder Sodhi, DVM; Carvel Tiekert, DVM; Thomas E. Van Cise, DVM; Pamela Wood-Krzeminski, DVM; Susan G. Wynn, DVM; and Michele Yasson, DVM.

I am particularly proud to have the voice of Norman Ralston, DVM, in this book. Ralston, a great holistic pioneer of veterinary medicine for more than fifty years, passed away in 1999. The holistic community misses him very much.

Special thanks to PJ Dempsey, senior editor at Crown Publishing Group, whose friendship, encouragement, and editorial astuteness did so much to shape the appearance and content of this book.

And to Bob Silverstein, of Quicksilver Books, a superb agent and caring friend.

Contents

Foreword xiii

Introduction xv

How to Use This Book xix

Part One — Natural Healing for Healthier Dogs   1

1. Why Alternative Veterinary Medicine?   3

2. The Ill-Health Epidemic   7

3. The Problem with Pet Food   10

4. Making the Switch to a Better Diet   15

5. Feeding Option #1—You want your dog to eat a better diet, but you are just too busy. . . all you can do is fill the bowl with kibble   22

6. Feeding Option #2—You're busy, but you can share table scraps and add meat and vegetables to your dog's diet   24

7. Feeding Option #3—The deluxe treatment: homemade meals   33

8. Nutritional Supplements   42

9. Herbs   47

10. Homeopathic Remedies   50

11. Flower Essences—Healing the Emotions   56

12. Veterinary Acupuncture   60

13. Veterinary Chiropractic   64

14. Massage Techniques   69

15. The Vaccination Question—How Often,
    How Much?   72

16. What to Do When Nothing Seems to Work   79

Part Two — An A to Z of Canine Problems   85

Introduction to Part Two   87
How to Give Your Dog Natural Remedies   87
Giving the Proper Dosage to Your Dog   88

Arthritis   89
Asthma   100
Back Problems   101
Bad Breath   104
Behavioral Problems   105
Cancer   109
Dental Health   122
Digestive Disorders (including constipation,
    diarrhea, vomiting, digestive enzyme
    deficiency, malabsorption, gas, irritable bowel,
    stool eating)   129
Ear Problems   141
Epilepsy (Seizures)   147
Eye Problems   151
First Aid   153
Fleas, Ticks, and Insect Pests   157
Food Allergies   164
Heart Problems   172
Heat Stroke and Hot Weather   178
Hip Dysplasia   180
Incontinence   185

Infectious Illnesses (Colds, Viruses, Bacterial
    Infections) 187
Kidney and Urinary Tract Conditions 193
Liver Disease 196
Motion Sickness 200
Neuromuscular Collapse or Paralysis 201
Obesity 202
Old Age 209
Parasites 212
Pregnancy, Nursing, and Beyond 219
Prostate 222
Skin Disorders and Allergies 223
Stress 240
Surgery 244
Toxicity and Drug Side Effects 248
Yeast Infections 251

Appendixes 255

A. List of Contributing Veterinarians 257

B. Resources: Holistic Veterinary Organizations and
    Natural Pet Product Manufacturers/Distributors 260

C. Recommended Reading 267

Index 271

Foreword

JUST AS YOU are ultimately responsible for your own health, and not somebody with an M.D. after his or her name, you are ultimately also responsible for the health of your animals. I am a veterinarian, a consultant, and a facilitator, and I can make all the recommendations in the world, but if you don't do the work at home and make it a team effort—both to try the recommendations and to report responses accurately—in many cases there won't be a proper resolution. You have to be involved.

Health is not a matter of taking a pill to get rid of a symptom or an operation to get rid of something nasty in the body. These things don't create health. It's what you do over your life or, when it comes to your pet, your pet's life, that counts. And what you do can create either chronic illness or chronic health. Unfortunately there are no magic bullets.

Western medicine is designed for acute care, and it is very good for that most of the time. It is also useful for diagnosis, and sometimes prognosis, and evaluating response to therapy. However, it doesn't have a good record for chronic disease. The problem is that it is oriented to the elimination of symptoms. In many cases, the symptom is the body's best response to a negative stimulus; for example, if you have pain in a joint due to arthritis, the body is telling you to take it easy. A conventional drug may make the pain go away, but the problem (inflammation) is still there, and you haven't helped the problem. Instead you may have aggravated it.

By comparison, when you use most natural therapies, if the pain goes away, it's because you have altered the course of the disease, *and the body no longer needs the symptom.*

Being an educated pet owner is important. The more you recognize what wellness is, the better you can understand illness. Know your animal. Look at your animal. Look at its ears, at its teeth. Look between the toes. Look underneath. Become familiar with what health is so that when you see changes you can act promptly. Anything that is abnormal is judged in the relationship to what is regarded as normal. And what may be normal for one animal may not be normal for another. By knowing your animal, you can help us to do our job as partners in your animal's health. This close contact will also improve your bond with your pet and make the experience of being guardian for a pet that much better.

What you will read in this book is information that can help you achieve better health for your animals; and if you use the information appropriately, you can even promote optimum health—that is, the very best health that the genetic programming of your animal allows. This book is unique. It contains recommendations and ideas based on the clinical experience of many veterinarians who have tried natural approaches to the health problems of animals and who know what works and what doesn't work.

Health writer Marty Zucker has done us all an important service by gathering this treasury of information and transforming it into a practical format for pet owners. His concept is to give you different options so that if one particular approach for condition "X" doesn't work, a second or third one might. Each animal, just as each person, is a different individual and has different needs. So if one option doesn't work, try another. Zucker gives you options that veterinarians have used in their own practices with good results. Given the individuality of all creatures, human or animal, this is a very practical idea. One remedy that might work for one animal may not work for the next.

As you use this book, keep one thing in mind. If you are dealing with what appears to be a minor problem, and an animal doesn't respond after you follow the advice in the book, don't wait until the animal is nearly dead before you take it in to see your veterinarian. Besides the fact that it could cost you a lot more money, there may be nothing that can be done at that point.

As I mentioned before, knowing your animal will help you as you consider the remedies and concepts in this book or, for that matter, any therapy your veterinarian recommends. I can't emphasize this point enough. You need to be able to evaluate progress or lack of it. You do that by knowing your animal.

Good luck in your search for health and wellness for you and your pet.

Carvel Tiekert, DVM, Bel Air, Maryland
Founder, American Holistic Veterinary Medical Association

Introduction

As a HEALTH writer who has coauthored three previous books on pet health with veterinarians, I have been asked many times by pet owners how they can make their animals healthier "naturally" and avoid the common side effects of medical drugs. These have been people interested in feeding a better diet and using vitamins, herbs, and other natural remedies, but they didn't know where to start or what to use. Often I would recommend consulting with a holistic veterinarian.

The many questions over the years inspired the idea for a book that would provide answers and introduce pet owners to the wide and wondrous world of natural healing as it applies to animals. The concept that eventually took root was to interview the leading experts of natural healing in the veterinary world—as many as possible—and translate their expertise into a practical how-to guide for pet owners.

When I finished my interviews, I had spoken to three dozen veterinarians with a combined clinical experience of nine hundred years—an average of twenty-five years in practice. Their insights and recommendations are contained in this book—and in a similar book for cat owners. It is my sincere hope, and the hope of the veterinarians who graciously shared their knowledge, that such clinically based information enables you to raise the health of your animals to the highest possible level.

Imagine a menu with multiple creations not by just one great chef, but by dozens of culinary masters. This book is like a "health menu of masters," filled with recommendations, commentaries, and recipes from veterinarians who have used natural healing methods for years. Just like a menu, these pages offer multiple options for preventing common conditions, enhancing the healing process, and improving health.

The major features of the book include the following:

- Dozens of natural remedies—and instructions on how to use them.

- A survey that reveals a startling epidemic of poor canine health.
- What's wrong with commercial pet food? Enough, according to veterinarians, to cause unwellness among animals.
- The absolute necessity of improving your animal's diet—the "mother of all natural remedies"—and how to do it. It's actually easier than you think.
- Pet foods most preferred by nutritionally oriented veterinarians.
- Recipes for weight loss. Obesity is not just a human health problem; it is also common among companion pets.
- Did you know that lamb and rice diets, for ten years the popular answer to food allergy in animals, are now being found to actually cause food allergies? From the co-developer of the original lamb and rice diets come the facts about this development and how to avoid the problem.
- The "HIT list"—foods "high in trouble" and most likely to cause allergic reactions.
- Why you must brush your animal's teeth, just as you do your own.
- How to revitalize older animals and keep younger ones healthy.
- How vaccinations frequently cause adverse reactions and ill health and what you can do about it.
- How you can learn to recognize stress—often the unrecognized cause of behavioral or health problems in animals—and take practical steps to alleviate fear, separation anxiety, grief, and other stressful emotions that animals develop.
- Revelations about a hormonal-immune "time bomb" in many animals that stems from disastrous contemporary breeding practices. When the "time bomb" detonates, it creates premature sickness and death and animals who do not respond to treatment. Read what you can do about it.

This book is not meant to replace professional veterinary care. If your dog is under treatment, you may want to share ideas mentioned in the book with your veterinarian. Generally speaking, the recommendations can enhance and support ongoing treatments. In using this book, always keep in mind that your animal is an individual. The remedies recommended here may be able to take you only just so far, to a certain level of wellness, after which you may need to consult with a veterinarian for individualized treatment. If you are interested in the services of a holistic veterinarian, contact the American Holistic Veterinary Medical Association in Bel Air, Maryland, at 410–569–0795, and ask for the name of one near you.

If an animal is in an obvious crisis, if a problem persists, or if symptoms appear to worsen after you initiate a remedy described in the book, consult with a veterinarian. Even though the recommendations in this book have been made entirely by veterinarians, such general advice can never substitute for a direct assessment and treatment offered by an experienced professional.

How to Use This Book

ALTERNATIVE MEDICINE EMPOWERS you to become an active partner in the health of your animals. Part 1 tells you why you need to become more active—and how. As revealed in chapter 2, there is a disturbing rise of serious illnesses among dogs. You must get more involved to protect your animals.

Among the major reasons for a genuine epidemic of unwellness is the general poor quality of commercial pet food. Pet food advertising is unadulterated spin for the most adulterated food product on the planet, holistic veterinarians say. You may think you are feeding prime cuts, but chapter 3 tells you otherwise.

You can't build a house on quicksand, and you can't build a healthy body—yours or your pet's—on poor-quality, highly processed food. Chapter 4 gives you the general guidelines on shifting to a better diet no matter how busy you are. Here you will also find a checklist that can tell you whether your dog is eating a healthy—or not so healthy—diet. In chapters 5, 6, and 7 you will find detailed, practical information on how and what to feed your animal depending on the time you have to do it. The options range from feeding a high-quality commercial food to creating home-prepared meals.

Part 1 also acquaints you with some of the major holistic approaches available to pet owners—such as acupuncture and homeopathy—and basics on vitamins, herbs, homeopathy, and flower essences. Some of the veterinarians have also shared wonderful healing massages that you can easily administer to your animals. Those are described in chapter 14.

Chapter 15 covers vaccinations. Guidelines are changing. Annual revaccinations are now in disfavor with researchers. Holistic veterinarians think too many vaccinations are administered to animals and their health suffers as a result. This chapter will review the changing vaccination scene and include recommendations on how to prevent or minimize vaccination reactions.

What if nothing you read in this book, and nothing your veterinarian tries, helps a suffering animal? Many dogs are so badly flawed because of horrendous breeding practices that they succumb to sickness early in life. In chapter 16 you will find information about two important tests that offer vital clues—and hope—for dealing with resistant, heartbreak cases.

Part 2, the main section of the book, covers many common conditions affecting dogs and gives you dozens of veterinarians' recommendations for natural remedies.

The section begins with *general guidelines on dosages* and other important points. *Please read this section before looking up specific conditions.*

Conditions are listed *alphabetically.* For each condition you will find individual recommendations grouped under the following categories: flower essences, herbs, homeopathic remedies, nutritional supplements, multiple approaches, and food and special diets. The nutritional supplement category includes vitamins, minerals, antioxidants, enzymes, glandulars, and "whole food" products.

The variety of recommendations for each condition gives you options for safe, nontoxic remedies that veterinarians have used repeatedly and successfully over many years. The recommendations include product names, where to obtain the products, and specific instructions for dosages. As a consumer you are exposed to many advertising claims. The broadside of information can be confusing. When I set out to write this book my goal was to help steer pet owners to effective natural remedies. I asked each of the veterinarians I interviewed: "What are the remedies you use that work well repeatedly?" You will find their answers in part 2. Each recommendation that appears is listed with the name of the veterinarian who has used it successfully in practice.

You will have choices. It is not possible to say which one of the several or more remedies listed under any given condition is the most effective. Each remedy or approach, however, has been used successfully by a veterinarian. Choose the option that fits your situation best. Keep in mind that each animal is an individual and may not respond to one particular remedy. That is why I included a variety of options for each condition. If one doesn't help, try another.

< PART ONE >

NATURAL HEALING

FOR HEALTHIER

DOGS

Why Alternative Veterinary Medicine?

Alternative medicine for pets may not be as widespread or well publicized as the human variety, but it's growing faster than a sprig of St. John's wort.

—Time *magazine, November 3, 1997*

VETERINARIANS SAY THAT our companion animals are suffering from an epidemic of poor health. Too many pets are becoming sick and dying well before their time.

The veterinarians also say that while great strides have been made in diagnostics, surgical treatments, and acute care, the overall ability of their profession to deal with widespread chronic disease leaves much to be desired. Conventional methods often just relieve symptoms temporarily but fall short of healing animals or effectively raising their levels of health.

Over the years, in veterinary as well as in human medicine, the shortcomings of a system emphasizing drugs and surgery have motivated many doctors to look beyond what they were taught in medical school. Increasingly, they have found answers in a global potpourri of healing arts collectively and popularly referred to as "holistic" or "alternative" medicine. More and more consumers, too, are turning to such practitioners for their own health, and the health of their pets, because they are wary of drug side effects and the invasiveness of surgery.

The veterinarians I interviewed for this book told me they became partially or totally alternative because of dissatisfaction with the results of surgery and drugs alone. They found that conventional methods often merely suppressed symptoms, while the cause of disease would rage on untouched, continuing to destroy tissue and life force at ever deeper and deeper levels. This is why they felt a need to expand their healing horizons by learning acupuncture, chiropractic, homeopathy, nutritional therapies using food, supplements, and herbs, and other methods not taught at medical schools.

Nino Aloro, DVM, of Virginia Beach, Virginia, has been practicing veterinary medicine for more than fifty years and long ago turned to alternative medicine because many clients told him they were discouraged with the side effects of drugs and the lack of lasting improvement in their animals. "Sometimes side effects are worse than the disease," he says. "Standard medications have the potential to cause frightening problems with the liver, heart, kidneys, skin, immune system, and digestive tract. And veterinarians know this."

Maria Glinski, DVM, of Glendale, Wisconsin, became frustrated early in her career with the limitations of medicine as she had been taught for the treatment of arthritis, cancer, and chronic conditions of older animals. She recalls treating an old, arthritic Collie whose owners would carry the dog up to their second-floor bedroom each night. The standard treatment she was using caused disturbing side effects without significant relief. The owners were interested in alternative medicine and heard that vitamin C along with an injectable combination of vitamin E and selenium might be helpful.

"I knew absolutely nothing about alternative medicine, but I figured there was no harm in trying," Glinski says. "The dog responded very favorably and was soon walking on his own up and down the stairs. This remarkable reversal so impressed me that I started learning more about holistic methods and have been involved with alternatives ever since."

Veterinarians like Aloro and Glinski say that after learning and applying alternative methods, they can often turn sick pets around, optimize their health, extend lives, and improve the quality of life of severely ill animals. Such practitioners use methods that harness and rally all the resources of the whole animal—the mind, body, and spirit—in an effort to encourage natural healing mechanisms. This approach revolves around a central concept as old as the art of healing itself: that each person, each living thing, possesses on a deep level the will and intelligence to be healthy and that these elements can and should be enlisted in effecting a cure.

The Western medical tradition tends to take control with invasive and powerful methods. Alternative methods nourish the whole body and its natural tendency for health and homeostasis.

It's important to understand, however, that no one single approach—neither conventional, with its powerful drugs and sophisticated surgery, nor alternative, with its less invasive, more natural "whole" body solutions—has all the answers. Increasing numbers of doctors and veterinarians believe that the future of medical practice lies in an integrative or complementary approach that uses the best of both worlds: the high-tech advances of Western medicine along with the natural methods that maintain and optimize health.

The faster that integration takes place, the better for all of us—human and canine patients alike. We can then start to expect that the practitioner we see will use the most effective and least invasive and toxic method, or combination of methods, he or she possesses. Such practitioners will choose from a menu of many choices—herbs, homeopathic remedies, vitamins, drugs, or surgery.

Many of the veterinarians whose comments you will read in this book have developed this practical, combined approach long before the term "integrative medicine" was popularized several years ago by Andrew Weil, M.D.

"There is a growing vision of a triad of complementary and conventional medicine, along with the element of the human-animal healing bond," says Allen M. Schoen, DVM, of Sherman, Connecticut, who operates an integrated practice. "The three combined is a powerful approach. I try to fit the particular program to the individual animal and the individual animal caretaker. If our highest goal is to help animals, we should look at whatever we can to help them."

DOING YOUR PART—KNOWING YOUR ANIMAL BETTER

Alternative veterinary medicine encourages pet owners to learn what makes their animals sicker or healthier and take appropriate action. Becoming involved is critical, and for many veterinarians the most important thing they can do is to empower and involve their clients in a health education process. They are glad to educate you about your dog.

People become part of their own health and healing process or they just take a pill, wish for the best, and go about doing the same things that got them sick in the first place. We can make healthy choices or not-so-healthy choices. But companion animals totally rely on us. We can feed them any cheap food and then get a prescription when they get sick. But that's not what being an active partner in your animal's care is all about. Involvement requires that you know your dog, a point strongly made in the foreword of this book. There is no substitute for knowing your animal and watching for signs that may indicate changes in health. You are the closest person to your dog, not your veterinarian. You can see changes that may not be obvious to others or are too subtle even for medical tests to pick up. When you see such changes, trust your observations and tell your veterinarian.

Keeping a journal is a practical and effective method for recording changes in the behavior or health of your dog. A move to another location or a dramatic event in the household could cause a problem related to stress or anxiety. If you make a diet change, log the date, and the details, and if your dog had a response. Observe your dog closely after treatments or vaccinations, which have the potential to create new symptoms.

Ask your veterinarian to show you how to routinely check your dog's teeth, ears, eyes, and other body parts. When you pet your dog, run your hand easily over the body in a search for any bumps, lumps, or anything abnormal.

The bottom line is this: The more you know about your dog, the better you can carry out your responsibility as companion and caregiver.

2

The Ill-Health Epidemic

IN DECEMBER OF 1994 *Time* magazine dedicated a cover article to "beastly beauty" and the shocking revelation that one out of four purebred dogs in this country has serious genetic problems. There is a national canine crisis of unwellness, said the magazine, citing an alarming litany of wretchedness:

- Sixty percent of Golden Retrievers develop a crippling dysplasia, and many are born with an undescended testicle, which may lead to cancer.
- German Shepherds have an even higher rate of hip dysplasia.
- Labradors, the most popular breed, are prone to dwarfism.
- At least 70 percent of Collies develop eye problems, and 10 percent go blind.
- Dalmatians are often deaf.
- Cockers tend to have bad tempers.
- Newfoundlands drop dead from heart attacks.
- English Bulldogs have such enormous heads that pups often have to be delivered by C-section.

Bred for looks, beauty, salability, and physical criteria to win ribbons at shows, many purebred animals have lost the hardiness and function they originally possessed. Inbreeding, where brothers and sisters, fathers and daughters, are bred with each other, and line breeding among cousins, grandparents, and grandchildren, are ram-

---

PUREBRED FACTORY FARMS—A NATIONAL DISGRACE

Michael W. Fox, DVM, Ph.D., of the Humane Society of the United States, describes the proliferation, especially in the Midwest, of purebred-dog-breeding factories that supply many pet stores with animals. "Parent dogs—the 'breeding stock'—often spend their entire lives in long, narrow wire cages elevated a few feet above their excrement," says Fox in his book, *Eating with Conscience—The Bioethics of Food"* (New Sage Press). "Their offspring are often riddled with diseases and genetic defects." The U.S. Department of Agriculture should close down most of these "puppy mill" factories, he says. "They are a national disgrace. So consumer beware, and never buy that puppy in the window that came from a breeding factory."

---

pant practices. "Puppy mills" churn out fashionable but often flawed creatures for sale to unsuspecting buyers.

The costs in terms of heartbreak, suffering, and veterinary bills for this genetic disaster are immense. Animals are being programmed not for life, but for death, simply because we humans have decided what a perfect dog should look like. Dogs are living shorter and sicker lives, the victims of breeders who have gone to extremes to accommodate the vogue. Great Pyrenees are dying at six or eight years instead of twelve or fourteen. Animals are developing bizarre autoimmune diseases that pit them in a life-and-death struggle not just against bacteria and viruses, but against the very food they eat, and their own deranged endocrine and immune systems. One authority estimated the medical costs attributable to breeding practices at $1 billion a year, according to *Time* magazine.

Veterinarians are incensed. They are faced with treating genetic cripples who are very difficult and frequently impossible to treat. Moreover, these genetic tragedies don't go away when you cross over into mixed breeds. Today, unwellness is not just pervasive among purebreds, it is growing as well among animals perpetuating purebred defects in their blood.

The veterinarians interviewed for this book—without exception—describe an alarming picture of declining health among dogs—purebreds and mixed breeds. Here is what they are seeing in their clinics across the country:

- More serious illnesses in young animals that before were seen only in older animals.
- More chronic diseases, such as cancer, at all ages.
- More animals with weakened or dysfunctional immune systems.
- More allergies.
- More skin problems.
- More behavioral problems, animals with anxiety, depression, and anger.

It isn't a pretty picture. To be sure, breeding is not the sole cause. According to the veterinarians, the other major factors contributing to widespread unwellness are these:

- Low-quality, highly processed, unfresh, unnatural commercial pet food. Often the same restricted diet is fed without change month after month. Deficiencies, imbalances, malnutrition, and malabsorption develop, leading to illnesses, a breakdown in resistance, and the loss of the ability to cope with environmental stresses of any kind. During a career spanning more than fifty years, the late Norman C. Ralston, DVM, of Mesquite, Texas, used to say that "most pets I treat have eaten themselves into ill health on diets of nutrient-poor food."
- Overvaccination. Animals are routinely injected with a broadside of powerful, multiple vaccines and then revaccinated unnecessarily—a practice undermining rather than protecting health.
- Environmental pollution. The proliferation of chemicals and toxic wastes has thoroughly infiltrated the air, water, and food. Both we and our pets are at risk from an increasingly poisoned planet.
- Unrecognized stress, caused, for instance, when animals are left alone for many hours at a time cooped up in an unnatural, confined environment.

Read on to learn how you can protect your dog from becoming part of what some veterinarians call a "massive health mess."

3

The Problem with Pet Food

UNTIL 1990 ANN Martin was a typical pet owner who purchased regular pet food for her dogs and cats from the store. When her two dogs became ill after eating a commercial pet food, she became concerned and started asking questions of people in the government and pet food industry, in both Canada, where she lives, and in the United States. The inadequacy of the answers she received motivated a seven-year investigation of pet food. Eventually she put her experience and findings into a book that every pet owner should read: *Food Pets Die For—Shocking Facts About Pet Food* (New Sage Press, Troutdale, Oregon).

Martin says her investigation revealed that "just about anything and everything is fair game for use in pet food. This includes condemned and contaminated material from slaughterhouse facilities; road-kill, dead, diseased, disabled, and dying animals; and, although the industry vehemently denies it, euthanized companion animals."

These are just the protein sources, she says. "Grains and fats, dregs from the human food chain, are also included. Labels do not indicate the hidden hazards that lurk in most cans and bags of pet food. Hormones, pesticides, pathogens, heavy metals, and drugs are just a few of the hidden contaminates. Sodium pentobarbital, for instance, is a barbiturate used to euthanize companion animals and, to some extent, livestock. When animals eat pet food that has gone through the rendering process, it is likely they are ingesting a euthanizing drug."

The vast majority of pet food companies purchase their raw materials from an outside source (rendering companies). Rendered material is dried matter comprising a wide variety of substances, all unfit for human consumption due to disease, high levels of drugs, hormones, and pesticides.

Martin was horrified to learn that euthanized dogs and cats are part of this rendered material used for meat meal in commercial foods. "Despite the denial by the industry that this is happening, none of the companies I have contacted actually test the raw material that they are using to ascertain the sources of the protein," she says. "Dogs and cats from shelters, pounds, and even veterinary clinics are ending up in pet food. Some people seem to feel that this is not a problem; after all, dogs and cats are a source of protein. What they neglect to consider is that 90 percent of these animals have been treated with high levels of drugs prior to their demise. These drugs, antibiotics, hormones, and so forth all withstand the rendering process and in fact can become more toxic. The companies selling the dyes and flavor enhancers are doing a landslide business, and as long as consumers are not offended by the smell and look of pet food, they assume it is good quality."

Martin once believed that herself—that she was buying quality. Now her opinion is that "most pet food is garbage—unregulated garbage." Her animals now are fed only home-prepared food.

In a book entitled *Home Prepared Dog & Cat Diets: The Healthful Alternative* (Iowa State University Press), Donald R. Strombeck, DVM, professor emeritus at the University of California at Davis's School of Veterinary Medicine, writes that "pet foods contain ingredients that people will not or cannot eat. Can a quality commercial pet food contain these ingredients and be wholesome? The sources for animal proteins, if known to the consumer, are likely to be objectionable to most."

PET FOOD—BIG BUSINESS WITHOUT GOVERNMENT QUALITY STANDARDS

The pet food industry is megabusiness—topping $10 billion a year in the United States alone. Competition is fierce among the major manufacturers seeking bigger market shares. Companies try to snare your business with hundreds of millions of dollars in advertising, slick TV commercials, meaningless and misleading nutrition claims, and cute names for products. In this competitive scramble, however, quality and good nutrition are often sacrificed to economics and profit. There are no government standards regulating quality, which changes even within single product lines of a company as cheaper ingredients are constantly sought to replace more expensive ones.

Pet owners have the well-being of their pets at heart, but they also want to feed their animals conveniently and cheaply. So they buy commercial pet food. But feeding conveniently and cheaply may cost you more in the long run—in veterinary bills. Cheap food means cheap ingredients. Poor-quality ingredients, fed over any length of time, leads to an increased incidence of obesity, skin and organ problems, behavioral symptoms, and chronic health disorders.

According to a 1996 report by the Animal Protection Institute of America, more than 95 percent of our companion animals derive their nutritional needs from a single source—highly processed commercial pet food. "Our report clearly shows that what you purchase and what the manufacturers advertise are two entirely different products," the institute said. "The difference is threatening your animal's health, cutting short any chance of him enjoying old age, and maybe even killing him now. The ingredients they are using are not wholesome, and the harsh manufacturing practices that make those nifty little shapes, the ones our companion animals surely love to eat, destroy what little nutritional value the food ever had."

The institute report described pet food manufacturers as "masters at getting dogs or cats to eat something they would normally turn up their noses at." One way they do this, according to the report, is to spray the kibble with discarded restaurant grease that has been stabilized with powerful chemical antioxidants. "Pet food scientists have discovered that animals love the taste of these sprayed fats," the report said. In addition, numerous other chemical additives are used that increase the palatability, extend the shelf life, and improve the appearance of the food, so it will look good enough to eat (but, more important, will look good enough for you to buy).

The pet food manufacturing process, in fact, includes a major infusion of some of the biggest names in chemical coloring of our time. Some of these dyes can actually make susceptible animals hyperactive. Sodium nitrite may be present to prevent fading of colors, or red dye #40 may be used to give a fresh, meaty look. Both these agents have long been linked to cancer or birth defects in laboratory animals and are even banned in some countries. Is color important to animals? Not as much as to you. The cosmetic effect is for you—the buyer.

Commercial pet food may be the most highly processed food on the planet—a tribute to the magic of food technology. Chemical additives enlisted to create the finished product include anticaking, antimicrobial, coloring, firming, flavoring, drying, pH control, and surface finishing agents, and emulsifiers, sequestrants, synergists, texturizers, lubricants, and sweeteners. The most common antioxidant preservative is ethoxyquin, which some pet food critics and veterinarians claim is a major cause of disease, skin problems, and infertility in dogs. In 1997 the U.S. Food and Drug Administration requested that manufacturers reduce the maximum level of ethoxyquin by half. The absence of ethoxyquin on the label of a product does not necessarily mean it is not in there. Suppliers to the manufacturers may use it in their processing of meat meal (or meat protein, as some companies are calling it), tallow, and fat. If that's the case, and it often is, the manufacturers don't have to list it on their labels. Ethoxyquin is not approved for use as a preservative in human food.

HOW HOLISTIC VETERINARIANS VIEW COMMERCIAL PET FOOD

Holistic veterinarians are keenly interested in nutrition and diet. They use both as primary healing tools. These animal doctors tend to be severely critical of the quality of most commercial food. They doubt whether the overcooked, chemicalized, refined, and "scientifically formulated" products you buy in stores can ever create radiant health or maintain a state of harmony in an animal. "The diseases we are treating is the food we are feeding," says Bill Pollak, DVM, of Fairfield, Iowa.

The critics point out that food has to be more than just the quantity of proteins, fat, carbohydrates, and added vitamins. It's the freshness, wholesomeness, energy, and digestibility of food that counts also. In these categories the veterinarians give failing grades to most commercial foods.

They say many animals cannot tolerate the ingredients. This rejection is often expressed in the form of violent illness or chronic health problems and often triggers a hypersensitivity and overreaction to flea and insect bites, pollens, soaps, sprays, and environmental contaminants. Dry food is a major offender because it is a concentrated collection of many of the foods that are the most allergenic for animals.

The veterinarians are most concerned about feeding inferior protein to animals ad infinitum. This burdens the kidneys and liver, leaving the system toxic and disease prone.

They are concerned about the level of fat. Contents are often 30 percent animal fat. In the wild, no animal prey carries that much. But fat is a cheap source of energy and it's also tasty, so manufacturers use a lot of it, as well as chemicals, to enhance the taste. The goal is for animals to eat their brand eagerly and in quantity. This, however, is a primary cause of obesity in companion animals.

If the pet food picture seems bleak, don't be discouraged. Increasingly, health-conscious consumers are demanding more quality. They are realizing that the food is causing many problems. Fortunately there is an industry response to this growing demand and awareness in the form of higher-quality products and more natural pet foods on the market. These and other dietary options covered in the following chapters will point you in the right direction for improving the health of your animal.

4

Making the Switch to a Better Diet

You ARE WHAT you eat and digest. The same holds true for our pets. Holistic veterinarians regard diet as the basis for health and treating any condition. It's the foundation. Everything else they do for an animal builds on this foundation. Some say they have treated dogs where all they could do was get the owner to switch from a mediocre commercial food to a higher-quality product, and that was enough, just a diet change, to see dramatic improvements in the health of an animal.

"I find that by changing diet I can make a big impact against many conditions," says Ron Carsten, DVM, of Glenwood Springs, Colorado. "A good diet provides me with a powerful pillar of support for all my treatments, even when I am treating very chronic and very sick cases."

The reason for this is simple and has been known since ancient times. In the words of Hippocrates uttered 2,500 years ago: "Let thy food be thy medicine and thy medicine be thy food." This is timeless advice, more relevant than ever in today's age of junk food and rampant chronic disease.

We all need to understand that the energy we call life animates the cells that make up our bodies and directs the countless biochemical functions in our bodies. Foods are the fuel of life. Poor fuel makes for little momentum in life. Our bodies do not function well on poor-quality foods, any more than a finely tuned automobile functions well on poor-quality gasoline. Many of the illnesses of people can be prevented or minimized through better nutrition, and it's the same for our pets.

But wait a minute here. You may be thinking: My dog has no problems, and all I do is feed it every day from the bag of food I buy at the supermarket. You may be right, because just like the person who smokes, drinks, and eats poorly and yet lives a long life without suffering from debilitating illness, many resilient animals seem to thrive and live long no matter how poor the quality of their food. "If you have such an animal, you may want to experiment with a better diet and see if you can notch up the level of health," says Christina Chambreau, DVM, of Sparks, Maryland. "Most animals are hugely benefited by being on a high-quality diet. The benefits show up as increased vitality, improved hair coat, and decreased illness."

Now that you have had a glimpse of some of the issues related to commercial pet food, this chapter is intended to help you shift your food choices in a healthier direction. Let's move on and consider your options from the angle of what type of food can you and should you feed your dog. Carvel Tiekert, DVM, a longtime observer of the pet food scene, has compiled a simple yardstick for judging the quality of food.

DR. TIEKERT'S SCALE OF NUTRITIONAL ADEQUACY IN PET FOOD

There is a whole landscape of pet food, from generic inexpensive to higher-quality "natural" products. The following guidelines are based on a scale of 1 (the poorest) to 10 (the best) to help you determine a better diet for your dog:

1. **All meat.** Animals in the wild don't eat just meat. They eat everything when they kill their prey, including the intestinal contents. In a rabbit, the intestinal vegetable contents amount to about 40 percent of body weight. Animals also eat bones, a source of calcium for the body.

2. **Soft-moist food.** These diets are high in sugar, chemicals, dyes, propylene glycol, and other additives to give them shelf life, softness, and an artificial look. Their labels make for interesting reading, and that's about the most you can say about them.

3 and 4. **Soft-moist and dry combinations—"generic brands."**
The cheap generic and store brands have been incriminated in
veterinary literature for their poor quality. They are infamous
for mineral deficiencies, particularly zinc.

5 and 6. **Standard commercial diets—the "name" brands.** They
are adequate in most cases for most normal, healthy, young to
middle-aged animals, but they are *not optimum*. They are merely
adequate. These products are reasonably well researched, but
quality comes second to price and palatability. They are made to
be competitive and are usually loaded with chemicals. An average thirty pound dog eating this food regularly will consume
nine pounds of chemicals a year!

7 and 8. **Top shelf lines.** These products, including Science Diet
and Iams, feature higher-quality ingredients but still have artificial preservatives and other chemical additives. I place some
"natural" products in this category because they are made with
inferior ingredients such as "wheat flour" (a euphemism for
white flour). If the product is made with whole grain, it will say
"ground whole wheat" or "whole-wheat flour." There are,
unfortunately a number of low-quality products that come with
high-sounding names.

9. **The so-called natural lines.** This category includes Precise,
Natural Life, and Verus, products made with the finest-quality
ingredients. They use vitamin C and vitamin E as natural
preservatives instead of using artificial preservatives, and the
added minerals are chelated with amino acids for better absorption. For most dogs, I recommend their "senior" formulas,
which contain lower quantities of protein.

10. **Homemade.** The very best food you can feed your animal is the
homemade diet made with fresh foods. *You can't do better for your
animal.*

Never feed a diet below level five. I recommend that you feed
either a homemade diet or a level nine food with supplementation,
to make sure you are giving optimum nutrition to your pet. You can
read all the labels and figure out the ingredients, but both good *and*

bad manufacturing plants are making these products. I can answer for some but not for others. So it is very hard to really know the absolute truth of what's inside the bags and cans. For a basic food, such as Precise, Natural Life, or Verus, I recommend switching from one brand to another. Buy one brand one time and another the next. That provides some variety in the basic ingredients.

The next three chapters are devoted to diet-improving options, starting with doing the minimum (for very busy people) to doing the maximum—that is, feeding an entirely home-prepared meal. You will find that within these options are practical approaches that will work for you and improve the health of your animal. Feel free to mix and match the options in whatever way is most convenient for you and that your animals likes. Always keep in mind that each pet is an individual with individual tastes and reactions. One dog may prefer chicken to turkey. One may like steamed vegetables. Another may not like vegetables at all. So in following the ideas here, always keep individuality and variety in mind as long as you don't forget quality.

Before introducing your options in the next chapter, it is worthwhile to consider two important points:

1. Switching the diet.
2. Preventive shopping—foods to avoid.

SWITCHING THE DIET

Many animals become accustomed and virtually "addicted" to a set diet. They may not appreciate overnight change. Also, sudden changes may cause digestive upset. This is especially true with the young and the old, and also with dogs that tend to vomit or have diarrhea. So go slow when you replace the old food with new foods. In most cases you can usually have your dog eating something different within a few days, but the recommendation is to make the switch over a period of seven to ten days. Here is a simple timetable to guide you:

- Add 10 percent new food the first day or two.
- Increase on subsequent days to 25 percent, 50 percent, 75 percent, 90 percent, and finally 100 percent.

When you improve your pet's diet, don't think you have to put a burden on your budget. Organic food is great, and many holistic veterinarians recommend it, but it's not necessary if you can't easily afford it. Some owners think they have to feed organic, range-fed meat and organic vegetables if they are going to do it "right." It's not true. Do what is comfortable for you. Straining for what is not easily obtained may cause stress and justification for stopping a more natural diet. Start from where you are and improve the level of nutrition for your pet comfortably and affordably. Don't forget the other vital things necessary for the health of your animals—the air, the water, the companionship, the exercise, and a nurturing environment. They all add into the equation of health.

PREVENTIVE SHOPPING—FOODS TO AVOID

Read labels, the veterinarians advise, and listen to the veterinarians' advice, and avoid products with chemical preservatives, dyes, and additives and, in particular, the following:

- **Cheap, plain-wrapped "generic" pet food products.** It is likely they contain highly questionable ingredients and are often reject or substandard chows sold "out the back door" by major manufacturers.

- **Semimoist foods.** These products appear red, moist, and pliable like real hamburger meat. They contain a full complement of sugar and chemical additives that you and I would avoid if we are truly interested in our health. They frequently cause allergic or allergiclike reactions and may contribute to pancreas or blood sugar problems.

- **Foods containing too much protein.** Dogs don't need as much protein as we feed them, and certainly not the kind of poor-quality protein used in most commercial foods. Excess, inferior protein stresses the immune system, kidneys, and liver. Many veterinarians suggest that 18 percent protein is adequate for most stages of life other than the puppy stage. You can feed perhaps even less protein to older animals. Just be sure the product contains high-quality protein. Read the labels. Switch to senior diets that offer no more than 18 percent protein.

HOW TO TELL IF YOUR DOG IS EATING
A HEALTHY DIET

Canadian expert Edmund Dorosz, DVM, of Fort MacLeod, Alberta, author of *Let's Cook for Our Dog*, instructs dog owners how to evaluate appearance, behavior, stools, and other signs, as a guide to feeding a good diet. Here's how to do it:

Appearance. Start with the skin—the largest organ in the body. A dull hair coat and shedding are typical signs of unhealthy skin below. If you part the hair and have a direct look at the skin, you will often find skin that is dry, flaky, and inflamed. This kind of a condition is associated with problems such as fleas, mites, ringworm, and inflammatory allergies.

Behavior. A healthy, properly fed dog receiving all the necessary nutrients and water it needs should be happy, active, and responsive. Always consider the diet if the dog is irritable, dull-appearing, hyperactive, nervous, or restless. Behavioral changes normally do not appear until several weeks after a new diet has been started.

Stools. A good-quality diet and properly functioning digestive system produces a small amount of formed, dark brown, firm stools. The small amount tells you the food has been digested and there is little waste left. Color may indicate food dyes, internal bleeding, or disease problems. If not enough water has been consumed, stools may be dry, hard, and difficult to pass. Poor-quality food results in undigested material passing into the large intestine, where fermentation from bacteria produces gas and loose stools. If the intestines are inflamed or infested with worms, the stools will be abnormal. Liver or pancreas problems cause digestive imbalances and also result in abnormal stools.

DR. DOROSZ'S GOOD FOOD–BAD FOOD CHECKLIST

SIGNS	GOOD	BAD
Eyes	Bright, alert, clear	Dull, cloudy, tearing, red
Nose	Cool, moist, clean, soft	Hot, dry, hard
Teeth	Clean, white, shiny	Dirty, yellow, foul-smelling
Ears	Clean, dry	Inflamed, waxy, foul-smelling
Hair	Shiny, soft, clean	Dull, dry, dandruff, hair loss
Skin	Soft, pliable	Dry, greasy, inflamed, itchy
Muscles	Firm, developed, defined	Soft
Condition	Can feel ribs	Obese, pot belly, waddles
Paws	Smooth, resilient	Cracked, sore, nails brittle
Anus	Clean, dry	Inflamed, itchy anal glands
Urine	Light yellow, average volume	Dark or clear, large amounts

5

Feeding Option #1

YOU WANT YOUR DOG TO EAT A BETTER DIET,
BUT YOU ARE JUST TOO BUSY...ALL YOU CAN DO
IS FILL THE BOWL WITH KIBBLE

I WON'T LAY a guilt trip on you, but if this is all you can do, then at least feed your dog the best possible product. What is the best on the market? Obviously you'll never know from the advertising claims. A number of health-conscious manufacturers do try to produce high-quality foods with few or no additives, and some of the veterinarians I spoke to had actually visited some of these plants and were familiar with the owners and their standards.

Because holistic veterinarians place such importance on nutrition, I asked each one I interviewed to name the brands he or she recommends to clients. Following are the results of this informal survey, with the brands most often mentioned listed first. My survey is hardly a scientific study of quality, but at least it gives you some better choices and the preferences of nutritionally oriented veterinarians. The list includes telephone numbers of companies in case you would like to obtain information on products and where to purchase them. Some of the brands are not widely distributed but can be shipped via UPS or other commercial carriers. You can often find a premium product on this list at a health food store, where pet foods tend to have higher quality and fewer chemical additives. Be sure to buy a product that turns over quickly and doesn't sit on the shelf for months.

VETERINARIANS' FAVORITE BRANDS

Wysong (517-631-0009)

Precise (800-446-7148)

Innova, California Natural
   (800-532-7261)

Natural Life (800-367-2391)

Flint River Ranch (909-682-5048)

Perfect Health Diet (800-743-1502)

Pet Guard (800-874-3221)

Solid Gold (800-364-4863)

Cornucopia (800-738-8280)

Verus (800-548-2899)

Lick Your Chops (800-542-4677)

Nature's Recipe (800-843-4008)

Nutro Natural Choice (800-833-5330)

Excel (800-592-6687)

Even if you feed a superior product, pet food manufacturers are not all-knowing, and there is probably going to be something lacking in any commercial diet you give your dog. "It's a good idea to change the brand every few months from one of the better products to another good product," advises Lynne Friday, DVM, of Lexington, Michigan.

FOR OWNERS OF GIANT BREEDS

Based on years of clinical observation and his own personal research, Carvel Tiekert, DVM, suggests that big animals do better on less protein. "Most people with giant breeds won't take the time to home-prepare for the animals," he says. "It's too much work. So if you feed a commercial food, go right to an adult food after weaning. Skip the puppy food. It has too much protein. And as soon as the animal is about full-grown, switch to a senior diet."

6

Feeding Option #2

YOU'RE BUSY, BUT YOU CAN SHARE TABLE SCRAPS AND ADD MEAT AND VEGETABLES TO YOUR DOG'S DIET

THIS OPTION REALLY gives you a powerful upgrade in the quality of the overall diet without taking much of a bite out of your time. The veterinarians I interviewed would prefer you did at least this much and not just rely solely on commercial pet food.

Here's what's involved:

- Feed the highest-quality pet food you can find and use that as the springboard, the base, for a better diet.
- To this base add things like broth, meat, fresh vegetables, and fruits. Add what you eat—if you yourself eat well.

"Animals will be a whole lot healthier if a portion of their diet contains fresh and raw food," says Pamela Wood-Krzeminski, DVM, of Boca Raton, Florida.

Even veterinarians who say they know a particular manufacturer, and respect the company's efforts to ensure quality, still recommend add-ons.

For instance, Wendell Belfield, DVM, of San Jose, recommends the Innova brand to his clients: "I know the people, the quality of their product, yet I still recommend adding some extra food to the diet—such as ground chicken, oatmeal, egg yolks, grated carrots. You really want your animal to have the extra nutrition and variety, even if you are feeding a better product."

The following easy-to-do suggestions provide practical ideas for simple diet upgrades and variety.

The Broth Plan—Joseph Demers, DVM

Even if you feed a good-quality, "natural" kibble, that by itself can be harmful over the long term. One of the major problems related to pet health is the overuse of dry, kibble food. I relate kibble to macaroni or rice you would take from the box and eat without cooking it. It is dehydrated food, and it causes dehydrated animals. It is too dry, too processed, with too many chemicals. It contributes to chronic disease. In Chinese medicine dehydrated food leads to what is called "internal heat." This overloads the kidneys over time as well as the spleen, the organ that governs the digestive system. It starts to heat up the liver, and eventually you see burping, throwing up of bile in the morning, and upset stomachs. You see thick saliva, dry stools, an animal panting after its evening meal even though the surroundings are cool. The animal is hot and has a lot of heat in the body to eliminate.

A simple solution, if you still want to feed just kibble and don't have time for much else, is to make the food wetter. Add some chicken or beef broth to the kibble. It is simple to add a bit of moisture or broth to the dry food. I suggest a minimum of 30 percent moisture.

I see many animals with dry, coarse coats and flaking dandruff who are shedding volumes of fur just as a result of eating a wholly dry diet. I turn many of them around within a month, just by having pet owners add broth to the dry food. The same animals often return with shining, healthy coats.

If you want to go a step further, add a good digestive enzyme product for pets to aid digestion, and a fatty acid supplement, such as flaxseed oil. Start with perhaps 1 drop for a small dog and 3 drops for a large animal. Gradually increase to a level equivalent to 1 teaspoon per fifteen pounds of body weight. Flaxseed oil is an excellent source of omega-3 fatty acids.

The Three-Minute Plan—Robert Goldstein, DVM

I have many clients who spend hours preparing recipes for their animals. But they aren't the majority, so I try to focus on people who don't have the time, who tell me basically this: "I have three minutes and then I have to go to work. What can I do? I want the maximum protection for my animal in that period."

Here's what you can do in three minutes:

- Use any of the following of my favorite dry dog foods as a base. I prefer lower-protein formulas—senior or light: California Natural, Cornucopia, Lick Your Chops Senior, Solid Gold Dog, or Wysong Senior.

- For added protein, use an already cooked, broiled rotisserie chicken (remove the skin and bones before feeding), cooked turkey breast, low-fat plain yogurt, low-fat cottage cheese, or a fertile egg yolk. Chunks of fresh tofu are another option. Tofu is especially useful if your animal has chronic arthritis or upper-respiratory infections. Such animals often have difficulty digesting heavy proteins from meat and chicken and may have an easier time digesting and utilizing tofu. Any one of these items can take the place of about one-quarter of your dry food. When using yogurt or cottage cheese, however, reduce and replace 15 percent of the dry content.

- For added carbohydrates, use a palatable portion of whole grains such as brown rice, oatmeal, or millet. They are rich in B vitamins and fiber to help keep the intestinal tract clean. If you don't have time to prepare or cook a meal, reach for a packet of "quick cook" oatmeal, which retains much of its nutrients and fiber sources even in instant form. For speed, you can use a parboiled brown rice, available in health food stores. Many animals are allergic to gluten, the concentrated protein fraction found in wheat. Millet is gluten-free, making it a good choice for hypoallergenic diets.

- Grated organic carrots and finely chopped broccoli are healthy additions. Sprouts are a good source of green, living foods, rich in chlorophyll that helps cleanse the blood. Sprinkle 1 teaspoon of chopped alfalfa sprouts onto the food of small animals. For larger dogs, use bean sprouts, up to 2 tablespoons. Wheat grass is another great source of concentrated nutrients. For small dogs start with 1 teaspoon of chopped wheat grass. Work up slowly to 1 tablespoon per meal. For larger dogs, use 3 tablespoons.

- Add a vitamin and mineral supplement. I suggest my own Daily Health Nuggets, available through Earth Animal (800-711-2292), or Dr. Goodpet's Maximum Protection Formula (800-222-9932).

- Add a good cold-pressed oil such as olive or flaxseed. Use a virgin olive oil for the oleic fatty acid that will promote energy and skin conditioning. If your animal is prone to inflammatory conditions such as chronic skin problems, use flaxseed oil, which is high in essential fatty acids such as linolenic and alpha-linoleic acids. Look for organic flaxseed products in dark containers, as this oil is quite fragile and will break down when exposed to light and heat. For small dogs, add 1 teaspoon of oil; medium dogs, 2 teaspoons; large dogs, 1 tablespoon; and giant breeds, 1 1/2 tablespoons.

Partially Raw Meat Diet #1—Carvel Tiekert, DVM

Every animal should have raw meat as a supplement. Raw meat is what they eat in the wilds, and I don't think we have bred out the need for it (see discussion on raw meat later in this chapter).

While I consider Precise and Natural Life in my experience to be high-quality foods, maybe as good as you can buy in processed foods, they are still processed. The enzymes and other natural factors that are alive in whole, raw foods have been killed in commercially prepared food.

I recommend supplementing the diet with raw, chunk beef, the cheapest stew beef you can find. I prefer that over hamburger, because when you grind up hamburger you take whatever bacteria there is on the outside and mix it into the inside. You damage the cells more. And if you let it sit in your refrigerator, you know what happens to it. Cut up the meat and freeze the pieces in plastic bags. I am not concerned about the fat. Raw fat in moderation is fine. Feed about 2 ounces to a small dog and up to 4 ounces to a large dog. I also recommend lightly steamed vegetables—all the animal will eat.

If you use a commercial diet of lesser quality (see "Dr. Tiekert's Scale of Nutritional Adequacy in Pet Food" in chapter 4) as a base food, then feed more raw meat and vegetables. Eggs may be substituted for meat on a periodic basis. If you can get them, and can afford them, organic products are best.

The use of a quality general vitamin/mineral is always a good idea. My favorite product is Lecizyme (made by Natural Animal Nutrition, 800-548-2899). I also recommend additional vitamin C. I suggest about 250 milligrams a day for a small dog, and up to 1,000 milligrams daily for a large dog.

Partially Raw Meat Diet #2—Thomas Van Cise, DVM

I consistently see good responses to a simple, partially raw diet. If possible, use organic food products for maximum quality.

Ingredients:

One-third raw meat, such as beef, chicken, or turkey. The meat you choose depends on your pet's tolerance for a particular food. Note that many animals may be allergic to a certain type of meat if it is cooked. However, in the raw form this doesn't seem to occur. It probably has to do with the enzymes that are destroyed by the cooking.

One-third lightly steamed or blanched grated vegetables, such as carrots, squash, beans, and greens like spinach and bok choy. This makes the vegetables more digestible without destroying nutrients and enzymes through cooking.

One-third Sojourner Farms' European-Style Dog Food Mix, a human-food-grade product with herbs, nuts, grains, and dried kelp added. Intended to be served with raw meat for a fully balanced diet, the food is soaked before using for a few minutes to make it more digestible. (Sojourner Farms: 888-867-6567.)

The Liver Plan—Edmund Dorosz, DVM

I regard liver as "nature's miracle food," rich in vitamins, minerals, fatty acids, and protein. Adding raw liver to your animal's regular diet is a simple step that yields major head-to-tail health benefits.

You will frequently see skin conditions improve just by supplementing the diet with liver alone. For small dogs, 1 tablespoon a day or 2 to 3 ounces a week is sufficient. For large dogs, 2 ounces a day or up to 6 ounces a week.

Vegetable, Yogurt, and Egg Add-Ons—Roger Dehaan, DVM

Add some raw vegetables daily. You don't need much, just 1 tablespoon for each twenty pounds of body weight. Typically you will have to start animals on the vegetable habit when they are young. You usually won't get a fifteen-year-old animal to start eating vegetables if he hasn't done it by then. My preferences are carrots, broccoli, beets, green beans, alfalfa sprouts, and dark green leafy vegetables.

Yogurt is an excellent add-on. Give 1 tablespoon per twenty-five pounds of body weight. Feed it twice to five times a week.

Feed 1 egg or egg yolk for each twenty-five pounds, twice a week.

TABLE SCRAPS: WHAT TO FEED, WHAT NOT TO FEED

Many veterinarians are influenced by the pet food industry, which discourages table scraps. Supposedly, table scraps can negatively affect the nutritional balance of a dog's "scientifically formulated" diet. That's a hard explanation to digest given the general poor quality of commercial pet foods. More likely the reason consumers are dissuaded is that table scraps can cut into pet food sales.

Holistic veterinarians generally favor adding table scraps, as long as the additions are wholesome and simple. Remember that all animals are individuals, with individual tastes and sensitivities. Make sure what you're feeding is not causing allergic reactions. And, of course, you don't want to feed your dog candy bars or chocolate ice cream or fill their water bowls with soda pop. One commonsense guideline offered by Norman Ralston, DVM, is this: "If the food on your plate is harmful for your pet to eat, maybe you should not eat it yourself."

Here are the veterinarians' suggestions:

- Share a little of what you are eating every day with your animals. That provides taste and nutritional variety.

- The volume of dry (commercial) food you normally feed should be lessened by the volume of table scraps you add.
- Don't feed leftover fat and remnants that may not be healthy. No bacon or bacon grease. Besides the high levels of nitrites, the high heat used in cooking bacon creates many other unhealthful compounds. It is best not to use any fat drippings.
- Vegetables are excellent, particularly carrots, anything in the broccoli family, and leafy greens. Dogs often like to chew on raw carrots. Cooked vegetables are okay, but raw vegetables in general should be mashed, grated, or aged. Vegetables and fruits can be pureed in a blender, then left to sit in the container for a day or two before feeding.
- Try different fruit. Many dogs enjoy the taste of bananas.
- Stay away from rich foods like ham, sauces, and cheese. They are invitations for trouble. The digestive tract of the dog is geared for simpler food than we eat.
- No spicy, salty, and fried foods. Unfortunately, some animals can get addicted to such fare. Also, no spicy chili, pepperoni, or luncheon meats.
- Pasta is okay, but without the spices and tomato sauce.
- A bit of olive oil is fine. It's good for the skin.
- Well-cooked rice (long-grained, but not the instant rice) and baked or boiled white potatoes are generally good.
- Do not feed sweets, cookies, and cakes. For sure, no chocolate. Certain compounds in chocolate—theobromine and caffeine—are toxic to dogs and can cause vomiting, excessive urination, hyperactivity, fast breathing, weakness, and seizures if enough is eaten.
- You can store unused leftovers in a plastic container with a loose cover. Don't refrigerate. Dogs like aged food that is warm. You can store for several days and use a bit at a time for flavor enhancing.

FEEDING RAW MEAT

Many holistic veterinarians recommend raw food, and particularly raw meat, as part of a regular diet for pets. They say that feeding raw restores vitality, even in very sick animals, and can improve many chronic health problems. Dogs, of course, evolved on raw food, including raw meat, and not on the highly processed, highly cooked commercial food eaten by domesticated modern pets. Raw foods contain their own built-in supply of enzymes, which facilitate the process of digestion. When food is cooked, the naturally occurring enzymes are destroyed, causing the body to activate its own enzymes to break down the food.

Bill Pollak, DVM, is an outspoken advocate of feeding raw meat, eggs, fish, and grated vegetables. "Foods lively with freshness, wholesomeness (proper for the species), and varied, give the greatest amount of life force to the animal," he says. "The genetic encoding of the raw food and the genetic encoding of your pet is a match. It is this energy incorporated into the body that creates and sustains health. Until basic healthy raw food is delivered to the system, higher states of health are near impossible or transient at best, and an animal functions suboptimally, in a constant state of unwellness. Processed food is appropriate for survival, not for health."

Not all holistic veterinarians are so keen about raw food. Some have reservations because of the risk of bacterial contamination that might cause gastrointestinal consequences. Poultry meat, in particular, has been associated with pathogens such as E. coli and salmonella, and some animals have been known to develop mild diarrhea. Some veterinarians also believe that many animals have lost the ability to digest raw meat after generations on cooked or commercial food and may throw up or absorb the nutrients poorly.

What should you do? Raw or not raw? Among the veterinarians I interviewed, the large majority have been recommending raw meat for many years and say they have encountered no problems. They argue that the benefits far outweigh the risk of contamination.

If you have any reservations about the safety of feeding raw, their advice is to lightly steam or sauté the meat until the redness is gone. Another option, suggested by Roger DeHaan, DVM, of Frazee, Minnesota, is to soak the raw meat in food-grade 3 percent hydrogen peroxide. Here's how to do it: Put a tablespoon of peroxide in a pint of water. Soak the meat for about twenty minutes. Then rinse off with water and feed. Don't be concerned about any residual hydrogen peroxide. A little bit can't hurt. In fact, it is helpful against yeast and any other parasites your animal may have.

If you decide to feed your dog raw meat, here is some helpful advice to do it safely:

- Start with a small amount and increase gradually. If your dog isn't used to getting extra morsels of meat, you may even want to start with cooked meat and then transition slowly to raw. Or you may want to chop up the meat in the beginning and with time move to chunks of raw meat.
- Make sure your source of meat is fresh.
- Keep the meat frozen in small chunks and thaw out only what you need.
- If the meat has an "off" odor or a questionable color, don't feed it.
- Don't feed raw pork.
- Don't use raw meat as kibble, which has been treated with preservatives, enabling you to fill your animal's feeding bowl with it and then leave for work. If your animal doesn't eat the meat in fifteen or twenty minutes, pick it up and toss it out. Then clean the dish.
- Be aware of the possibility that some dogs, once they are fed raw meat, might begin to regard livestock in terms of prey. This may be a problem if you live on a farm or in a rural setting. The taste of raw meat could possibly increase a tendency in certain animals to go after chickens, piglets, or other small livestock. (Some dogs, of course, might be prone to do this even if they are eating standard kibble.)

7

Feeding Option #3

THE DELUXE TREATMENT—HOMEMADE MEALS

THERE'S NOTHING LIKE homemade meals, for us and, yes, for our pets as well. If you have the time to prepare entire meals without the inclusion of commercial pet food, this is the way to go. It's the deluxe treatment. And, as you will see, it doesn't really take that much time.

Why should you even go to the trouble? The pet food industry is constantly changing. One company with a high-quality product now may, in six months, start cheapening its food to save on cost, and soon it is not the same quality as before. Moreover, the way commercial foods are processed pets may not get all the nutrients they need to have. Nothing works as well as fresh food that you prepare yourself, my veterinarian sources say, and the result is thriving dogs who consistently look better than dogs eating store-bought food.

In this chapter you will find a sampling of perspectives, guidelines, and recipes from veterinarians. While the recipes vary, the basic message from the experts is the same:

- Keep it simple—there's no need to get fancy.
- Fill the diet with fresh and wholesome foods.
- Find a formula that works well for you and that your animal likes. Remember, each animal has different taste preferences.

- Don't feed the same thing every day. Constantly feeding the same foods increases the risk of a food allergy over time. Rotate different ingredients in and out of the basic diet to provide nutritional variety.
- Add a good pet multiple vitamin and mineral supplement to help achieve optimum nutritional intake.

If you have any doubts about how your animal is doing after you start a homemade diet, refer to chapter 4 for tips on recognizing the signs of a good or bad diet. For additional information on home-prepared diets, check out appendix C for a list of excellent books that contain many more recipes.

The Best and the Most Inexpensive—Carolyn Blakey, DVM

Giving the best care possible to your pet means feeding food you yourself prepare. Homemade meals are the best and most inexpensive—period! The expense is with time, not money. It's obviously more time-consuming to make good food for yourself or your pet than it is to buy preprepared food.

The following simple recipe contains basic proportions from the three major food groups.

> *Ingredients:*
> One-half of the diet can be cooked whole grains (such as brown rice and oatmeal).
> Up to a quarter or a third should be high-quality proteins, namely real meat, and some of it raw if your animal will eat it.
> Up to a quarter with vegetables or fruits (lightly steam or grate the veggies).

This isn't a hard recipe to put together. Most people find pets will readily eat this kind of a dish when prepared as a casserole or stew. Add a good pet vitamin/mineral supplement and a digestive enzyme to the food before feeding to ensure that all the nutrients the animal needs are present and are well absorbed.

The only pet food I like to add to the recipe is Sojourner Farms' European-Style Dog Food Mix, a blend of human-quality grains, herbs, dried sea vegetables, and ground nuts. It is very easy to prepare and adds solid nutrition. The product is available at many

health food and pet stores or through Sojourner Farms at
888-867-6567.

Simple Fresh, and Varied—Norman C. Ralston, DVM

The diet can be very simple. The important thing is to use fresh
ingredients. Fresh doesn't mean expensive. Use a simple rule of
thumb for proportions, and vary ingredients according to your situation, availability, nutritional need, season, and weather. For animals,
as well as for humans, a healthy variety of food is the key to success.

Tailor the diet to your animal's particular needs, don't just take it
out of a book or mechanically apply a formula or recipe. If it is not
convenient to prepare food daily, several days' rations can be prepared in advance and placed in the refrigerator, though this will
reduce its vital energy. Add a little warm water and possibly some
fresh leftovers from the table, and you have a warm meal.

During one period of time, I cooked for dogs every day for 3 1/2
years. I was looking for the best-possible diet. I came up with the
following formula, which I found beneficial most of the time. Keep
in mind that some individual ingredients will work better or be
more palatable for one animal than for another. That is something
you can find out only by trial and error.

Ingredients:
- 50–60 percent grain (brown rice, corn, barley, buckwheat,
  amaranth, wheat). Be sure to cook the grains thoroughly and
  then blend them or run them through a food processor. That
  will enhance digestibility. Animals tend to gulp food down.
- 25 percent raw or barely cooked meat.
- 25 percent steamed fresh vegetables along with seaweed (dulse
  or kelp) for organic trace minerals, including calcium. Blend
  or chop into small particles. If possible, choose vegetables in
  season and grown in the region where you live.
- Add an essential fatty acid (omega 3) supplement.

V.J.'s Recipe—Mark Haverkos, DVM

The late V. J. Keating, DVM, a pioneer of holistic veterinary medicine who practiced in Oregon for many years, always recommended
that you try to simulate what the animals eat in the wilds. This, he
felt, stimulates the life force and helps animals become healthier. I

have found his concept works well. V.J.'s simple recipe was that the food should be about one-third each of protein, carbohydrates, and vegetables.

Ingredients:
Protein should be from the normal game range, if possible: turkey, chicken, rabbit. Try to avoid beef or pork.
For the carbohydrates, use brown rice or any other palatable whole grain.
Use any vegetables the dog will eat. Vegetables provide good fiber.

Directions: The meat can be either raw or cooked. Mix with cooked vegetables and add over the brown rice.

The Time-Saver Recipe—Karen Bentley, DVM

Time is the great dictator on how much preparation you can put into a meal for your animals. I am often pressed for time in the morning and find that oatmeal alone works quite well as a quick A.M. meal. Years ago I developed the following recipe for evening feeding that provides good-quality nutrition while taking up a minimum of time to prepare.

Ingredients:
Cooked chicken thighs (no bones) or raw beef if animal has no allergic tendencies to beef. Small dogs, feed 1/4–1/2 cup; medium dogs, 1 cup; larger dogs, 2 cups.
Mixed vegetables, same amounts.
Tofu. Small and medium dogs, 1 tablespoon; larger dogs, 1/2 cup.
Pumpkin pie filling (a good source of fiber). Small dogs, 1 tablespoon; medium dogs, 1 1/2 tablespoon; larger dogs, 1/2 cup.
A good kelp meal product. Small dogs, 1/4 teaspoon; medium dogs, 1/2 teaspoon; larger dogs, 1 full teaspoon.
To this mixture add two multi-vitamin/mineral supplements— Mega C Plus, from Orthomolecular Specialties (408-227-9334) and Maximum Protection Formula from Dr. Goodpet (800-222-9932). Besides providing important vitamins and minerals, Maximum Protection helps keep intestines clean.

For small dogs, use half the label dosage of each product. For large animals, use the full recommended dosage for each.

The Natural Raw Meat Diet—William Pollak, DVM

Start your pets on this type of diet slowly. An animal transitioning from a previous all-commercial food diet may have severely weak digestion. A water fast of one or two days can ease the transition. Follow the fast first with the meat portion of the diet for several days, then add the vegetables (for two more days), and then the grain portion. This will reduce the occasional side effects of diarrhea arising from too much internal purification occurring from the new diet.

Ingredients:

Protein: 65 percent raw meat. Use turkey, chicken, beef, and lamb. Begin with the meat chopped. For convenience, it is okay to serve the same meat for three to four days. Then switch, if possible. Steady feeding of the same food can lead to sensitivities. If you decide to cook the meat, know that you are cooking it because of your own feelings of discomfort and not because cooked is better for your pet. Raw is best, so cook the meat as little as possible until you feel more comfortable. Eggs are an excellent source of protein. Feed one to several eggs (depending on the size of the dog) twice a week. Raw is fine with the shells broken into small pieces. Or lightly scramble the eggs with butter. Be cautious with milk and milk products, another source of protein. Pasteurized cow's milk can cause diarrhea, gas, and discomfort in a less vital animal. Cottage cheese or cultured dairy products are usually okay. Raw milk can be well tolerated if introduced slowly into the diet once the animal has become accustomed to raw meat.

Vegetables: 30 percent raw grated or chopped vegetables. Use whatever is fresh at the grocery. Dark green leafy veggies, cauliflower, string beans, broccoli, zucchini, carrots, and turnips are good choices. Add any favorite, healthy greens such as watercress, dandelion, and cilantro.

Carbohydrates: 5 to 10 percent grains. Dogs love oatmeal. Rye, millet, couscous, quinoa, buckwheat, and wheat are all fine. Cook if desired or crumble raw and sprinkle over the meat.

Fats: Cold-processed olive oil, sesame oil, butter, ghee (clarified butter), and canola are all fine.

Nutritional supplements: Use a pet multi-vitamin/mineral formula, human-quality bone meal, colloidal minerals or kelp, and extra vitamins C and E.

Directions: For convenience, grains can be cooked and mixed together with other ingredients once a week. Freeze mixtures in containers and use on a daily basis. Add supplements daily.

How to feed: Feed adult dogs once a day. One cup a day of food by volume for each 35 pounds of body weight is usually sufficient. Amounts will vary with activity, age, and digestive ability. The best way to know whether you are feeding too much or not enough is to look at your dog. The backbone and ribs should be felt easily without layers of fat in between. Your animal will lose its previous "doughy" appearance, and a more compact, solid conformation takes its place. You will notice less voracious feeding behavior. The eyes become bright and clear. There is overall greater energy and vibrancy. There is almost always less drinking, with less urination and stool. This is natural. These characteristics become more prominent as higher-quality nutrition saturates the cells of the pet, a process that can take weeks to months. If more weight is needed, increase the food ration. Generally speaking, after some time on a natural diet, your dog will eat half (or less) the amount previously eaten on a diet of commercial food. An animal doesn't need a lot of food if what it eats is quality. Today, animals on most commercial diets are simply being overloaded with low quality—and with a disastrous impact on the organs.

If your dog is very active, you can increase the quantity of food, as well as raise the carbohydrate (grain) level. Puppies require double the amount of food normally eaten by adult dogs. Lactating and pregnant dogs also require more frequent feeding and slightly higher protein, mineral content, and dairy in the diet.

> ## BE ALERT FOR HEALING EPISODES—
> ## WILLIAM POLLAK, DVM
>
> Some 15 to 20 percent of animals develop a "healing episode" as a result of purification of the system brought on by purer and more nutritious food. This may manifest in such transient symptoms as diarrhea or skin sores. The body is simply expelling accumulated impurities. This situation is, in a sense, a transition to a higher state of balanced health. The frequency, intensity, and duration of such episodes is totally dependent on an individual animal's health, nutritional state, age, and breed. As long as the animal is clear-eyed, bright, and full of the energy of life, these periods (should there be any) will quickly pass. The need for medical intervention is rare. (For more details on feeding a raw diet, see Pollak's Web site at www.healthyvet.com.)

CAN YOUR DOG BE A VEGETARIAN?

Yes, it's possible, but not easy. Most veterinarians say don't do it. Dogs are meat eaters by nature. They have the tooth structure of a carnivore and do better if at least a third of their diet is meat. Best consult with a nutritionally savvy holistic veterinarian if you want to try, but ask yourself first, who are you doing it for, you or your animal?

Here's what veterinarians tell me about vegetarian dogs:

- They are missing ingredients in their food that they naturally get in the wilds.
- Their coats are dull.
- They seem to develop odd kinds of illnesses.

Carvel Tiekert, DVM, tells the story of a woman who once brought in a Newfoundland mixed breed that was a sorry sight. "The dog was saggy and baggy, head down, and depressed," he relates. "The owner thought the animal had a disease. I asked what she fed it. She had become a strict vegetarian and was feeding the dog similarly. I suggested that she feed him some meat, but she was reluctant. I then suggested some eggs. She could handle that. She returned a month later with a new dog. Eyes bright. Tail wagging. Energetic. That's all I did for the 'disease'—prescribe some animal protein."

WATER—DON'T LEAVE (YOUR DOG) HOME WITHOUT IT!

Dogs drink about ten times a day, so always have clean, fresh water available at all times, especially when the weather is hot. A dog of about forty pounds will drink about a quart of water daily. Dogs eating only dry food need more. Always consider the temperature of the water—too warm or too cold may discourage the dog from drinking. A nursing female needs more water, as does a sick dog with a fever, diarrhea, or kidney disease.

You can tell if a dog isn't drinking enough water by the stool. You will see hard, dry, foul-smelling stools. Sunken eyes and dry nose mean your dog is dehydrated. Severe dehydration can occur with fever, diarrhea, or heat stroke.

HEALTHY SNACKS ONLY

Try to find natural products. Read the labels. Avoid products with artificial coloring agents, sugar, chemical additives, and wheat flour, a nice-sounding substitute term for devitalized white flour. Whole-grain products are okay. Raw carrots make great snacks. They contain beta-carotene, which has anticancer properties, and also provide some friction to keep the plaque down on the teeth.

BONE ALERT!

Be careful with bones. In the wilds animals don't really go for the bones but will eat the gristle, cartilage, and the covering of the bones. Bones can break teeth, especially the rear teeth.

One potential problem with eating large amounts of bones is that the pieces may compact into a mass and cause blockage in the intestine. Some people recommend that bones be cooked thoroughly and then crunched into crumbs. "The problem is you can miss a piece, which can possibly cause some damage," says Nancy Scanlan, DVM. Over the years Scanlan has pried many bone splinters out of gums and intestines. With this in mind, don't feed cooked bones. And don't feed pork bones, which splinter easily. (Moreover, dogs frequently become sick from pork.)

Many people feed raw bones to their dogs without problem. The

bones should be big enough so that animals are just chewing off cartilage and scraps without splintering the bone. The knuckle end of
a big bone should be okay as long as the actual bone isn't being broken down. Another option is to ask your butcher to cut some long
beef bones into smaller "rings." Freeze them and give as a tasty
treat.

FEEDING WITH LOVE—ROGER DEHAAN, DVM

Is love a particle? A nutrient? Is food prepared with love better than one prepared
in a corporate kitchen? If the ingredients are the same, is there still a difference? I
doubt if we'll ever discover a love nutrient in a test tube, but it sure shows up in
growth, health, and repair. Without love, babies and animals die. We all know moth-
ers who cook with love. Do you add love to your pets' food? Or do you slop the food
in a dish, expecting it to be 100 percent nutritionally complete—but without your
involvement and blessing?

8

Nutritional Supplements

DOGS BENEFIT FROM many of the same nutritional supplements that we humans take—vitamins, minerals, essential fatty acids (oils), digestive enzymes, and amino acids. Holistic veterinarians routinely recommend supplements as part of their treatments and to improve the general health of their patients.

Nutritionally oriented doctors say that good health is created primarily by eating wholesome food. This helps explain why so many of us, people and animals alike, are in such poor health. We eat too much devitalized convenience food and feed our pets the same way.

Before 1990 vitamins and minerals were viewed narrowly by the medical establishment as vital elements in food that prevented certain nutritional-deficiency diseases. The mainstream attitude was that supplementation was unnecessary—and a waste of money— because a balanced diet provided you with all the good nutrition your body needed. For decades a minority of holistic physicians vociferously contradicted this notion and advocated supplements as a potent, safe, and inexpensive way to help treat illness and create optimum health.

Reality, along with scads of research, has set the record straight. Nutritionists now acknowledge that huge numbers of people fail to eat anything closely resembling a balanced diet. Moreover, much of the food reaching our tables these days is grown on soil degraded by years of intense commercial farming and agrochemicals. Many studies now show that individual nutrients at supplemental doses higher than those usually present in the diet can have a profound preventive and therapeutic impact on cancer, heart disease, and other serious illnesses.

Research has demonstrated, for instance, that vitamin E supplementation blocks arterial plaque formation and strengthens immune function. The research has validated the clinical observations of Canadian physicians Wilfrid and Evan Shute, who more than fifty years ago first discovered that vitamin E helped ailing hearts. While the medical community rejected the Shute brothers, it was their persistent reporting of positive, and often dramatic, results with patients that led to the popularity of vitamin E today. Wilfrid Shute, by the way, was an ardent breeder of Doberman Pinschers and used vitamin E to keep his dogs vital and healthy. Today many holistic veterinarians are doing the same.

Among our pets there is a crisis of health that parallels the human predicament. The mirage of the balanced diet is promoted by the pet food industry in the form of so-called complete and balanced diets. Ideally pets should get all the nutrients they need in food, but standard pet food sources are highly questionable and the end products usually low in freshness and high in additives.

The pet food industry generally offers your pet nutrient levels in their merchandise that are minimum amounts designed to maintain adequate health. But today the contamination of the environment and the chemical additives in many commercial pet diets lessen the likelihood that minimum nutrition will maintain good health.

"We need more nutrients provided by supplementation if we are to raise our animals to the level of optimum health and also sustain them through the stresses of pregnancy and disease," says Wendell Belfield, DVM, of San Jose, who has been prescribing vitamins and minerals for more than twenty-five years.

The more removed animals are from good, natural homemade diets, the more they need supplementation. But even with solid home cooking or a better commercial food, they thrive with the addition of certain supplements. Veterinarians report dramatic changes in dogs after supplementation is started. Shaggy hair coats become lustrous. Health and vitality zooms.

SUPPLEMENT GUIDELINES

What supplements should you use? The marketplace is full of products, and trying to find the right one for your pet can be confusing. Your best bet is to find a nutritionally oriented practitioner to customize an effective supplementation program for your dog based on its individual health status, age, diet, and stress level. Different conditions benefit from different supplements that require an expert's know-how. In addition, some dogs have extra nutritional requirements. For example, the breeds that originated in the northern latitudes such as the Akita and Husky tend to need more zinc.

There is another good reason to seek professional guidance: You don't want to overdo it. "I have had clients come in with shopping bags full of supplements they are giving their dogs," says Donna Starita Mehan, DVM, of Boring, Oregon. "After a while the client becomes confused because the animal may not be making progress. I will do a muscle test on an animal with these supplements and sometimes find that one or two products will do the job and the others are unnecessary, an overkill that may even be hampering progress. This is where the individualized treatment that a holistic veterinarian can offer is invaluable in fine-tuning the needs of a particular dog."

Remember this: Supplements are not meant to replace good food. Improve the diet first. Then add the proper supplements. Until you have advice from a professional for your dog's particular condition, here are some general supplement recommendations:

- **Multivitamins.** A product with a wide spectrum of nutrients fortifies the diet. In recent years an increasing number of excellent products have been formulated for pets and are available in health food and pet stores or through veterinarians. Look for a supplement containing a wide range of minerals as seabed or marine-type mineral compounds. Such minerals are typically missing from the diet.

- **Calcium.** Be cautious. Oversupplementing can cause problems as animals get older. "In large dogs, it can contribute to sore joints," says Nancy Scanlan, DVM. "The rule of thumb is to supplement if you are feeding homemade meals, and not to add calcium if you are using strictly a commercial food." The recommended dosage for toy dogs is 100 milligrams daily; small dogs, 200 milligrams; medium dogs, 300 milligrams; larger dogs, 500 milligrams. Large puppies can use 10 percent more.

- **Digestive enzymes.** Holistic veterinarians frequently recommend plant-based enzymes to optimize digestion, even for healthy dogs, and routinely prescribe them for digestive disorders. These products also aid older animals with slowing or diminished enzyme production. Digestive enzymes for pets are widely available.

- **Essential fatty acids.** Veterinarians frequently prescribe these supplements to improve the skin and combat exterior problems. There are many fatty acid products for pets on the market. If your animal is prone to inflammatory conditions such as chronic skin problems, use flaxseed oil, which is high in beneficial fatty acids. For small dogs, add 1 teaspoon of oil to the diet; medium dogs, 2 teaspoons; large dogs, 1 tablespoon; and giant breeds, up to 2 or 3 tablespoons. You will find the flaxseed oil in the refrigeration section of a health food store. Look for organic products in dark containers, as this oil is quite fragile and will break down when exposed to light and heat. Buy a small bottle. Use it up and then buy another small bottle. That way the oil will be fresh.

- **Vitamin C.** Most people don't think about this nutrient for their animals, but it is very beneficial, particularly for the skeletal growth of large-breed dogs and animals under any stress. Vitamin C levels in the body decrease with stress. Give 250 milligrams a day for small dogs and up to 1,000 milligrams daily for large dogs.

- **Vitamin E.** This is particularly useful for older dogs. Give 100 to 200 international units (IU), according to the size and condition of the animal.

HOW TO GIVE SUPPLEMENTS TO YOUR DOG

Supplements are widely available as powders, capsules, and tablets. In part 2 of this book you will find specific recommendations for products and how to administer them.

Powders are mixed directly in the food. It is always a good idea to start with a small amount and then work up slowly to the suggested level. Start low. Go slow. This gives the dog a chance to become accustomed to a new taste.

Many dogs will take a capsule or tablet directly into the mouth. For smaller animals you may need to empty the contents of the capsule or crunch up a tablet and mix into the food.

HOW TO FIND A NUTRITIONALLY ORIENTED VETERINARIAN

Contact the American Holistic Veterinary Medical Association, 2214 Old Emmorton Rd., Bel Air, MD 21015 (phone: 410-569-0795). If you have Internet access, use the directory of veterinarians on the alternative veterinary medicine Web site at www.altvetmed.com.

9

Herbs

MEDICINAL HERBS HAVE been used since time immemorial for healing purposes. In recent years medical research and clinical usage of herbs have soared as modern science validates many of the traditional applications and explores new ones. Today herbal supplements are riding high atop a huge consumer wave of interest in natural healing.

Experts say the natural compounds in herbs—called phytochemicals—may offer the best protection we know of against the diseases that plague society. There is much yet to learn about the tissue-specific way these compounds work. But in time they are expected to play a major role in antiaging medicine and how we prevent and treat disease.

HOW TO GIVE HERBS TO YOUR DOG

- Use whichever form of a recommended herb is easiest for you to administer. Herbs are available as tablets, capsules, and liquid tinctures.
- Herbs are best given apart from a meal. Most are absorbed better this way. However, medicinal herbs often have a bitter or unpleasant taste. It is okay to mix them into food if that is the only way your pet will take them.
- Some herbs have the potential to cause slight nausea. If there are signs of that, or an animal loses appetite when on herbs, administer on a full stomach.

- Unless you are knowledgeable about herbs, be very careful when mixing herbs. Stick to tried-and-true formulas.

HERBAL DOSAGES

In part 2 you will find many herbal recommendations among the natural remedies offered by veterinarians. The recommendations include Chinese herbs, Ayurvedic herbs from India, South American herbs, and North American herbs. Each recommendation includes directions on how to dose the herb and where to get the specific herbal product used by the veterinarian. Be sure to follow the instructions. In the current boom of interest in holistic health, people are jumping on the herbal bandwagon. However, it is advisable to be cautious when giving herbs to pets. Even though herbs are natural and can do a lot of good, there is still potential for harm if they are given inappropriately or excessively.

There are no precise doses for animals. Many veterinarians extrapolate their dosage from human usage. Generally speaking, if a human takes a whole capsule for a particular herb, then give a small dog a quarter capsule and a medium or large dog a half. For herbal tinctures, use considerably less than the capsule or tablet form. In a dog, 4 to 8 drops twice a day should suffice.

Start with a small amount and work up slowly to avoid the possibility of stomach upset. Decrease or increase the dose depending on the size of the animal. Many times a low dose is enough and you don't have to go higher. An animal will resonate with the frequency of the herb, or the herb just isn't giving the animal what it needs. Giving more doesn't necessarily enhance the effect. Herbs heal by their frequency, not necessarily by their quantity.

THE "HEALING CRISIS"—MARK HAVERKOS, DVM

Herbs are capable of creating powerful healing effects in the body and may trigger a "healing crisis." This term, used by holistic healers, refers to a wave of purification generated by the natural medicine. Unlike conventional drugs, which suppress symptoms, herbs activate and fortify the body, like recharging a battery, helping it to cleanse itself of toxins and pathogens. In this process symptoms may temporarily intensify as a result. Things may get worse before they get better. It is then advisable to back off from the herb and let the body do the job it has now been activated to do. Improvement usually follows. You can then resume the remedy at the same or lesser level, depending on the situation. However, if the animal doesn't get better when the remedy is stopped, then you should seek professional advice, preferably with a holistic veterinarian familiar with herbs.

HOW TO FIND A VETERINARIAN WHO USES HERBS

Contact the American Holistic Veterinary Medical Association, 2214 Old Emmorton Rd., Bel Air, MD 21015 (phone: 410-569-0795). If you have Internet access, use the directory of veterinarians on the alternative veterinary medicine Web site at www.altvetmed.com.

❦ 1 0 ❦

Homeopathic Remedies

HOMEOPATHY, A POPULAR form of natural healing throughout the world, is rapidly gaining adherents in North America among health-conscious individuals interested in helping themselves and their pets as well. Serving these animals are several hundred veterinarians who use homeopathic remedies exclusively, or along with other treatment techniques, for problems ranging from trauma to chronic diseases. The veterinarians say that just about every condition encountered in a general practice can be treated wholly or in part with homeopathy. Often the animals they see have undergone conventional treatment that hasn't worked or has caused too many side effects. Homeopathy offers a safe alternative. It is also an excellent complement to surgery and is frequently used to reduce postsurgical pain and accelerate the healing process.

Ideally, homeopathic veterinarians like to see animals treated homeopathically from early on. "Pets cared for this way live long, healthy lives and do not develop as many nagging health problems or serious illnesses," says Christina Chambreau, DVM. "Also, many breed-related problems can be prevented. At the end of their lives, these animals tend to die from a very short-term illness. As far as treating disease is concerned, homeopathy doesn't just relieve symptoms. It can restore health!"

In part 2 of this book you will find many recommendations for homeopathic remedies that you can safely use on your animal.

These natural medicines are available at health food stores, pharmacies, and holistic pet stores.

HOW HOMEOPATHIC REMEDIES WORK

Homeopathy utilizes remedies made from diluted amounts of natural substances—such as herbs, bark, seeds, berries, minerals, and animal matter. The remedies activate the body's own healing mechanisms according to a principle known as "like cures like." It works this way: If you were to give these substances in large doses to healthy individuals or animals, they would produce the same symptoms that they help heal when given in diluted homeopathic doses.

Two examples will help illustrate the point. A large amount of coffee can cause nervousness and prevent sleep. In homeopathy, a remedy made from coffee is used to calm the nerves and help promote sleep. Sulfur, in a large dose, can cause a rash. In homeopathic amounts, it helps heal rashes and skin problems and is a popular remedy for those conditions in animals.

Homeopathic remedies are so diluted that there is virtually no trace of the original substance. For this reason they are not toxic. Homeopathy works as an "energy medicine." The healing power comes not from the substances themselves, but from matching the energy vibration of a specific remedy to the energy pattern of the patient.

"Homeopathic remedies provide information to the body," says John Limehouse, DVM, of North Hollywood, California. "Imagine those card keys that open your hotel room. The right information on that magnetic strip will open the door. Similarly, homeopathic remedies contain magnetic resonance information. The right remedy contains the right information to stimulate the body's vital forces to do the work of healing, repair, and maintenance in a more efficient way."

How do homeopathic medicines compare to pharmaceutical drugs?

Powerful pharmaceutical drugs suppress symptoms and potentially lower the health status of the body by driving the disease deeper. Instead of suppressing symptoms, the correctly prescribed homeopathic remedy will safely, gently, and permanently elevate the health of the body.

WHAT A HOMEOPATHIC VETERINARIAN DOES

Conventional veterinarians typically prescribe cortisone or a non-steroidal anti-inflammatory drug to a dog with a painful arthritic joint. The drug is meant to stop the inflammation—that is, treat the symptom. But in the process it often creates side effects and new symptoms. Frequently a second drug is prescribed to prevent the side effects of the first drug. Moreover, the underlying cause of the inflammation is not addressed in this approach. When the drug is discontinued, the original symptoms return.

Homeopathic veterinarians treat the whole animal and not just a single symptom or disease. They prescribe specific remedies based on a variety of details, such as the color of a discharge, an animal's behavior and need for companionship or solitude, how it reacts to pain, when the pain is worse, or factors that aggravate an illness.

"We seek clues to give us the right homeopathic remedy," explains Charles Loops, DVM, of Pittsboro, North Carolina. "If you select the correct remedy, not only do the symptoms of pain and inflammation go away in the case of arthritis, for instance, but the animal is likely to be more energetic and feel better overall. Usually, if there is not a lot of tissue damage, you need to give the remedy for only a short period of time and then go months or even years without having to use it again. Compare this to a drug that you have to use continually, running the risk of side effects and negative changes to the physiology. Basically, with homeopathy there are no side effects, only side benefits."

Homeopathic veterinarians typically prescribe a remedy or series of remedies with a single ingredient. Over-the-counter homeopathic remedies include single remedies as well as user-friendly combination formulas for people with little knowledge of homeopathy. Such combinations include products for pets that have multiple ingredients to cover such problems as flea bite allergic reactions, scratching, stress, motion sickness, and diarrhea. If you find that a combination does not help, it should be discontinued and the right single remedy found.

To effectively deal homeopathically with serious disorders, it is advisable to consult with a knowledgeable veterinarian. That's because it often takes skilled detective work to sort out the clues and select correct remedies. "Many conditions are aggravated by multiple, confusing factors, such as poor nutrition, vaccinations, and conventional drugs that suppress symptoms to begin with," says Joseph Demers, DVM. In addition, expertise is often needed to prescribe different remedies or potencies for changing conditions and symptoms.

Homeopathic specialists emphasize the importance of good nutrition and say that true healing is difficult without it no matter how many remedies they prescribe. Some degree of illness is always going to be present unless an animal has a good nutritional basis.

Homeopaths also advise that it is best not to resort to quick-fix pharmaceutical treatments of a symptom while using a homeopathic remedy because you will not know if an animal is improving or not.

UNDERSTANDING HOMEOPATHIC POTENCIES

Homeopathic remedies are identified by a name and number, such as Arnica 6X or 30C. The number tells you the potency—that is, the strength—of the particular remedy.

Homeopathic medicines are created by a special process of consecutive dilutions in distilled water followed by succussion (vigorous shaking). X potencies refer to substances diluted 1 part to 9 parts of water. The designation 6X means the remedy was diluted and shaken 6 times. C potencies mean a substance has been diluted 1 part to 99 parts water. Thus, 30C means a remedy that underwent thirty rounds of dilution and shaking.

This process is called "potentization." The more a substance is potentized—that is diluted and shaken—the longer and more deeply the remedy acts in the body and the fewer doses are required for treatment.

Stores generally carry potencies of 30C or less. Higher potencies should be used cautiously and, ideally, under the guidance of a professional. That's because higher potencies are more likely to trigger what is called a "healing crisis," in which symptoms may at first appear aggravated before they improve.

HOW TO GIVE HOMEOPATHIC REMEDIES TO YOUR DOG

Remedies come in several forms—liquid, pellets, and hard and soft tablets. There is no difference in effectiveness.

To give liquid remedies: Pull the lower cheek away from your dog's teeth. Using the dropper from the bottle, apply drops into the space between the gums and teeth. Do not touch the dropper to the skin or gum tissue. If you do, wash it afterward with boiling water before reusing. Liquid remedies contain a small amount of alcohol, which veterinary homeopaths say is not a problem, even for smaller animals. Occasionally the alcohol may cause a dog to foam at the mouth. If this happens, dilute the remedy until there is no foaming. Because this is an energy medicine, such dilution does not alter the effectiveness.

To give pellets and hard tablets: Spill out the pellets or tablets from the container onto a piece of white paper or an index card. Fold paper repeatedly and then crush the pellets/tablets with the back of a spoon or a glass. Sprinkle the powder into the front of your animal's mouth or into the space between the gums and teeth.

To give soft tablets: These tablets dissolve readily and do not need to be crushed. Simply place into the mouth.

HOMEOPATHIC DOSAGES

The quantity of the remedy you administer is the same regardless of the size of your dog. Give enough so that you are sure some of the remedy goes into the mouth and becomes absorbed. A general rule of thumb is several tablets, or 3 to 5 tiny pellets, or half a dropperful of liquid.

When giving remedies on a regular basis, continually evaluate how your dog is doing. Keep a record of symptoms. If most symptoms become worse, or your animal is not feeling happier and more active, then the remedies aren't working. This is the time to consult with an experienced homeopath. A onetime single dose should always be administered directly into the mouth. For repeated doses, the remedy can be dissolved in drinking water, if it is not easy to give by mouth.

It is best, especially for single doses, to not give the remedy within an hour before or after feeding.

Unless you are being guided by a specialist, don't give the same remedy on a daily basis for more than about two weeks. Constant administration of a remedy can create the symptoms or toxic effects you are attempting to counteract.

FOR MORE INFORMATION ON HOMEOPATHY

- *The Consumer's Guide to Homeopathy*, by Dana Ullman (Tarcher-Putnam), an excellent introduction to homeopathic healing. For this and other books, contact Ullman's Homeopathic Educational Services, 2124 Kittredge St., Berkeley, CA 94704 (phone: 510-649-0294).

- The following books from England, also available through the Homeopathic Educational Services, offer specific information about homeopathy and companion animals:
  The Homeopathic Treatment of Small Animals by Christopher Day.
  Dogs: Homeopathic Remedies, by George MacLeod.
  The Treatment of Dogs by Homeopathy, by K. Sheppard.

- Write to Christina Chambreau, DVM, 908 Cold Bottom Rd., Sparks, MD, 21152, for information on homeopathy seminars for pet owners.

HOW TO FIND A VETERINARY HOMEOPATH

Contact the Academy of Veterinary Homeopathy, 751 N.E. 168th St., N. Miami, FL 33162-2427 (phone: 305-652-5372).

Contact the American Holistic Veterinary Medical Association, 2214 Old Emmorton Rd., Bel Air, MD 21015 (phone: 410-569-0795). If you have Internet access, use the directory of veterinarians on the alternative veterinary medicine Web site at www.altvetmed.com.

₩ 11 ₩

Flower Essences—Healing the Emotions

IF YOU BELIEVE in the mind-body connection, you're going to love flower essences. This unique healing system was developed by an English physician, Edward Bach. During the 1930s he discovered that many of the nonpoisonous wild plants, bushes, and trees in the English countryside exerted genuine therapeutic effects on the emotions, which in turn promoted physical balance in the body. He believed that by thus correcting emotional dysfunction, you could help heal physical dysfunction.

Bach identified and developed applications for thirty-eight individual English flower essences plus the well-known five-flower combination called Rescue Remedy. Since his time many more flower essences have been added. Today there is even a whole new breed of products called "nature essences" that work on the same principle and are prepared from gems, minerals, and animal matter. The original essences, as well as the newer additions, are available at most health food stores and come in a liquid form.

Each individual remedy relates to a specific mental and emotional state. Bach once declared that disease is a kind of consolidation of a mental attitude...and that behind all disease lies our fears, our anxieties, our greed, our likes and dislikes.

Flower remedies have been most widely used for humans, where stressful and negative emotional states are known to weaken the immune system and contribute to the disease process. Veterinarians, too, have been using and prescribing these essences for many years and in increasing numbers find them highly beneficial to help heal the emotional and physical ills of animals.

Jean Hofve, DVM, of Sacramento, has extensively studied and used flower essences for many species of animals. "They often bring remarkable results in cats, dogs, horses, and wildlife," she says. "We know that in humans, mental and emotional upset can have deep and lasting physical effects, far beyond what used to be referred to as 'psychosomatic illness.' Animals, too, have an active mental and emotional life. They can similarly manifest not only behavioral but physical problems that have their roots in emotional trauma."

Writing in *Complementary and Alternative Veterinary Medicine* (Mosby, 1998), Stephen Blake, DVM, of San Diego, points out that he has used flower remedies effectively for more than ten years. "Most pet owners and veterinarians would agree that behavioral problems are a major concern," says Blake. "They often accompany or precede physical disease as well. The dramatic positive changes in the animals' behavior demonstrates the effectiveness of the noninvasive way the remedies work…[to] alleviate the emotional stresses in veterinary patients."

HOW FLOWER ESSENCES WORK

Flower essences basically correct a negative emotional state by "flooding" the patient with the opposite, positive quality that is the particular essence of that flower. For instance, the essence of the flower Holly is love. Therefore you would use Holly in situations where there is a lack of love, as in times of jealousy, anger, or hatred. Rock Rose, another essence, holds the quality of courage and is used in times of deep fears, panic, and terror.

With flower remedies you aren't treating specific behavior. You are working on a subtle emotional level instead, trying to create a new mental state that is peaceful and happy. Hofve says that while flower essences can be used for physical conditions, she believes their greatest application is to help correct behavioral problems, many of which are based on emotional or mental disturbances. She has found that these remedies work between 70 and 100 percent of the time.

Flower remedies are generally considered an "energy medicine," as are homeopathic remedies. Essences, however, are not prepared in the same way as homeopathics. Part of the essence processing, for instance, involves infusion of the liquid extract with sunlight.

Experts say flower remedies enhance the effectiveness of any form of medicine, conventional or alternative, without any interference. They cannot be overused or misused, and if you administer the wrong remedy, it will simply not have any effect. Essences are safe and nontoxic.

In part 2 of this book you will find a number of recommendations from veterinarians for behavioral problems. If you do not have a successful result, seek out a veterinarian knowledgeable in the method.

HOW TO GIVE LIQUID FLOWER ESSENCES TO YOUR DOG

1. **By mouth.** The liquid doesn't need to be swallowed. It is enough just for the liquid to contact the mucous membranes of the gums or tongue. Try not to contaminate the dropper by touching it to the animal. In case this occurs, rinse the dropper in boiling water before returning it to the bottle.

2. **Applied topically,** usually around the head and ears. You can even put a few drops in your hand and pat your dog on the head.

3. **Added to wet food or water.** There is no loss of potency from dilution.

4. **Add a dropperful to a spray bottle filled with spring water.** Spray rooms, carriers, cars, houses, trailers, or stalls.

FLOWER ESSENCE DOSAGES

Generally you give from 4 to 8 drops at a time. For most behavioral problems, give three to four times a day for two to four weeks. If the response is adequate by then, you can decrease the frequency.

In crisis situations, such as the loss of a loved one, a tornado, or some sudden fearful event, the remedy can be given as often as needed, even every few minutes. For chronic behavioral problems, such as dogs not getting along well, you may need to add a dropperful to the drinking water or give one or more times a day longterm. The speed of response generally depends on the condition and how long it has been present. Usually you should notice a change within two weeks.

FOR MORE INFORMATION ON FLOWER ESSENCES

- Additional remedy options and instructions on how to mix your own combinations are found in an Internet article by Hofve at the Critter Chat on-line newsletter at www.critterhaven.org/critterchat/bach.htm, or visit her Web site at www.spiritessence.com.

- Flower Essence Society, P.O. Box 459, Nevada City, CA 95959. Phone: 800-736-9222 or 530-265-9163. Web site: www.flowersociety.org.

- Nelson Bach USA, 100 Research Dr., Wilmington, MA 01887. Phone: 978-988-3833 for information; 800-314-BACH for orders. Web site: www.bachcentre.com/.

HOW TO FIND A VETERINARIAN USING FLOWER ESSENCES

Contact the American Holistic Veterinary Medical Association, 2214 Old Emmorton Rd., Bel Air, MD 21015 (phone: 410-569-0795). If you have Internet access, use the directory of veterinarians on the alternative veterinary medicine Web site at www.altvetmed.com.

☘ 12 ☘

Veterinary Acupuncture

THE YEAR WAS 1981 and the dog was an eleven-year-old Black Labrador with severe arthritis of the elbows, hips, and back. The owner had brought the dog to veterinarian Allen Schoen's clinic in Sherman, Connecticut, to be euthanized. All the standard options available at the time had worked temporarily. Now the dog was unable to walk, was crying in pain, and could not sleep through the night.

"I was just about to attend an intensive introductory course in acupuncture and felt that possibly the knowledge I would gain might be able to help the animal," recalls Schoen. "I certainly couldn't claim to be an acupuncturist after the course, but I suggested to the owner that we give another injection of cortisone to buy a few days' time and then see if I could help the animal. There was nothing to lose. Amazingly, the dog responded to the treatments and after six sessions was up and about and playing. The dog lived another three years, in fact. When your first case works so well, you get very excited about a new method."

Schoen went on to become a certified veterinary acupuncturist and joined a growing society of animal doctors trained in this amazing and ancient Chinese healing art. Today he also teaches the widely accepted technique at veterinary medical schools.

WHAT IS ACUPUNCTURE?

Acupuncture is based on the concept of *qi* (pronounced "chee"), which loosely means "energy," and its effect on how well the body functions.

In an acupuncture treatment session, needles, with or without microelectrical currents attached, are inserted at specific bodily locations along meridians of energy. The needles stimulate sensory nerve endings that send impulses up through the spinal cord to the different areas of the brain, causing both local- and central-acting effects. By stimulating these points, acupuncturists seek to restore normal energy flow and in the process stimulate the body's ability to heal itself. On the local level, the technique relieves muscle spasm and increases circulation. Systemically it causes release of different neurotransmitters and hormones throughout the body.

Veterinarians trained in acupuncture say their technique puts an animal's energy back in balance whether they are treating a kidney, liver, pancreas, or arthritic condition.

You may be wondering whether it is painful for dogs to be stuck with needles, and will they sit quietly for it. Pet owners always ask those questions before their animal receives a first treatment. Well, the experts say, you can relax. Dogs normally don't mind it.

When an acupuncture needle is inserted, it pushes tissue out of the way, causing very little, if any, discomfort. This is due in part to specially designed fine wire needles that have no edges. The needle literally slips into holes that lead to the actual acupuncture point. When a needle reaches the correct depth it may produce a feeling like a dull ache or pressure. And relief. "Pets become so acclimated to treatments and so relieved by the effects that they often fall asleep after the first few visits," says Thomas Van Cise, DVM, of Norco, California.

Veterinary acupuncturists say that occasionally they encounter an overanxious pet and in such cases are usually able to calm the animal, and proceed with the treatment, by using natural relaxants such as flower essences, homeopathics, or herbs.

HOW ACUPUNCTURE CAN HELP YOUR DOG

The kind of remarkable results Dr. Schoen witnessed in his very first case using acupuncture is experienced daily and routinely by other practitioners. They find they frequently are able to enhance the quality of life—and even extend life—for cases where other veterinarians have nothing more to offer.

"Much of my acupuncture activity is spent on serious, chronic internal problems, such as liver and kidney failure, and chronic colitis," says Joseph Demers, DVM, of Melbourne, Florida. "These are cases where pet owners are often given the sole option of when to put the animal to sleep. With acupuncture, we can improve the function of the kidneys, for example, and sometimes extend the lifetimes of animals a year or more."

Acupuncture can help in many cases of nongenetic hearing loss that often occurs in geriatric dogs. "I can usually restore about 50 percent of the hearing with four to ten treatments," says Lynne Friday, DVM.

Acupuncture is clearly not just for people alone. It renders wonderful relief and curative benefits for numerous canine conditions that do not respond well to customary treatments. It works for many acute and chronic disorders and pain conditions and also is a powerful tool for preventive health care and maintenance.

Acupuncture can often eliminate the need for surgery. For instance, it is helpful for large dogs who develop anterior crucial problems. This is where one of the two ligaments that crosses the knee tears or partially tears. It is fairly common among overweight or very active animals. The sign of such an injury is sudden limping on one hind leg. Surgery is typically used for this knee problem; however, acupuncture can often substitute for surgery. It stops the pain and promotes healing.

The following situations are the most responsive to acupuncture:

- **Pain relief.** Some veterinarians say it is the best pain reliever of all the alternative therapies, especially for chronic pain.
- **Relief of musculoskeletal problems,** such as arthritis, disc disorders, lameness, and stiff backs in older dogs. Experienced

acupuncturists say they can effectively help more than three-quarters of the cases they treat.

- **Certain neurological problems,** such as hindquarter weakness, partial paralysis, and epilepsy.
- **Gastrointestinal disorders,** such as chronic vomiting and diarrhea.
- **Immune system enhancement.**
- **Postponement of surgery in high-risk cases.** Acupuncture can help patients gain strength.
- **Postsurgical promotion of healing.** After an operation, some animals will have lingering pain or discomfort at the site of surgery and start chewing or licking the spot. Acupuncture can often stop it. After surgery involving the legs, animals will sometimes have trouble walking. Acupuncture can help restore full motion.

HOW MANY TREATMENTS ARE CUSTOMARY?

Individual acupuncture sessions last anywhere from a few seconds up to an hour. Your pet's condition and response determine the number and frequency of office visits required. Each veterinarian acupuncturist I spoke to has his or her favorite story of a dog who hadn't been walking for months and after one treatment got right up and walked out. In general, the longer a problem has existed, and the more serious it is, the greater the number of treatments necessary. Some severe cases may respond dramatically to one treatment, while others that seem to be quite mild may require several treatments. Sometimes the results of a single treatment are long-lasting. Other times a series of treatments is necessary for a long-lasting effect. No two cases are the same.

HOW TO FIND A VETERINARY ACUPUNCTURIST

Contact the International Veterinary Acupuncture Society, P.O. Box 1478, Longmont, CO 80502 (phone: 303-449-7936).

Contact the American Holistic Veterinary Medical Association, 2214 Old Emmorton Rd., Bel Air, MD 21015 (phone: 410-569-0795).

If you have Internet access, use the directory of veterinarians on the alternative veterinary medicine Web site at www.altvetmed.com.

Veterinary Chiropractic

CHIROPRACTIC FOR DOGS? A resounding *yes!*

In recent years many holistic veterinarians have become trained in chiropractic methods and apply them therapeutically for many conditions, either as a primary or a supportive treatment.

WHAT IS CHIROPRACTIC?

Most people think of chiropractic as a natural method for effective relief of back pain. However, chiropractic offers much, much more—not just for humans, but for pets as well. It involves a system of locating spinal and joint misalignments throughout the body and "adjusting" them through a series of treatments that reduce the stressful impact on the nervous system and organs. Such misalignments pinch nerves and cause pain as well as disturbances to normal behavioral and physical functioning. Misalignments commonly occur from injury, birth trauma, and wear and tear of the body. They can also result from malnutrition and toxicity, often present to some degree in chronic diseases. Thus, in many cases of prolonged illness, an undiagnosed misalignment may be present that is contributing to the problem.

Without chiropractic evaluation, such misalignments may never be diagnosed and may produce a lifetime of suffering. The aim of chiropractic is to restore the normal structural alignment of the body so that energy flows better and moving parts work more optimally.

"I use chiropractic to get animals to feel better and give them more ease and flexibility," says Mark Haverkos, DVM, of Oldenburg, Indiana. "When they feel better, they function better. I often see immediate results after an adjustment—dogs walking differently, stretching out, shaking, and wagging their tails. Often the owner will stand there and say, 'I haven't seen my dog do that in years.'"

Veterinary chiropractors sometimes combine chiropractic with acupuncture. They use the acupuncture first to relax the muscles of an animal, after which it is possible to make more effective realignments.

HOW CHIROPRACTIC CAN HELP YOUR DOG

Veterinarians use chiropractic techniques most typically to treat dogs for musculoskeletal problems stemming from hip dysplasia, arthritic changes, and injury. Dogs hit by cars, for instance, may suffer joint misalignments in addition to more obvious effects of trauma such as bone fractures or lacerations. Even the constant tugging on a leash can create a problem in the spine that may benefit from chiropractic treatment.

Chiropractic benefits older animals with joint stiffness and problems in the back, the result of a lifetime of minor trauma from jumping and running. Such small injuries are not apparent at the time they occur, but they add up and may eventually slow an animal down.

Many dogs suffer from slight misalignments undetected by X-rays. Though subtle, they have the potential at any time in life to upset the normal biomechanics of motion and cause inflammation and degeneration of tissue. These situations are often resolved by gentle chiropractic adjustments. Lameness, for which the cause has not been found, is an example. Either the hips or the forelegs may be involved. Frequently the pet owner believes the cause is arthritis, yet X-rays are negative. The problem instead may stem from a nerve impingement from a spinal or joint misalignment that develops pain or reduces nerve supply to a leg, similar to sciatica in humans.

Veterinarians are often able to relieve the so-called Beagle neck syndrome with chiropractic adjustments. With their heads continually to the ground during intense hunting activity, Beagles and other hunting animals stub their noses so many times that they frequently develop traumatic misalignments in the cervical spine (neck). As a result, they may not be able to raise their necks without pain.

Behavioral problems have many causes. Among the most overlooked are misalignments in the skull bones. The skull is not one solid piece of bone. Rather, it comprises plates that actually move, akin to the way the geological plates in the earth move. When you breathe in and out, for instance, the skull bones shift microscopically. Head or neck trauma can cause the bones to lock along the suture lines—the fault lines, so to speak—that separate the plates. Inadequate prenatal nutrition and difficult delivery can also cause misaligned cranial bones. Whatever the cause, the resultant loss of movement can create neurological disturbances, stress, abnormal function, and symptoms. This is a hugely overlooked source of problems.

Roger DeHaan, DVM, has found that about 30 to 50 percent of the behavioral cases he sees involve misalignments of the skull bones. "There is a jamming or pinching of the cranial plates, which can lead to headaches, irritability, hyperactivity, or depression," he says. "I have dramatic, and sometimes instant, success in many of these cases using chiropractic cranial adjustments."

Many dogs with epileptic seizures who do not respond well to standard anticonvulsant drugs may have a misalignment of the first vertebra in the neck. A misalignment there can exert an array of adverse effects on the nervous system, including seizures. Adjustments often improve the control of the condition and may even stop the seizures. This type of problem usually requires multiple treatments and regular maintenance because there is so much movement in the neck bones, which heightens the potential for a misalignment to recur.

HOW MANY TREATMENTS ARE CUSTOMARY?

Ron Carsten, DVM, recalls the dramatic case of a six-year-old Labrador who had been lame in a foreleg for about nine months. On examination, the veterinarian determined the presence of a misalignment in the shoulder and adjusted the joint. The owner left with the dog and then returned excitedly a few moments later. "She said she couldn't believe what had happened," Carsten says. "The dog had jumped up into the back of her pickup truck, something he hadn't done since the problem started."

Dramatic success after one treatment, of course, doesn't happen in every case. The number of treatments depends on the condition. However, veterinary chiropractors say they are often able to restore normal alignment in situations like this with three or four sessions, sometimes even fewer.

HOW TO TELL IF YOUR DOG CAN BENEFIT FROM CHIROPRACTIC TREATMENT

Misalignments can occur at any time in a dog's life and cause a variety of problems. For minor misalignments of the extremities you can often easily correct the problem yourself. For instance, if a dog has just jammed a toe, it can be corrected by jiggling the joint just as if it had happened to your toe. Use the same kind of tension. Many times the joint will snap right back in place. If you have an animal that is supersensitive about one particular toe when it is getting its nails trimmed, the problem could be a jammed digit. That could also be the case when an animal chews at one toenail and there is no infection or broken nail there. Again, just try jiggling it gently and you may hear it snap back.

Misalignments of the head, ribs, or spinal column call for a proper evaluation and treatment by a veterinarian trained in chiropractic. Lynne Friday, DVM, offers the following checklist to help you tell if your dog is affected:

The neck may be misaligned if:

- The head is cocked to one side or the other.
- The dog is reluctant to raise its head or flex the neck without crying.

The jaw may be misaligned if:

- A pup becomes cranky and appears uncomfortable when nursing.
- There is sudden behavioral change, particularly after the dog has undergone teeth cleaning, oral surgery, or has been intubated.

- There is shaking of the head or scratching of the face or ear, especially on one side. This could also be a sign of cranial misalignment.
- Seizures occur and medication does not help.
- The mouth is sore when you try to open it.
- The dog is reluctant to chew its biscuits or chew sticks.
- The dog has a distressed look or is acting depressed. The head may be down. This could indicate a headache. If you are sensitive to your pet, you can tell there is pain by looking in the eyes.

The ribs, thoracic (upper back) vertebrae, or breastbone may be misaligned if:

- The dog walks almost on its tiptoes, as if walking on high heels. You can confirm this if you lift the animal with your hands under the chest and it cries out.

A spinal misalignment in the lower back may be involved if:

- The dog walks like a camel, with its back humped. This is called "splinting," an effort to hold itself together to take away pressure from the spinal cord as it stretches out. The dog is guarding its lower back.
- The dog cries when it sits and acts as though it is sitting on a cactus.

The pelvis or hip may be out of line if:

- The animal sits off to one side.

HOW TO FIND A VETERINARY CHIROPRACTOR

Contact the American Veterinary Chiropractic Association, 623 Main St., Hillsdale, IL 61257 (phone: 309-658-2920).

Contact the American Holistic Veterinary Medical Association, 2214 Old Emmorton Rd., Bel Air, MD 21015 (phone: 410-569-0795). If you have Internet access, use the directory of veterinarians on the alternative veterinary medicine Web site at www.altvetmed.com.

⚜ 14 ⚜

Massage Techniques

This CHAPTER INTRODUCES four gentle hands-on techniques you can do on your own that generate healing energy and improve the physical health of your dog. The importance of human contact cannot be overemphasized. Petting and stroking keep you connected to your dog, creating an interchange of love and energy benefiting both you and your animal companion. Massages are a good way to take physical contact to a level of healing. If, through your massage activity, you detect a growth or area of extreme sensitivity or pain to your dog, be sure to bring it to your veterinarian's attention.

The Daily Health Massage—Norman Ralston, DVM
Start with gentle stroking of the ears in a circular, clockwise fashion. As you gently massage the ears, which are rich in acupuncture points, you are in a sense stimulating or treating every major organ in the body. You are sending a minute electrical impulse to each organ. Near the base of the ear is located the thermostat of the body. By massaging here, we also increase the temperature of the body. You can experience this by rubbing your own ears.

Once you have raised the energy by massaging the ears, gently stroke the animal from head to tail to direct the energy flow. Do this daily for a house pet, if possible. Often when a problem is developing, a sensitivity will appear in an associated acupoint or meridian, sometimes twenty-four hours before symptoms show up. By understanding this and being aware that your pet has suddenly developed a sensitivity at a given point, you can, through gentle massage, cause the energy to flow to the part and stimulate healing before a major problem arises.

Massage for Back Pain and Stiffness—Nancy Scanlan, DVM

This light touch massage covers various acupuncture points on the body and acts in a sense as a very mild acupuncture treatment, releasing spasm and possible trigger points. For dogs with pain and stiffness in the back, this massage generates more limberness.

Make small circles with two fingers of both hands, starting at the base of the ears, and slowly work your way down along both sides of the spine. Make two or three circles on the skin at each spot as you move down just to the right and the left of the spine, along the big muscles. Don't exert a lot of pressure and push on the muscles. Be delicate. You just want to move the skin over the muscles with a light touch. As time goes on a bigger dog may enjoy a deep massage. But always start light, so the muscles will relax. If you start massaging too hard, the muscles tense up, and the dog will want to get away, because it is painful.

Massage gently in this light touch manner down to the base of the tail and then back up again. If you hit a point where you notice an actual release of heat, that is an area of muscle spasm that has just relaxed. If you encounter this phenomenon, concentrate on the area. It will feel as if you have been on a heating pad at that spot.

Spinal and Disc Massages—Roger DeHaan, DVM

A gentle massage of the muscles along the spine helps work out tension and increase blood flow for dogs with arthritis, mild disc problems, or injuries and also serves as a general massage. The technique is simple and involves kneading or massaging the muscles in small clockwise circles. This puts energy into the body.

To massage trouble spots along the spine, run the palm of your hand slowly just over the surface of the coat. Move your hand from front to the rear, from the shoulder to the tailbone. Do this several times. Quietly notice if some areas give off an increase in heat. Any animal who has arthritis or trouble walking will give off more heat in certain spots. Those are areas of spasm or tension. You will be surprised how easy it is to feel the areas of heat. If you don't detect any heat, move your hand higher to about one to two inches above the body and again slowly move it from front to rear. Now you are attempting to detect radiant heat that may be emanating from the animal.

A second technique I call "the 4–4–4 rule" will help generate relief for any animal with mild disc and lumbar problems. Check with your veterinarian to be sure that there are no contraindications.

Hold the middle of the tail with your strong hand. Use the other hand for leverage, and hold on to the shoulder. Now *gently* tug on the tail for four seconds, as if it were a rope and you were pulling it away from the animal's body. Apply very mild pressure, the equivalent of pressing a bathroom scale to read one or two pounds. Then release the pressure for four seconds.

Do the maneuver a total of four times, increasing the traction *slightly* each time. Sometimes you will hear a pop, even in the tail, when a misalignment goes back into place. When doing this procedure, never apply too much pressure and never jerk the tail. If the animal doesn't like it, don't do it. Most like it, however.

All the vertebrae that run down the spine are connected, like a rope. This simple action opens microspaces along the length of the spine, allowing a bit more room for blood vessels and nerves that might otherwise be pinched. If there is a disc problem, it will create more space for the disc to return gradually to its normal position.

Use this technique until the animal improves. I generally recommend it daily for a week, then two or three times for two weeks, and then as needed.

The Antianxiety Massage—Pamela Wood-Krzeminski, DVM

A simple method for calming anxiety or aggressive behavior is to massage an acupressure point on the head. If you have an acupuncture chart handy, it is point GV20. Specifically, it is located in the central indentation on the top of the skull that runs from front to back and just forward of a make-believe line connecting the ears. This is considered an energizing point for the front of the body.

Massage the point daily for thirty seconds to a minute in a clockwise direction. This has been shown in many cases to calm a nervous or aggressive animal. If you do this with an aggressive animal, just make sure you don't run the risk of getting bitten.

⚜ 15 ⚜

The Vaccination Question—
How Often, How Much?

IDEAS COME. IDEAS GO. Now, in the going stage, is a hallowed concept of veterinary medicine—annual vaccinations. In recent years a steady stream of evidence from leading researchers has challenged the effectiveness and scientific validity of the practice. Experts say that almost without exception there is no requirement for annual boosters. Immunity to viruses persists for years or for the life of the animal, and successful vaccination to most bacterial pathogens produces long-term protection as well. While defending the critical role that vaccines play in preventing, controlling, and eliminating diseases in dogs and cats, prominent researchers say that the goal of the veterinary profession should be to vaccinate more animals but vaccinate them less often and only with the products that the animal needs.

Based on current findings, a new generation of vaccination guidelines has emerged. At the time of the writing of this book, the new thinking is this:

- For the most clinically important vaccines, the duration of immunity is at least three years and probably more than five.
- Vaccinations for young dogs should be spaced out over two to four weeks. Thus, vaccinations should be split up and fewer done at one time.
- Give an annual booster at one year and then boosters every three years unless required more often by law. (In some states

and municipalities, rabies vaccines are required. Check with your animal control authority for local regulations, as well as when traveling out of state.)
- Monitor antibody levels annually between boosters.
- Older animals usually do not require boosters.

WHAT VETERINARIANS DON'T TELL YOU ABOUT VACCINATIONS

Alternative practitioners have long criticized standard vaccination practices as the source of much woe among companion animals. Many adverse reactions, allergies, and illnesses are triggered by vaccines, they say. Even though the new guidelines represent a paradigm shift for the profession as a whole, the current recommendations still call for more vaccinations than most holistic veterinarians would like to see. They consider the shift as an overdue recognition of overvaccinating, a practice, in their opinion, that has helped sow the seeds of rampant disease throughout the pet population. Generations of overvaccinated animals, they say, have contributed to weakened offspring who today suffer the penalty of this medical abuse. Of course, vaccinations help eradicate or reduce the incidence of severe, acute diseases, but the by-product has been to plague animals with insidious, chronic diseases that are very difficult to treat.

"We have been destroying the immune systems of animals," says Roger DeHaan, DVM. "What began as an answer to widespread life-threatening diseases, such as distemper, parvo, and panleukopenia, evolved into shotgun 'cocktail' multiple vaccine shots for every pet, whether there was significant danger of exposure or not. 'Just in case,' was the byword. House pets, pound, and show animals were all treated alike. All breeds were treated alike. The 'what's good for one is good for all' syndrome took over."

Adds DeHaan: "Over the years, it has become increasingly clear that some vaccines are ineffectual or unnecessary; that some of the diseases being vaccinated for are not life-threatening; that some vaccines are dangerous, even causing symptoms of the disease they are supposed to prevent; that some vaccines cause immunosuppression, or interactions among different components of the vaccine when mixed together; and that some vaccines, once useful, are no longer needed but still included in the 'cocktail.'"

There is some research evidence that overvaccination causes immune suppression and opens the door to various acute and chronic diseases. DeHaan cites an English study involving 2,700 dogs that found that the incidence of illness in dogs treated with more than one vaccine at the same time was significantly higher than when only a single vaccination was administered. Moreover, the study said, dogs boosted annually were more likely to become ill than those that were not boosted annually.

ONE PERSPECTIVE ON VACCINATIONS— CHRISTINA CHAMBREAU, DVM

Yearly, or more often, a typical veterinarian has been recommending a combination injection of distemper, hepatitis, leptospirosis, parainfluenza, and parvovirus. The veterinarians and kennels require Bordetella (kennel cough) vaccination before boarding. They often suggest corona vaccine, and Lyme disease vaccine as well. Annually, this adds up to at least four to eight viruses, in addition to rabies.

Would you rebel if your doctor told you to have measles, mumps, rubella, diphtheria, pertussis, tetanus, hepatitis, and rabies shots every year of your life until you died, instead of only a few doses as a child?

A healthy animal or person is unlikely to become ill (or very sick) even if exposed to infectious agents. Ideally we would never vaccinate if we fed our animals only wonderful fresh food and treated the early symptoms of imbalance or infection with natural means, such as with homeopathy. Vaccinating an animal does not necessarily protect it from the very diseases for which it is vaccinated. Instead it may render the animal weaker overall and trigger symptoms and illnesses.

Many of the veterinarians interviewed for this book told me they routinely treat dogs, often brought to them as a last resort, who develop challenging health problems days, weeks, and even months after vaccination. These problems include the following:

- **Life-threatening autoimmune crises,** where the body's immune system attacks healthy tissue.
- **Chronic skin allergies** or conditions that destroy a dog's quality of life.

- **Weak animals going from bad to worse.** These are dogs, unwell to begin with, now suffering from thyroid disease, adrenal malfunction, or even cancer, after vaccinations.

Michele Yasson, DVM, of Rosendale, New York, regularly sees animals who have never been vaccinated and in old age are healthy and robust. "They seem to have a much lower incidence of chronic, debilitative, degenerative diseases such as diabetes, hypothyroidism, and cancer," she says. "Vaccines are like any dis-ease influence—a harsh stimulus to the body. Some animals are more susceptible than others. I have some patients who have never been well since they were vaccinated."

Holistic veterinarians do not speak with one voice on the issue of vaccinations. Some say that the best way to achieve optimum health is to feed a diet rich in fresh foods and raw meat and avoid vaccinations. Others suggest just vaccinating puppies once for distemper and parvo. No boosters. Some say don't vaccinate until an animal is three or even four months of age because vaccinations are much more stressful on an underdeveloped immune system. There are differing shades of opinion.

Nancy Scanlan, DVM, expresses concern about people who are against all vaccinations. "I am seeing more distemper and parvo in nonvaccinated dogs," she says. "I fear that if people stop vaccinating, we may see these infectious diseases make a comeback."

The definitive scientific verdict on the frequency and need of vaccinations lies in the future. In the meantime, talk to your veterinarian, who should be aware of the new ideas. If your vet isn't up-to-date, and simply recommends annual booster shots, you need another veterinarian. Whatever your decision regarding vaccination, holistic veterinarians make the following recommendations:

- Vaccinate only healthy animals. Weakened animals are more prone to develop reactions.

- Unless absolutely necessary, you probably shouldn't vaccinate an animal with a history of reactions to vaccines. If necessary, consult the guidelines in this section for preventing reactions.

- Always ask for killed-cell vaccines, and never have modified-live vaccines. The former are generally less damaging to the immune system and tend to produce fewer side effects. The killed-cell versions are, in fact, less expensive.

- Be watchful for growths at, or near, the site of the vaccine injection. Strange tumors may develop within a couple of months of vaccination, the result of a compromised immune system.

THE PROMISE OF ANTIBODY TESTS

Tests known as "antibody titers" have become available to determine the strength of an animal's immune system to a particular disease. These tests are seen by many veterinarians as a promising way to assess the need for additional vaccinations. "Practically speaking, dogs should have antibody titers against canine distemper and canine parvovirus evaluated annually until we know how long the vaccination-induced antibodies actually last in the blood," says Susan Wynn, DVM, of Marietta, Georgia. "These annual tests will provide some peace of mind, while at the same time helping to establish just how long vaccinations actually protect the average animal. This is critical knowledge that will guide us how to more safely and judiciously vaccinate our pets and at the same time save many pets the ordeal of iatrogenic illnesses."

Nevertheless, these tests are not universally agreed upon as accurate and foolproof assessments of immune status. Low levels, as well as adequate levels, guarantee nothing, Wynn cautions, "just as simply giving a vaccination guarantees nothing in terms of an animal's immune response."

REMEDIES FOR PREVENTING AND RELIEVING REACTIONS TO VACCINATIONS

Thuja for Reactions—Charles Loops, DVM

Thuja is the leading homeopathic remedy to deal with vaccinosis—that is, adverse reactions to vaccination. Examination of the individual animal might result in selecting a different remedy, but generally Thuja is an excellent choice. Consider this remedy if a problem develops within a few weeks after vaccination.

Once I treated a dog who had developed irritable bowel within five days of being vaccinated. For six months the dog's owners tried unsuccessfully to control chronic diarrhea with standard prescriptions from other veterinarians. When they came to me, I recommended Thuja. After one dose the diarrhea began to ease. Within a few days it was entirely gone and never returned.

DOSAGE
• **Thuja 30C:** Once a day for five days.

Thuja for Prevention—Karen Bentley, DVM

I recommend one dose of Thuja 30C within twenty-four hours of vaccination to prevent adverse reactions. It can make a big difference. I recall the case of a nine-year-old Poodle vaccinated repeatedly over the years by another veterinarian. There were always bad reactions. Within a few days of vaccination the dog would usually run a fever, not feel well, and go on to have several months of serious skin problems. The day after the last vaccination the owner called me and asked my advice. I suggested Thuja. The woman called back sometime later to say that no fever or illness had developed. Neither did the dog experience the usual skin problems.

FOR SEVERE REACTIONS
For animals who develop more severe vaccine reactions, I recommend a combination homeopathic remedy called Vaccine Detox Tabs, by Natramed. It contains Thuja, Sulfur, Arsenicum album, Pulsatilla, Silicea, and Antimonium. The formula was developed by Asa Hershoff, ND, a Southern California homeopathic physician. The product can be ordered in the United States through Dr. Hershoff's Santa Monica office (310-829-7122); in Canada, through Actiform in Markham, Ontario (800-668-0066).

DOSAGE
• 1 or 2 tablets daily, starting a week before vaccination. Finish the entire bottle. To remedy ongoing chronic problems resulting from past vaccines, give 1 tablet up to three times daily for two weeks or more.

ALTERNATIVES TO VACCINES—NOSODES

When pet owners ask about alternatives to vaccines, one possibility is a nosode, a homeopathic remedy prepared from an isolate of the particular disease agent. However, properly controlled studies have yet to be conducted on the effectiveness of this method, according to *Complementary and Alternative Veterinary Medicine*, the major reference book on holistic practices.

Among holistic veterinarians, opinion is divided. Some recommend nosodes and say they have had good results. Others do not recommend them. If you are considering nosodes, consult with a holistic veterinarian who is familiar with them.

⚜ 16 ⚜

What to Do When Nothing Seems to Work

IF YOU AND your veterinarian are at wits' end, when nothing seems to work to help a suffering dog, consider the two unique tests described in this chapter. Developed by veterinarians, they can reveal critical clues for developing effective hormonal and nutritional therapies. The tests can also be used to detect deficiencies and imbalances before problems occur so that a preventive strategy can be worked out by your vet.

TEST #1: THE ENDOCRINE-IMMUNE TEST
FOR GENETIC PROBLEMS

Sitting atop each kidney is the tiny, thumbnail-shaped adrenal gland, part of an exquisite network of glands called the endocrine system. The role of glands is to produce minute quantities of hormones, chemical substances with powerful regulating effects on the body's operation. The adrenals pump out a staggering array of important hormones, including estrogen, adrenaline, and cortisol. Cortisol regulates the activity of the white blood cells known as lymphocytes, immune cells that produce antibodies to counteract viruses, bacteria, disease, and toxic substances. Cortisol, in turn, is regulated by a hormone produced by the pituitary gland. This hormone controls cortisol production depending on whether there is too much or too little cortisol circulating in the body.

The pituitary-adrenal relationship is just one of many finely tuned feedback mechanisms within the endocrine system that governs a major branch of the body's defense forces. When the system is operating smoothly the white blood cells naturally recognize the difference between friend and foe. They turn their chemical weapons on the enemy. They do not attack healthy tissue. The hand of man, however, has overturned this remarkable arrangement in many of our dogs.

"Years of inbreeding and line breeding in a one-pointed attempt to achieve certain cosmetic appearances for sales or show ribbons have upset the precision of these systems and perpetuated the breeding of genetically flawed animals, contributing in a big way to today's epidemic of disease among companion animals," says Alfred Plechner, DVM.

Plechner, a Los Angeles veterinarian who has investigated this issue for more than twenty years, believes that the critical regulating mechanisms linking the endocrine and the immune systems have been seriously damaged. Many animals can't produce enough cortisol, or what they do produce is inactive. Their other hormones are out of balance as well. The flaws are passed down from generation to generation, from purebreds to purebreds, from purebreds to mixed breeds, and from mixed breeds to other mixed breeds.

COMMON TYPES OF ENDOCRINE-IMMUNE DISORDERS

The end result is the proliferation of animals programmed for self-destruction, says Plechner. Their internal systems are out of control. They have all the medical diseases that the veterinary profession has trouble treating:

- Severe hypersensitivity.
- Relentless skin allergies with inflammation, ulceration, and itchiness.
- Chronic vomiting and diarrhea.
- Generalized mange.
- Aggressiveness, rage, and weird behavior.
- Seizures and head shaking.
- Chronic liver, pancreas, and urinary tract problems.

Moreover, dogs with genetically based hormonal-immune imbalances may not develop protective antibodies from vaccinations. Vaccines may be worthless for them.

"These animals need improved diets, the right supplements, and help with acupuncture and other natural means, but none of these good methods may work well unless you consider and rectify their hormonal mechanisms," Plechner says. "It's wonderful if you can enhance a system naturally that is suppressed, depressed, or screwed up some. I believe you can often do this with remarkable results. But many animals are too genetically defective, too far gone, and there is nothing you can do but replace the missing hormonal links—synthetically, with drugs. There is nothing there but a vacuum, and you can't enhance it, you can only fill it."

For many conditions, veterinary medicine relies intensely on a family of important synthetic cortisol drugs commonly called "steroids" or "cortisone" (such as Prednisone, Medrol, and Vetalog). They are anti-inflammatory and anti-itching agents that work well for a certain period of time, but when given in powerful pharmaceutical doses they can cause suppression of the adrenal glands and many side effects. If used properly, these drugs can keep many genetically flawed animals on an even keel, and indeed for some of them may be all that can keep them alive, says Plechner, adding that the key is using them properly, in doses that are physiologically relevant.

DETERMINING ACCURATE HORMONAL
REPLACEMENT LEVELS

To determine accurate dosages, Plechner champions a blood test that, among other things, measures the level of cortisol an animal is producing. The test is called "the E-I One" test and is available to veterinarians at the National Veterinary Diagnostic Services, 23361 El Toro Rd., Suite 218, Lake Forest, California 92630–6929 (phone: 949-859-3648). The criteria and range of normal values for the test were developed by Plechner.

The test monitors a critical range of hormonal and antibody activity: resting cortisol, total estrogen, testosterone, progesterone,

T-3, T-4, IgA, IgM, and IgG. Comprehensive tests such as these are not done routinely by veterinarians.

Veterinarians tend not to measure cortisol and simply prescribe steroids that are often too strong or not appropriate. This results all too frequently in side effects. Plechner strongly recommends measuring the level of a patient's ability to produce natural cortisol and if a deficiency exists, to treat it *physiologically*.

"That means treating it at levels that are appropriate, and that usually means tiny amounts," he says. "You correct the body's own deficiency, and you don't get the side effects. I recently corrected a 140-pound dog totally out of sync with 1 milligram of Medrol, much less than a standard pharmaceutical dose of 4 to 8 milligrams."

One of the other important elements of the test is the measurement for total estrogen. Standard tests, by comparison, look only at a component of estrogen, called "estradiol."

"I have found total estrogen to be a more accurate measurement of this one particular hormone," Plechner explains. "Estrogen can exert a dramatic blocking effect on cortisol and thyroid hormones, and just a slight variation out of the normal range is enough to cause a cascade of hormonal and immune complications."

Your veterinarian can also arrange for the laboratory to do a more comprehensive test (called "the E-I Two") that includes the E-I panel plus complete blood count and blood chemistry. "With this more elaborate test you can connect—and then correct—abnormalities in endocrine-immune activity to irregularities in organs or other systems in the body," according to Plechner. "Hormonal imbalances can be addressed by simple hormonal replacement therapy, which helps restore normal immune function. This is an important first step in therapy. It allows the veterinarian to make an accurate correction and manage it long-term. True genetic imbalances require lifelong management, in my opinion. Acquired imbalances can occur as a result of exposure to toxic chemicals, anesthesia, heavy metals, or pollutants. They may require only temporary management or, in some cases, management for a lifetime. This test is extremely beneficial in providing clues for intractable cases or where there have been substantial health problems early in an animal's life. It also has great benefit as a prevention tool in helping to determine which animals should or should not be bred."

Yet another test, called "the E-I Three," looks at four hormonal levels. Plechner recommends it for any individual considering the purchase of a puppy. The greater the hormonal imbalances revealed by this test, the greater the loss of control over the immune system and the earlier in an animal's life one sees health problems.

"If you find such imbalances, your choice is to put the animal on hormonal replacement or not accept the animal," Plechner says. "I would very much like to see breeders use passing marks in this test as criteria for future breeding of animals. Fortunately, I have increasing numbers of breeders who are using it. As they breed hormonally healthier animals they are finding fewer health problems in the offspring. This type of test offers a solution to the current nightmare. We have a great urgency to do something, and this is something we can all do."

Plechner says these special tests have allowed him, and other veterinarians who use them, to help animals who otherwise remain untreatable or who are walking time bombs just waiting to explode.

For individuals who may be philosophically opposed to using pharmaceutical drugs and synthetic hormones, Plechner says this: "I have found in so many cases that there is nothing you can do for these pitiful creatures other than replace synthetically what is genetically missing in their bodies. I am all for correcting the diet, feeding the best possible food, and adding supplements, but do this, too. This is what the term 'holistic' should be all about. Looking at the whole picture. At least do these tests. Get the information."

The information, he says, provides something to think about for cases that may not respond to anything good, well-meaning, and natural you do for your animal.

TEST #2: THE BIO-NUTRITIONAL ANALYSIS

In his veterinary career, which has spanned three decades, Robert Goldstein, VMD, of Westport, Connecticut, has seen "the worst of the worst cases," many of them brought to him as a last resort after all other methods failed.

To help such seriously flawed animals, Goldstein, and his veterinarian brother, Martin, developed the Bio-Nutritional Analysis. The program utilizes data from an animal's blood tests, medical histories, and diagnoses to determine individual deficiencies and imbalances. With this information, an individualized strategy of effective diet and nutritional remedies is developed to address weaknesses and build up an ailing animal.

The Bio-Nutritional Analysis is offered to veterinarians through Antech Diagnostic Laboratories. Veterinarians can choose to have the nutritional analysis along with other standard blood tests performed by Antech. The program also offers an option of purchasing specific supplements that are recommended in the analysis for resale to pet owners. For more information, contact BioNutritional Diagnostics, Inc., at 800-670-0830.

"We have been using this analysis for more than twenty years, with impressive results, even for many cases where animals have been 'written off,'" says Goldstein. "Many have been animals so defective that even improved diet and natural remedies previously had little more than Band-Aid effects."

Obviously, he adds, "we must begin properly breeding animals with stronger immune systems and cut out this mass breeding just for the money. The puppy mills produce animals that are sicker and sicker at a younger age and more difficult for veterinarians to treat. This test provides a higher level of analysis than what is presently available, allowing practitioners to create an effective nutritional program for hard-to-manage patients."

‹ PART TWO ›

AN A TO Z
OF
CANINE PROBLEMS

INTRODUCTION
TO PART TWO

PART 2 IS divided alphabetically into the many different conditions that commonly affect dogs. Under each condition you will find commentaries and recommendations from the veterinarians with detailed instructions on how to use specific natural remedies (for general information on using natural products, refer to the appropriate chapter in part 1).

Many of the recommended supplements and remedies are available at health food stores, pet stores, and drugstores or through natural pet product distributors or manufacturers. Some remedies, as noted in the text, are sold only to health professionals. You will have to ask your veterinarian to purchase such products for you.

For your convenience, the names and telephone numbers of manufacturers and distributors are included in the text in case you have difficulty locating a product in a nearby store. The addresses of these companies are also listed in appendix B.

If your dog doesn't get better after you try various recommendations and remedies presented in the book, be sure to see your veterinarian.

HOW TO GIVE YOUR DOG NATURAL REMEDIES

Give nutritional supplements with food, unless directed otherwise. Herbal supplements should ideally be given apart from food. If your dog won't take the herbal product alone, mix it into the food.

Supplements and remedies are available in different forms. Use the following guidelines for administering them:

- **Powdered supplements.** Mix into the food.

- **Capsules and tablets.** Give directly. Smear the pill in butter if the dog won't take it readily. That disguises the flavor and makes the pill slippery. You can also empty the contents of capsules into the food. Or you can crunch up tablets and mix into the food.

- **Pilling a dog.** Ask your veterinarian for a pill dispenser or to demonstrate the best way to pill your animal.

- **Liquids.** Give directly in the mouth or add to the food, as directed. To give in the mouth, make a pouch on the side by pulling out the lower lip slightly. Add the drops in the area of the molar teeth. Pets generally prefer the side route rather than a straight-down-the-middle, under-the-nose approach.

GIVING THE PROPER DOSAGE TO YOUR DOG

The veterinarians interviewed for this book have provided dosage instructions along with each of their recommendations. The dosages are generally to be given daily, unless otherwise noted.

As a rule of thumb, start low and go slow. If the particular taste of a supplement or herb is bitter, for instance, start with a very small dose and then build up slowly to the recommended amount. For some fussy dogs, this is a necessary strategy. If an animal is reluctant to take a supplement because of the taste, camouflage the supplement in liver, sardines, cottage cheese, peanut butter, baby food (meat), or a favored aromatic food.

Many dosage recommendations are given according to the size of the dog. In such a case, use the following guideline: small dogs, up to twenty-five pounds; medium dogs, up to seventy-five pounds; large dogs, up to one hundred pounds; and giant breeds, over one hundred pounds.

Some of the remedies recommended in the book are products sold primarily for human consumption but that have been safely and effectively used by veterinarians. Unless specific dosages are given for the remedy, figure the amount to be taken by your dog according to its weight as compared to a 150-pound adult.

In the book you will sometimes encounter veterinarians recommending different dosages of the same supplement for a particular condition. If you have any doubts about how much to use, it is best to go with a lower dose and, if needed, increase to a higher recommended level.

Dosages of individual flower essences and homeopathic remedies are generally the same—that is, the amount of the remedy you give is standard; only the frequency changes. General guidelines for these types of remedies are found in part 1. Follow the guidelines unless other instructions accompany a particular recommendation.

VITAMIN C AND THE BOWEL TOLERANCE CONCEPT

Many holistic veterinarians recommend giving vitamin C to "bowel tolerance" therapeutic levels for certain conditions. What this means is slowly raising the amount of the supplement you give the animal in its food until you see the stool becomes soft. When you reach that level, reduce the amount slightly. Tolerance varies among individual animals. Try to give the vitamin C in divided doses throughout the day with food. The most economical and convenient form of vitamin C for these megadose quantities is buffered (nonacidic) sodium or calcium ascorbate crystals, which can be sprinkled onto food. Many years of clinical experience among both veterinarians and physicians who use megadoses of vitamin C demonstrate that the vitamin has powerful therapeutic properties when used in this manner. A quarter of a teaspoon of crystals is equal to 1,000 milligrams (1 gram).

ADVERSE REACTIONS

If, after starting a particular supplement, an adverse reaction occurs (such as diarrhea or throwing up), stop the supplement. Sometimes you may avoid the reaction with a smaller dose. If that doesn't help, try a different supplement. Some animals are particularly sensitive. In such cases it is prudent to introduce supplements at levels lower than the recommended dosages and slowly increase the amount.

⚙ Arthritis ⚙

See also Hip Dysplasia

Wear and tear of the joints of the body leads to arthritis, also known as degenerative joint disease or osteoarthritis. Just as in people, arthritis in dogs causes pain, stiffness, lameness, slowness of movement, and a reluctance to walk as far as usual. Arthritis of the hips and spine most commonly affects older dogs and particularly the heavier breeds.

Arthritic degeneration can also occur in young animals, especially if there has been traumatic injury to the joint or to the bone, or the animal has developed canine hip dysplasia.

Many things contribute to arthritis, including traumatic injury, toxic damage, scar tissue, genetic weaknesses, and nutritional deficiencies.

Many holistic veterinarians recommended acupuncture and/or chiropractic treatment for animals with arthritis.

HERBS

Ayurvedic Herbal Combination—Tejinder Sodhi, DVM
The combination of the two well-known Ayurvedic herbs boswellia and ashwaganda works wonders on animals with arthritis. These herbs are available in health food stores or through Ayush Herbs (800-925-1371). The liquid form of these herbs can be purchased through Ayush only.

Boswellia is a potent anti-inflammatory shown to help relieve the stiffness and pain of arthritic patients. It effectively shrinks inflamed tissue, the underlying cause of pain in many conditions. It also improves the blood supply to affected areas and promotes repair of local blood vessels damaged by proliferating inflammation.

Ashwaganda acts on the musculoskeletal and nervous systems, generating energy and vitality. It works somewhat in the manner of ginseng as an adaptogen—that is, it helps counteract the effects of stress. It is also a potent anti-inflammatory and contains a natural chemical that has an anabolic effect in the body. This means it can help build up muscles that have atrophied around diseased joints.

In a majority of cases you start to see significant improvement with this herbal combination within fourteen to twenty-one days, although in very severe cases it may take three months.

Dosage
- **Boswellia:** Dogs up to twenty pounds, 10 drops of liquid boswellia twice daily for each ten pounds of body weight; dogs

up to thirty pounds, one 500-milligram capsule or tablet twice daily; dogs up to sixty pounds, 500 milligrams three times daily; larger dogs, 1,000 milligrams twice. Give after feeding.

- **Ashwaganda:** Dogs up to twenty pounds, 10 drops of liquid ashwaganda twice daily for each ten pounds of body weight; dogs up to thirty pounds, one 500-milligram capsule or tablet twice daily; dogs up to sixty pounds, 500 milligrams three times daily; larger dogs, 1,000 milligrams twice. Give after feeding.

Chinese Herbal Formula—Joseph Demers, DVM

A classical Chinese herbal formula called Du Huo Jisheng Wan has worked very well for the garden-variety arthritis cases I have treated. The formula, which comes in tiny black pills, contains ginger, cinnamon, angelica, Chinese foxglove, and licorice root. It can be purchased in Chinese groceries or pharmacies.

The formula tonifies the liver, kidney, and blood. The Chinese say it dispels wind and dampness in the joints, lower back, and knees that cause weakness, pain, and stiffness. It is as effective as aspirin or other drugs I used previously for animals who are limping, lame, having a hard time getting up or down, chilled in the winter, or achy whenever the temperature changes.

Often you see improvement within days. I recommend taking the product for one to three weeks and then as needed.

DOSAGE
- Give twice daily. Small dogs, 2 to 3 pills each time; medium dogs, 5 to 6 pills; larger dogs, up to 10 twice daily.

HOMEOPATHIC MEDICINES
(See chapter 10 for general dosage guidelines.)

Rhus Tox Plus Ruta—Mark Haverkos, DVM

For less severe stiffness, sore joints, or a hard time getting up or going up steps, use Rhus tox and Ruta, two homeopathic remedies. In many cases you will see more ease of motion within two weeks.

DOSAGE
- Each remedy once daily. Administer them at the same time. Use potencies ranging from 6C to 30C. After two weeks use remedies only as needed. (See chapter 10.)

NUTRITIONAL SUPPLEMENTS

Whole-Food Antioxidant—Thomas Van Cise, DVM

Dismutase, made by Bio Vet International (800-788-1084), is a whole-food antioxidant supplement prepared from specially grown wheat and soy sprouts. I have used the flavored veterinary version but find that the product for humans works better.

Dismutase counteracts free radicals, molecular renegades in the body that contribute to accelerated aging and disease. The action of this supplement helps put a brake on the destruction of cartilage. It also reduces inflammation.

I expect a response in about three weeks, but it can sometimes happen faster, within days. Animals generally walk, run, and jump more normally. They may move in a strange manner if there has been considerable structural damage to the joint caused by the condition. The supplement will not remake damaged joints; however, the flexibility and energy it generates are often phenomenal. You frequently see older animals displaying the energy of a much younger dog.

DOSAGE
- A forty-pound dog, 6 tablets daily; giant breeds, up to 10 tablets. Give for at least one month. Afterward slowly reduce dosage to an effective maintenance level for the animal. Give tablets on an empty stomach.

Sea Jerky Nutritional Treat—Carolyn Blakey, DVM

An excellent treat that dogs really love and that has a remarkable effect on arthritic joints is Sea Jerky, made by Coastside BioResources (800-732-8072). The product contains a blend of sea cucumber, crab meat, kelp, glucosamine sulfate, beef, and vitamin E.

I recommend Sea Jerky for any sign of discomfort in the joints. That could mean stiffness, slowness to move, limping, or an animal not wanting to move as far as it used to. When I usually see a case, there is already some erosion of the joint health. Most of these animals don't turn around to healthy joints again. But I am able to relieve them substantially with this product.

Dogs have much less apparent pain after they start on Sea Jerky. They move more easily instead of hesitating or being lame. My clients say their dogs are acting like puppies again. I see that in my own dog.

There is often significant improvement within two weeks. The results suggest this product may replace other nutritional supplements used for arthritis.

DOSAGE
• Follow label instructions.

Goat's Whey—Michele Yasson, DVM

For the stiffness, lameness, and pain involved with osteoarthritis, I use a product for humans called Capra Mineral Whey, made by Mt. Capra Cheese (800-574-1961). This is an easily absorbed natural whole-food supplement in powder form from dehydrated goat's milk. Dogs like the taste.

The product is a rich source of important minerals, including biologically active sodium—not to be confused with inorganic sodium that is part of salt. Bioactive sodium is stored in various tissues of the body, primarily the walls of the stomach and small intestine, and the joints. Long-term use helps loosen up joints and appears to dissolve osteophytes (calcium deposits). The mode of action is believed related to restoring missing sodium to joint tissue.

When dealing with hard tissue as in osteoarthritis, improvement takes time. Be patient. We put animals on the product for up to three months and then monitor results to determine their minimal effective maintenance dosage. In general, results are very good. I see freer motion and less stiffness and pain.

DOSAGE
• Dogs under twenty pounds, give one-quarter the full human dose on the label; dogs up to fifty pounds, one-half the label dose; dogs over fifty pounds, full label dose. Mix powder into food.

MSM—Mark Haverkos, DVM

For severe arthritis and joint disorders, I recommend methylsulfonylmethane (MSM), a source of biologically active sulfur. The product is widely available and comes in either powder or capsule form.

I have used MSM for about a dozen years and find it more potent than other popular arthritis supplements, but it usually takes a while to see improvement. Most of the time people tell me MSM works fantastically or it doesn't work at all. In more than about five hundred cases I have seen good results about 60 percent of the time. Improvement often becomes apparent in six to eight weeks and sometimes within two or three weeks. If the condition isn't getting better by eight weeks, I try something else. Improvement means more ease, flexibility, and apparent comfort.

One dramatic success involved a fifteen-year-old Weimaraner bitch. She was limping on a foreleg, the result of an old injury that had turned arthritic. I treated her with acupuncture and other remedies, with fairly good results, but it was when we turned to MSM that there was a big change. After one month on MSM the dog was strong in the leg without any sign of limping.

Since that time the owners would occasionally run out of MSM. If the interval was more than a week, the signs of limping would return. After supplementation was resumed, the limping would disappear within days. This is fairly typical with MSM. Once you stop the supplement, symptoms return. Long-term maintenance on MSM is usually needed. The Weimaraner is strong on all her legs now, and it's three years later.

DOSAGE
- A thirty-pound dog, give 1/8 teaspoon of powder or one 500-milligram capsule twice daily for one week; dogs sixty pounds or over, 1/4 teaspoon. After one week reduce to one dosage daily. MSM is bitter to the taste, so mix well into food.

Vitamins, DLPA, Sod, Glucosamine—Nancy Scanlan, DVM

You can obtain good results with a number of supplements available in health food stores. If the case is mild, I recommend vitamins C and E and dl-phenylalanine (DLPA), an amino acid excellent for pain and especially useful where animals have hind leg weakness. These three are also good for conditions that are more muscle-related or where there is no clear X-ray evidence of arthritis.

If the case is more severe or not responding to the C, E, and DLPA approach, add sodium oxide dismutase (SOD), an antioxidant with good anti-inflammatory properties, or any one or more of the popular antiarthritis supplements, such as glucosamine sulfate, chondroitin sulfate, and green-lipped mussels. If the dog is in much pain, then you need the additional firepower from these supplements. Each acts in a somewhat different way, and often you don't know which one is the main source of relief. Remember that each animal is individual. Some do better on glucosamine sulfate than on chondroitin. Others benefit more from the green-lipped mussels.

Start slowly. Don't begin all the supplements at once. You don't want to overload the system; you might cause some diarrhea. If this happens, cut back on the supplements, particularly vitamin C and SOD.

Improvement frequently is seen in about two weeks, but the range can be anywhere from one day to one month. It is not possible to predict the speed of improvement from an X-ray or the animal's condition when first brought in. If you want to speed the healing process, I strongly recommend acupuncture with a qualified veterinary specialist. You can also help with regular massaging (refer to chapter 14).

DOSAGE

- When an animal improves on this program, cut back the dosage of the supplements, such as going from twice to once a day. Some animals, however, may require a full dose on a long-term basis. If an animal starts to show signs of deterioration when you reduce supplement levels, return back to the higher level.

- **Vitamin C:** Give twice daily. Small dogs, 125 milligrams each time; medium dogs, 250 milligrams; large dogs, 500 milligrams; giant breeds, 1,000 milligrams.

- **Vitamin E:** Small dogs, 50 international units (IU) once daily; medium dogs, 100 IU; large dogs, 200 IU; giant breeds, 400 IU.

- **SOD:** Small dogs, 100 milligrams once daily; medium dogs, 200 milligrams; large dogs, 300 milligrams; giant breeds, 400 milligrams. If no improvement, increase to twice daily. Go slow so as not to cause diarrhea.

- **DLPA:** Give twice daily. Small dogs, 100 milligrams each time; medium dogs, 200 milligrams; large dogs, 400 milligrams; giant breeds, 600 milligrams.

- **Glucosamine sulfate:** Give twice daily. Smaller animals, 250 milligrams each time; larger dogs, 500 milligrams.

- **Chondroitin sulfate:** Give twice daily. Smaller animals, 200 milligrams each time; larger dogs, 400 milligrams.

- **Green-lipped mussels:** Small dogs, 150 milligrams once daily; medium dogs, 300 milligrams; large dogs, 450 milligrams; giant breeds, 600 milligrams.

Cartilage-Protective Supplement—Pedro Luis Rivera, DVM

I have been using a product called Arthri-Soothe, available through NaturVet (888-628-8793). In my opinion the formula works better and faster than other cartilage-protective agents on the market. The product consists of chondroitin sulfate, perna mussel, yucca, and boswellia. It helps provide building blocks for the joint fluid and cartilage, as well as for the collagen matrix in general, thus giving strength also to the ligaments and tendons. Depending on the severity of the case, I have seen animals respond within two weeks of starting the supplement.

DOSAGE
- Follow label instructions.

MIXED AND MISCELLANEOUS APPROACHES

Homeopathy Plus Liver and Digestive Care—Ron Carsten, DVM

To help reduce the pain and stiffness of arthritis, try Arnica and Ruta, two homeopathic remedies. At the same time, always give your animal nutritional and liver support when dealing with arthritis. Feed a high-quality food without chemicals and preservatives that can stress the digestive tract.

Be aware also that toxins produced by intestinal disorders and poor liver function often cause disruption of normal processes leading to inflammation in the joints. Digestive enzymes and probiotic supplements with beneficial bacteria can help restore normalcy and health in the gut (see section on digestive disorders for comments on enzymes and probiotics).

For the liver, consider using the herb milk thistle to strengthen and nourish a sluggish or sick organ (see Carsten entry in liver section).

DOSAGE
- Arnica 30C in the A.M. Ruta 30C in the P.M. Give for ten days. If condition improves, determine an appropriate maintenance cycle. An example is ten days on and five days off. Remember that each animal responds differently and for a different duration. If signs of arthritis return after the animal has been off the remedies, start them again.

- Use a good pet digestive enzyme and follow label instructions.

- Use a probiotic supplement and figure dosage according to weight of animal as compared to a human.

Homeopathy Plus Supplements—Carvel Tiekert, DVM
I strongly recommend switching to a better diet with less protein as the first step of any treatment program. Arthritis has an immune component to it. The poor-quality protein typically found in many commercial diets challenges the immune system on a daily basis. When you switch to a better diet, the animal has more ability to deal with the arthritis.

For older dogs with lameness and degenerative joint disease, I often begin treatment with a homeopathic combination of Rhus tox 6X and Bryonia 6X. This is an inexpensive approach that is often very helpful. If the two don't work, they at least won't do any harm. I find, however, they often help the older guys who have bad days when the weather is damp. Rhus tox is a good remedy for the animal who tends to be stiff on getting up. Bryonia is a remedy for the animal who tends to get stiffer with activity. I find that animals generally respond better to the two remedies in combination than to each alone. There is a significant improvement in about 40 percent of cases and some improvement in many others. Buy the individual remedies and then mix them together.

Another option is to purchase combination homeopathic products with these and other ingredients. Several such products are Dr. Goodpet's Arthritis Relief (800-222-9932), HomeoPet's Arthritis (800-434-0449), and Newton Laboratories' Rheumatic Pain (800-448-7256). These products are available in many health food stores or through distributors such as Morrill's New Directions (800-368-5057) or PetSage (800-PET-HLTH).

DOSAGE

- **Rhus tox–Bryonia combination:** A half dropperful three times daily.

- **Other combinations:** Follow label instructions.

My overall program also includes acupuncture, chiropractic, and supplements. For the supplement aspect, I recommend two formulas that have been helpful for many of my patients. They can be used along with the homeopathics.

One formula is A.C.A., made by Natural Animal Nutrition (800-548-2899), containing alfalfa, calcium ascorbate (vitamin C), selenium, vitamin E, and chromium. I use this powder supplement for milder cases. I recommend the half-pound size, and if I haven't seen a response by the end of the container, I conclude it won't work.

In severe cases I turn to Cosequin, made by Nutramax (800-925-5187). This product is sold through veterinarians only, but a similar formula is sold in health food stores for humans under the brand name Cosamin. Among the many glucosamine products for arthritis now on the market, I find Cosequin the best, even though it is expensive. Cosequin is a neutraceutical—that is, a nutritional supplement that acts in almost a pharmaceutical way. It contains glucosamine hydrochloride and chondroitin sulfate, substances similar to natural compounds found in healthy cartilage tissue. If at the end of six weeks there is no significant improvement, I try something else. Research has shown that the amount of hip dysplasia is reduced in growing puppies who take this product.

A.C.A. and Cosequin have helped in about 80 percent of cases. These are products given long-term. A.C.A. may be more beneficial than Cosequin for the long term. Arthritis is a chronic, progressive process. Unless you are dealing with an immune-related arthritis in a younger animal, you don't "cure" arthritis. You manage it. These products help manage the condition.

DOSAGE
- **A.C.A.:** For prevention, 1/2 teaspoon daily in food per twenty pounds of body weight. As a therapeutic dose for older animals with arthritis, 1 teaspoon per twenty pounds.

- **Cosequin:** For prevention, 1 capsule daily of the normal-strength formula for puppies under forty pounds; larger puppies, 2 capsules. Give product until puppy is full-grown. For animals with arthritis, follow label instructions.

FOOD AND SPECIAL DIETS

The Antiarthritis Diet—A. Greig Howie, DVM
I believe acupuncture is the number one method for arthritis. Number two is homeopathy. Seek a holistic veterinarian who is skilled in either of these techniques for an individualized treatment and maximum results.

At a veterinary acupuncture course years ago I learned about a special arthritis diet, which I subsequently have recommended to clients. Many animals improve on this diet alone. I suggest also adding a good vitamin/mineral supplement and digestive enzymes. Often I will treat animals two or three times with acupuncture in the beginning and then send them home with the diet. It is amazing how well they do within a month's time. Normally they don't need much follow-up.

Ingredients:
2 cups brown rice
2 cups barley (pearls)
1 cup lentils

2 cups carrots
1 cup celery
1/2 cup parsley
2 cups spinach
2 cups lamb or beef heart
2 garlic cloves
8 to 12 cups water

Directions: Combine ingredients in a large pot. Bring to boil and then simmer for 1 1/4 hours. Keep pot covered. Stir every fifteen minutes. Add water if needed. Feed daily for a month or until significant improvement. Afterward you can make changes and even feed it just part of the time, although it can be used as a maintenance diet if you don't mind going to the trouble. Later you can vary ingredients, such as changing meats and rotating vegetables. The diet also helps for weight loss and energy.

⚘ Asthma ⚘

Asthma is an inflammatory condition of the airways leading into the lungs. The airways become inflamed and spasm, causing excessive amounts of clogging mucus to build up, which in turn sets off a contraction of surrounding muscles. Asthmatic flare-ups can cause extreme difficulty in breathing. This condition is seen more frequently in cats but also occurs in dogs. Airborne allergens are often involved in asthma.

NUTRITIONAL SUPPLEMENTS

Stabilized Oxygen—Thomas Van Cise, DVM

I recommend an oral stabilized oxygen product for any lung or allergic condition. There are many available in health food stores. I use Earth Bounty Oxy-Max from Matrix Health Products (800-736-5609). This product oxygenates the whole body, including the lungs, and helps to clear out toxins generated by allergies.

You should see improved breathing within four to five days. Older pets, or animals who have been long-term on medication such as steroids for allergies, may take two weeks.

DOSAGE
• Dogs under twenty pounds, 3 drops; dogs up to forty pounds, 5 drops; dogs up to sixty pounds, 8 drops; larger dogs, 10 drops. Add drops to food. Apply twice daily if condition is severe.

⚓ Back Problems ⚓

Primary causes of back problems are arthritis (see section on arthritis), disc disorders, and spinal myelopathy.

"Slipped discs" are common among Dachshunds. Discs are gelatinous "shock absorbers" between the bony joints of the spinal column. When they "slip," the fibrous shell of the disc ruptures and the jellylike substance inside spills out. The body attempts to contain this leakage and resultant inflammation in the area with a wall of scar tissue. Limping and hindquarter weakness may develop as a consequence.

Spinal myelopathy involves a degeneration of spinal cord nerves and progressive weakness in the hindquarters.

HOMEOPATHIC MEDICINES
(See chapter 10 for general dosage guidelines.)

Dachshund Slipped Discs—Thomas Van Cise, DVM
Arnica, the popular homeopathic remedy, works well for the slipped discs that often affect this elongated breed. The remedy is useful whenever there is irritation and loss of some nerve function from localized swelling, regardless of whether the disc problem occurred recently or long ago. Arnica does not restore the disc to its previous position, but it helps repair injuries, even old ones, as well as old surgical wounds. It helps also to restore nerve function.

After interference with the nervous system and the development of scar tissue, animals start limping, dragging their hindquarters, or showing signs of pain. It is at this point that veterinary help is usually sought. By then there is often considerable calcification of the inflamed tissue around the affected joint. Unless an animal is treated surgically within twenty-four hours after a fall or accident or some other incident that damaged the disc, chances of a successful operation are minimal. Usually veterinarians don't see animals that soon because pet owners are not immediately aware of any changes.

DOSAGE
- If the disc just "slipped," use Arnica 12C. Place a few drops or pellets in the mouth twice a day. Usually improvement is seen after the first or second dose. Within a few days animals often appear normal again. If so, stop remedy. If no improvement is seen after second dose, and you are considering surgery, consult with a veterinarian immediately.

- For existing conditions, use Arnica 30C long-term. Place a few drops or pellets in the mouth once or even twice a day for first week. Watch for an effect. You may not see a major difference at first. But something as subtle as a dog wagging its tail, where it wasn't doing that before, is a sign of improvement. Then stop the remedy and observe if the improvement continues. You may have to administer the Arnica again.

NUTRITIONAL SUPPLEMENTS

Glutamine, Enzymes, for Myelopathy—Ron Carsten, DVM

I see many German Shepherds with this problem. The standard treatment includes anti-inflammatory and steroid drugs, but results are mediocre. Moreover, I have found that steroid treatment tends to make animals less responsive to other supportive approaches.

I am able to slow down the progression of this condition and start the healing ball rolling with an approach that nourishes the digestive tract. It features the amino acid glutamine, digestive enzymes, and a good probiotic supplement. I strongly believe that gut disorders play a big role in this problem. These supplements can be given along with whatever individualized treatment program your veterinarian may recommend.

DOSAGE
- **Glutamine:** All animals, 500 milligrams twice daily with meals.

- **Digestive enzymes:** Follow label instructions for pet products.

- **Probiotic:** Adjust the dosage according to the animal's size if using a human product.

Manganese, Vitamin C, for Disc Health—Carvel Tiekert, DVM

I treat this condition, as in arthritis, with a broad approach of acupuncture, chiropractic, diet, supplements, and homeopathy (see Tiekert's entry under arthritis).

Vertebral disc disease is usually caused by arthritis. Long-backed dogs such as Dachshunds are particularly susceptible, as are small breeds such as Shih Tzus, Lhasas, and Poodles. As spinal tissue becomes inflamed, animals develop pain and stiffness in the hindquarters. This can progress into paralysis. If the condition becomes acutely painful, see a veterinarian immediately.

Manganese and vitamin C are beneficial for animals with this problem. In my practice I use Vetri-Disc, made by Vetri-Science (800-882-9993). It is a product sold through veterinarians and contains a synergistic combination of manganese and vitamin C, plus other minerals and bovine tracheal cartilage, a source of chondroitin sulfate. These supplements may have a preventive effect, so I recommend them for animals prone to disc disease.

DOSAGE
- **Chelated manganese:** 5 to 10 milligrams per day.

- **Vitamin C:** 250 to 500 milligrams.

- **Vetri-Disc:** Follow label instructions.

⚜ Bad Breath ⚜

Halitosis (bad breath) is generally caused by two things: dental problems or poor digestion.

NUTRITIONAL SUPPLEMENTS

Digestive Aids—Lynne Friday, DVM

First, look in the mouth. The problem may be bad teeth or gums, cancer of the mouth, or bones stuck between teeth.

If the mouth isn't the problem, look to the digestion. Give your pet digestive aids such as digestive enzymes, ginger snaps, or Chlorets. I use Chlorowin, made by Wintec Inc. (314-257-5400), a digestive aid with chlorophyll, mint, and liver for palatability. The product helps combat bad breath as well as odors during heat. Another good supplement is chlorella, available in health food stores.

DOSAGE
- **Chlorowin:** Follow label instructions.

Enzymes Plus Green Vegetables—Carvel Tiekert, DVM

If the teeth are clean, purchase pet digestive enzymes for your animal. The enzymes help the animal break down and absorb food. Green vegetables in the diet are also helpful. The veggies contain, among other things, lots of chlorophyll, a natural detoxifier. If halitosis persists, see a veterinarian. There may be a liver problem.

Peppermint Oil—Jan Bellows, DVM

Peppermint oil, available in health food stores, has a minty scent and is antibacterial and anti-inflammatory. It will not cure periodontal disease (see section on dental health), but it will help with the breath. Other options for bad breath include natural toothpastes, baking soda, lemon juice, and finely ground rubbed sage.

Dosage
- **Peppermint oil:** Add a few drops of this or spearmint essential oil to a cup of distilled water and use as a mouth spray.

FOOD AND SPECIAL DIETS

Food Allergies?—Alfred Plechner, DVM

Bad breath, without dental disease, may mean you are looking at a problem of food that doesn't agree with an animal. The immune cells in the mouth are overreacting to foodstuffs and you get a kind of "dermatitis of the mouth" and a bad smell. A red flare, or line, above the teeth, or even an entire oral cavity that appears inflamed, is a major sign that the problem is being caused by imbalances in the endocrine and immune system that often lead to food allergies and other disorders (see section on food allergies; also see chapter 16 on what to do when nothing seems to work).

⚜ Behavioral Problems ⚜

Many holistic veterinarians recommend liquid remedies made from flower essences to help normalize behavioral problems of pets. Commercial pet food can often be an unsuspected cause of hyperactivity and other behavioral problems, as a number of the following commentaries indicate.

FLOWER ESSENCES
(See chapter 11 for guidelines on using flower essences.)

Separation Anxiety

In early 1999 the U.S. Food and Drug Administration announced approval of the first "antidepressant" drug for dogs. The drug, Clomicalm, was designed for canines who suffer from separation anxiety when, for instance, their owners leave all day to go to work. For some anxious dogs left alone, abandonment can trigger prolonged barking, gnawing on a leg or other body part, or destructive behavior in the house. Nicholas Dodman, of the Tufts University

School of Veterinary Medicine, says as many as 10 percent of dogs may have this problem, and "it is serious in 40 percent of these," according to a 1999 front-page report in the *Los Angeles Times*.

Flower Remedy Alternatives—Carolyn Blakey, DVM

A number of flower options can be tried, depending on the circumstances, instead of drugs. They include Agrimony, for anxiety hidden by a mask of cheerfulness, as when you don't see the anxiousness that is triggered by the impending departure; Aspen, for an animal that might be fearing the unknown; Chicory, for getting attention through negative behavior; Holly, for feeling cut off from love; Sweet Chestnut, for strong despair; and, always, the beloved Rescue Remedy, sometimes known as Five Flower Formula, for general anxiety.

For any major changes in the life of an animal that are of an upsetting nature, the essence Walnut is helpful. Examples of such changes are a new addition to the household, a death, whether animal or human, or a physical move.

These remedies are safe to try for an animal, but for best results you may want to work with an experienced veterinarian or a practitioner specializing in flower essences.

DOSAGE
- Give frequently, perhaps three to four times per day, if possible, over an extended period of time.

Red Chestnut for Separation Anxiety—Jean Hofve, DVM

The flower essence Red Chestnut is often useful for the anxious dog who worries about being abandoned or neglected the minute the pet owner walks out the door. I have a dog who screams if I leave him for thirty seconds outside a store, even if he can see me inside. "Willie" still lets me know when I return that I left him alone, but the remedy has made a huge difference in the decibels of his complaint.

For serious cases, ask your veterinarian about behavioral training techniques that can also help lower the anxiety level of your dog.

DOSAGE
- Put the remedy in the animal's drinking water. Also add some of the remedy in a small bottle of water. Then, as you are about

to leave the house, put some in your hand and pet your dog's head with it. That puts the remedy directly in the place where it needs to be at the moment it needs to be there.

Zinnia for Sad Dogs—Donna Starita Mehan, DVM

Zinnia can restore playfulness and lightheartedness to animals and their human companions alike. I use the product made by the Flower Essence Society (800-736-9222). This is a wonderful remedy for all creatures who are depressed and heavy and who have forgotten how to have a good time. People tell me it brings back smiles to their faces, humor to their hearts, and friskiness to their animals.

DOSAGE
- 1 drop twice a day in water or food, or rub a drop on the ear of the animal.

Essences for Rescued Dogs—Jean Hofve, DVM

In conjunction with animal communicators Kate Solisti Mattelon and Patrice Mattelon, I developed a set of liquid remedies that are very helpful in assisting dogs to overcome their past circumstances and move into their new lives with courage and joy. The remedies contain a combination of flower and other natural essences. The products are available through Flower Essence Therapy for Animals, P.O. Box 22302, Sacramento, CA 95822, or through my Web site at www.spiritessence.com.

The remedies and their applications are as follows: Abandonment, for dogs left behind, given away, lost, or separated from their families; Abuse, for dogs who have endured physical or emotional abuse; Neglect, for dogs left outside, alone, tied up, poorly cared for, without love or human companionship; Fear, for dogs who are fearful, shy, timid, excessively submissive, mean, closed, unfriendly, jealous, territorial, or aggressive; Transition/Travel, for dogs going to new homes, being boarded long- or short-term, or traveling in airplanes, trains, or automobiles; Appropriate Elimination, for learning or remembering appropriate elimination behavior, as well as for dogs who mark territory indoors or who urinate in fear or submission.

HOMEOPATHIC MEDICINES
(See chapter 10 for general dosage guidelines.)

Ignatia for Grief—Michele Yasson, DVM

Any time a dog loses a companion animal or human, it can experience grief just as we do. Behavioral or health problems may develop. Ignatia, a dependable homeopathic remedy for grief, is often helpful.

DOSAGE
- **Ignatia 30C:** For an older pet, one dose usually works. For a middle-aged animal, give twice a day for two days, if needed. For a younger animal, give three times daily for two days.

MIXED AND MISCELLANEOUS APPROACHES

Homeopathics Plus Diet for Hyper Dogs—Roger DeHaan, DVM

For animals who are hyper or who become agitated by loud noises, there are a number of natural remedies that work well in a large percentage of cases. They include the following:

- **Rescue Remedy,** or other calming flower essences.

- **Calm Stress,** a homeopathic combination remedy from Dr. Goodpet (800-222-9932).

- **Aconite 30X,** a single homeopathic remedy.

Often these remedies will calm an animal immediately after a single dose or within a few days of giving them two or three times a day. Try them for at least a month. If you don't see results, consult with a veterinarian to sort out the causes.

Feeding commercial "junk" food always has the potential to cause problems, among them hyperactivity. Be sure to feed a good natural diet that does not contain the poor-quality ingredients, chemicals, and preservatives that might trigger agitation or hyperactivity.

One animal trainer told me that when he encounters hyperactive animals he will always change their diet, and 75 percent of the time that solves the problem. Food can often be part of the underlying cause of nervousness and hyperexcited animals.

Food and Exercise for Hyper Dogs—Lynne Friday, DVM

Hyperactivity is multifactorial. I have traced many hyperactivity problems to the preservatives, synthetic dyes, and flavorings used in commercial foods. Avoid foods with these additives. Stay away from highly processed foods. They are basically "junk" and not fit for a regular diet. Try different natural food products preserved with vitamins C and E. I have seen many animals turn around just on this alone. Try a natural food for a week, and you will often see a calmer animal.

Don't forget to give your animal enough regular attention and exercise. Animals need both. Sporting breeds, in particular, need to run. They should have a long run three times a week.

Diet Plus B Complex—Carvel Tiekert, DVM

Look at the diet. Food allergies can cause abnormal behavior. Make sure there are no chemicals and preservatives in the food. These can be major behavioral triggers.

Keep the protein level down (see Tiekert's comments in chapter 3 on too much protein) and the B-complex level up. Many animals can be helped with a regular stress B-complex formula alone, particularly if the problem is antisocial behavior such as aggression and short temper. Try the supplement for a month. In my experience, this inexpensive supplement works in about 30 to 40 percent of cases.

If these simple approaches don't work, consult with an animal behaviorist or your veterinarian to see if deeper issues are involved.

DOSAGE
- **B complex:** 1/4 to 1 capsule/tablet daily of a human supplement, depending on size of animal.

❧ Cancer ❧

Cancer, an uncontrolled growth of cells on or inside the body, is common in pets. According to the American Veterinary Medical Association, dogs get cancer at about the same rate as humans. The incidence increases with age and accounts for almost half of deaths over the age of ten years. However, many veterinarians interviewed for this book expressed concern about seeing more younger animals than ever before developing cancer. "When I started in practice more than twenty-five years ago, cancer was a disease of older animals," says Robert Goldstein, VMD, who regards cancer as an epidemic disease among pets. "Now you see it regularly when they are one, two, and three."

The incidence of cancer is attributed by holistic veterinarians as a failure of the immune system in the face of genetic weaknesses fostered by contemporary breeding practices and a constant onslaught of poor diet, medication, toxic chemicals, vaccines, and stress. The disease is seen as a systemic affliction that may appear locally as skin tumors in one patient or breast cancer in another. But the underlying problem, in the holistic viewpoint, is a failure of the body's defenses to stop abnormal mutating cells from growing rapidly.

Just as their human medicine counterparts, veterinary oncologists (animal doctors specializing in cancer treatments) recommend the standard approaches of chemotherapy, radiation, and surgery. For some forms of cancer, surgery is the best option. Skin tumors, for instance, can often be eliminated cleanly by surgery, especially when treated early, veterinarians say. Drugs and radiation are also beneficial when used appropriately. For lymphomas and lymphosarcomas, chemotherapy can be very effective and should be considered as an option.

Natural healing methods, unlike conventional treatments, are not invasive. They emphasize strengthening the body's weakened healing resources. Natural methods can be used in two ways:

1. In combination with standard treatments to reduce side effects and speed healing. Animals undergoing chemo or surgical procedures do much better if they are on nutritional and natural supportive therapies.

2. As the major modality, under the care of a holistic veterinarian, and bypassing standard therapies.

Cancer is a life-threatening condition. The following commentaries and anticancer programs provide general information for helping affected animals; however, the most effective approach is an individualized plan of natural "immunotherapy" structured by a qualified holistic veterinarian to extend and improve the quality of life and enhance the chances of recovery.

Alternative treatments are highly varied and multifaceted. As Roger DeHaan, DVM, points out, "There is as yet no 'magic bullet' that kills cancer cells. The holistic approach tries to build up the immune system and improve nutrition. Any time you do these things you are going to help the animal—or the person—combat cancer. Working on these critical fronts is basic to any anticancer approach, whether it is medical or natural. I am for building the body's defense mechanisms. The normal pet's body is equipped to kill or discard unhealthy cells. My goal is to fortify this natural ability. I believe this is the best way to tackle cancer."

General points made by the veterinarians include the following:

- **Good nutrition is critical.** Food as medicine is particularly important for very sick animals. An anticancer diet does not include commercial pet food. Cancer patients need a home-made diet emphasizing fresh, wholesome food and lightly steamed vegetables (see chapter 7). Avoid chemical additives. "Unless this is done, animals don't have a fighting chance," says Joseph Demers, DVM.

- **Use of supplements.** Holistic veterinarians recommend multiple nutritional supplements to fortify the immune system. They suggest starting the supplements at a lower dose and working up slowly to recommended levels. You will find that here in this section on cancer different veterinarians recommend some of the same supplements at somewhat different dosages. Your best bet is to select and apply one particular veterinarian's program and work with it. These recommendations are general guidelines that can be used in virtually all cases, even if your animal is being treated conventionally.

- **Stress depletes the body of important cancer-fighting vitamins,** interferes with digestion and the nervous system. Stress thus weakens the immune system and the defense cells that kill or neutralize cancer. Is there a lot of stress in your animal's life? (See discussion on stress later in part 2, starting on page 240.)

- **Last resort.** Holistic veterinarians say they unfortunately tend to see animals who have been previously treated with chemotherapy and who are then brought to them as a last resort. "Even though they may be near the end we can frequently improve their quality of life for the time that is left," says Tejinder Sodhi, DVM, of Bellevue, Washington.

- **Meditation, prayer, and forgiveness.** Do not burden yourself or your beloved pet with guilt, which only blocks healing. Enjoy the time that's left.

SPAYING/NEUTERING AND CANCER—NANCY SCANLAN, DVM, SHERMAN OAKS, CA

Domestic animals are bred for maximum fertility. They go into heat more frequently and produce more offspring than their wild counterparts. In addition, the high-protein and high-caloric foods they eat stimulate more eggs and hence more offspring. Canines in the wild go into heat once a year and have a single litter. A female dog nurses her young longer and expends considerable energy hunting down food. This tends to delay the next heat period.

If you own an unspayed female who keeps coming into heat, and you do not breed her, she will have a tendency to develop cysts on the ovaries and be more prone to cancer, especially breast cancer. If you spay before the first heat, the risk of breast cancer is reduced by about 95 percent; before the second heat, up to 60 percent less. In addition, spayed dogs have no chance of developing pyometra, a potentially fatal infection of the uterus.

Male dogs can develop enlarged prostates. Neutered animals are much less prone to develop prostate cancer, which is somewhat common in older dogs.

MIXED AND MISCELLANEOUS APPROACHES

Natural Diet Plus Supplements—Roger DeHaan, DVM

Even when we do the best for our pets, cancer may still strike. Here are some personal recommendations when this happens:

- Get a full veterinary diagnosis, including a biopsy, and surgery if relevant.

- Feed a natural diet of whole foods that minimizes or eliminates chemical additives. Feed live foods, such as yogurt.

- Supplement the diet with important antioxidant and protective nutrients. Among them I recommend coenzyme Q_{10}, an important antioxidant, especially in cases involving mammary and lung tumors, and noni (morinda), a healing tropical fruit from Hawaii. (The noni product I use, from Nature's Sunshine, is available through Holistic Veterinary Services, at 218-846-9112.)

DOSAGE

- **Coenzyme Q_{10}:** 1 milligram daily for each pound of body weight.

- **Noni.** 1 capsule daily for each twenty-five pounds of body weight.

- **Digestive enzymes** (to support the pancreas and digestion): Follow label instructions.

Antioxidants Plus Chinese Herbs—Nancy Scanlan, DVM

(Note: Scanlan has written a comprehensive book on cancer in pets—*Cancer, All the Options: A Wholistic View of Cancer Therapy*, available through Hibridge Press in San Jose, California, at 800-860-9422. This book offers the latest information on cancer treatment, both conventionally and holistically, for dogs and cats.)

Whatever course of treatment you choose, support it with a strong supplement program to protect and reinforce your animal's immune system. Antioxidant supplements, such as vitamins C and E and coenzyme Q_{10}, will do this, as well as exert specific anticancer benefits. They should be part of any anticancer strategy. Antioxidants also offer protection against the side effects of chemotherapy.

Omega-3 fatty acids, as found in fish liver oils (containing eicosapentaenoic or decosahexaenoic acids), also give nutritional support. Animal studies have shown they inhibit tumor growth and metastasis.

I also recommend two Chinese herbal formulas made for humans that have anticancer properties. They are extremely helpful in dealing with cancer in animals. Both are made by Health Concerns (800-233-9355) and are available through health professionals or veterinarians. I use Power Mushrooms, one of the formulas, for any kind of cancer as well as to boost immunity in animals with weak defenses. I have used Regeneration, the other formula, for its anti-cancer properties as well as its ability to help counteract the side effects of chemotherapy.

DOSAGE

- **Vitamin C:** Build up slowly to bowel tolerance level. (See note to reader at beginning of part 2 on how to give vitamin C in this manner.) Sicker animals need more—and tolerate more—vitamin C than healthy animals.

- **Vitamin E**: Small dogs, 50 international units (IU); medium dogs, 100 IU; large dogs, 200 IU; giant breeds, 400 IU. You can safely double these doses in serious cases. Don't exceed 800 IU.

- **Coenzyme Q$_{10}$:** Small and medium dogs, 20 milligrams; large dogs, 40 milligrams; giant breeds, 60 milligrams. You can use even higher amounts, but watch for possible signs of gastric upset or decreased appetite.

- **Omega-3 fatty acids**: Small dogs, 250 milligrams daily; medium dogs, 500 milligrams; large dogs, 750 milligrams; giant breeds, 1,000 milligrams. Do not use omega-3 fatty acids that are combined with omega-6 oils.

- **Power Mushroom and Regeneration:** Give twice daily. Dogs under fifteen pounds, give 1/4 to 1/2 tablet each time; dogs up to thirty-five pounds, 1 tablet; dogs up to fifty pounds, 1 1/2 tablets; dogs up to eighty pounds, 2 tablets; larger breeds, 2 1/2 to 3 tablets.

Homeopathy, Herbs, and Supplements—Charles Loops, DVM

Seventy percent of my cases involve cancer. Homeopathy offers an effective alternative to conventional approaches for this devastating disease. In general, you can accomplish with homeopathy the same results obtained with chemotherapy, radiation, and surgical treatments. Often we can accomplish more. However, I strongly recommend that you consult with an experienced veterinary homeopath because the remedies used must be skillfully individualized.

We do get cures with homeopathy. More than 50 percent of animals go into remission if treated early enough, but even with more
advanced cases we have results that are similar to invasive therapies,
yet without the side effects. In general, the tumors that respond the
best to chemotherapy and radiation are the same that respond to
homeopathy.

In my opinion, homeopathy helps pain better than any drug. The
animal will feel much better right up to the end. Homeopathy seems
to ensure a dying process that is more natural, as compared with that
of an animal being treated with drugs. Often with homeopathy we
are able to extend the lives of animals given only a short time to live
by other veterinarians. This is because homeopathy uplifts the
animal's life force.

In addition to homeopathics, there are many other remedies you
can apply to strengthen an animal diagnosed with cancer. I have
found the following to be particularly helpful.

DOSAGE
- **Chinese astragalus:** This herb is an excellent immune stimulant that can be used indefinitely on a daily basis. It is available
  as an herbal tincture or in capsule form. Give twice daily. Small
  dogs, 3 drops or 1 capsule each time; larger dogs, up to 6
  drops, or capsules up to the human dosage depending on size
  of animal.

- **Grapeseed extract:** 1 milligram per pound of body weight
  twice daily.

- **Multi-vitamin/mineral:** Pro VitaMix or other quality formulas available through Morrill's New Directions (800-368-
  5057). Follow label instructions.

- **Vitamin C:** Give twice daily. Small dogs, 500 milligrams each
  time; large dogs, 1,000 milligrams.

- **Vitamin E:** Small dogs, 200 IU daily; large dogs, 400 IU.

- **Omega-3 fatty acid fish oils (such as salmon):** 1,000 to
  2,000 milligrams daily, depending on size.

Multiple Supplement Program—Tejinder Sodhi, DVM

The following supplements are basic elements in a nutritional program to help support animals with cancer. Start low and build up to the recommended levels. The supplements can usually be mixed into the food.

One supplement you may be familiar with as a spice, but not as a nutritional aid, is turmeric. This popular Indian spice contains curcumin, a natural substance that acts as a strong anti-inflammatory in the body. It also helps boost the immune system. Turmeric is available at most supermarkets, health food stores, and for sure at any Indian store.

DOSAGE

- **Vitamin C (sodium or calcium ascorbate powder):** Use the bowel tolerance concept. (See note to reader at beginning of part 2 on how to give vitamin C in this manner.) Remember that tolerance varies.

- **Vitamin E:** Small dogs, 100 IU, giant breeds, 800 IU.

- **Digestive enzymes:** Use the pet products made from plant sources. Follow label instructions.

- **Coenzyme Q$_{10}$:** Small and medium dogs, up to 30 milligrams daily; large and giant dogs, up to 120 milligrams.

- **B complex:** Small dogs, give a supplement that has up to 25 milligrams of the major B components; medium to large dogs, 50–milligram potencies; giant breeds and dogs with special needs, 75 milligrams. Special needs refers to dogs debilitated from the illness or who suffer weight loss due perhaps to inflammatory bowel disease and other associated problems.

- **Essiac tea tincture:** 10 drops, two or three times daily.

- **Turmeric:** Small dogs, 1/4 teaspoon. Giant breeds can take up to 1 teaspoon twice a day. Mix into food. Start low and increase gradually.

Whole-Food Supplements—Joseph Demers, DVM

There are a number of potent products available at health food stores that have substantial anticancer properties. Among them are natural whole-food supplements such as kelp and barley grass. Start with a pinch and increase slowly to the recommended label level over two weeks. The ones I particularly recommend are the following:

DOSAGE AND OTHER IMPORTANT DETAILS

- **Sea Meal,** a kelp formula made by Solid Gold (800-DOG-HUND). Kelp nourishes the thyroid gland, which in turn helps to stabilize the endocrine system.

- **Barley Dog,** made by Green Foods Corporation (800-222-3374), containing chlorophyll, antioxidants, amino acids, and enzymes.

My other anticancer recommendations include the following:

- **Essiac tea,** an alcohol-extract product from New Action Products (716-873-3738). Small dogs, 4 to 8 drops daily; medium dogs, 8 to 10 drops; large dogs, 1 to 2 full droppers.

- **Antioxidant supplements.** Find a good product with vitamin A or beta-carotene, vitamins E and C, and selenium. I like to add some of the potent antioxidants such as pycnogenol or grapeseed extract. The daily dosage for these is one-quarter of the recommended human level for small dogs and up to a full dose for very large dogs.

- **Organic flaxseed oil.** This type of product contains important fatty acids believed to combat cancer. Animals don't like the taste. Start with 1 to 2 drops and mix into the food. Slowly increase to 1/2 teaspoon daily for small dogs and as high as 1 tablespoon for giant breeds.

- **Digestive enzymes.** Cancer patients need help with their digestion. Enzymes will enable them to extract the maximum nutrition from the food they eat. Follow label instructions on pet products.

Pau d'Arco Plus Vitamin C—Maria Glinski, DVM
Pau d'arco is a primary herb I use for all species diagnosed with cancer, immune disorders, or chronic yeast infections. It is a powerful

immune-stimulating agent from Brazil, where it is widely used for cancer patients. I recommend the glycerin-based liquid product from Gaia Herbs (800-831-7780), available at health food stores.

The most dramatic effect I have seen was with a group of ferrets with cancer I was treating for a rescue organization. Ferrets are very prone to colds. About five years ago a terrible virus was ravaging the older rescued ferrets. The only ones that did not come down with upper-respiratory symptoms were the ferrets with cancer that I was giving pau d'arco!

I also recommend buffered vitamin C powder (in the form of calcium ascorbate). I have had wonderful results with this combination for animals given little time to live. Many have gone on to live for years. This is a safe and beneficial long-term program.

DOSAGE
- **Pau d'arco:** Give twice daily. Small dogs, 10 drops each time; dogs up to fifty pounds, 20 drops; larger dogs, use the capsule form and give 500 milligrams each time.

- **Vitamin C:** Start with 500 milligrams and slowly increase the dosage to bowel tolerance. Mix powder directly into food. If animal balks at the taste, mix it with yogurt.

CHINESE HERBS FOR MAMMARY GLAND TUMORS
Once an animal is diagnosed with this form of cancer, the conventional opinion is that it will live about six months if you do not remove the tumor. And if you remove the tumor, the prognosis is death within two years from recurring cancer. In my clinic I recommend surgical removal of the tumor, followed by natural remedies on a long-term basis to help prevent recurrences. With this approach many animals live on for years, in the end dying of causes other than cancer.

For such mammary gland tumors, I enhance my supplement program with a traditional Chinese multiple herbal formula called Chih-ko and Curcuma, from Seven Forests (distributed through I.T.M., 800-544-7504). The Chinese name for this formula is Xiao Zhong Liu Pian. It is used extensively in China for cancer and comes in the form of an oval tablet.

DOSAGE
- **Chih-ko and Curcuma:** Give twice daily. Small dogs, 1/2 tablet each time; medium dogs, 1 tablet; large dogs, 2 tablets; giant breeds, 3 tablets.

Extending Life Naturally—Thomas Van Cise, DVM

In many cases we attain good therapeutic results using a variety of different natural approaches where pet owners chose not to subject their animals to chemotherapy, radiation, or surgery. Frequently tumors go into long-term remission. In general, animals that eventually succumb to the disease live much longer than expected and usually more comfortably, without any of the serious side effects associated with conventional treatment.

The type of natural treatment a holistic practitioner selects depends on the severity of the condition, the tissues involved, and what the owner expects. My approach is basically threefold:

1. Acupuncture, probably ten sessions or more, to stimulate the body to fight off the cancer. This technique works well to protect animals against side effects from radiation treatments.

2. Shark cartilage. I recommend Benefin shark cartilage made by Lane Laboratories (1-800 LANE-005). I have little confidence in other shark cartilage brands for cancer therapy. Most companies limit the expected benefits to arthritis.

   One old pitbull I treated years ago was a descendant of "Pete," the dog who appeared in many *Our Gang* comedies. The animal had been previously diagnosed through biopsy with two types of tumors: a hemangiosarcoma, a blood-borne cancer that frequently settles in blood-filled organs such as the liver and the spleen, and an oral fibrosarcoma so big that he couldn't close his mouth. Another veterinarian had recommended the dog be put to sleep.

   First, I surgically removed the oral tumor. Then, sometime afterward, I prescribed shark cartilage, which cleared up the other tumor and also dramatically improved the animal's arthritic condition. The dog was eventually euthanized, not because of his cancer, but because he was feeling so good that he started running after female dogs and severely damaged his arthritic joints!

3. Either uña de gato (cat's claw), a South American herb with a powerful effect on tumors, or Dismutase. The choice is often based on the form (tablet, capsule, liquid, or powder) of the supplement available or on the preference of the pet or owner.

   Una de gato is an antioxidant and adaptogen—a substance that helps the body against stress. I have seen tumors disappear over time when this herbal is used. It is also an excellent agent for reducing or eliminating the serious side effects that accompany chemotherapy. I have found Rainforest Bio-Energetics' una de gato to be a reliable herb (available through Van Cise's clinic at 909-737-1242).

   Most owners of cancer patients are reluctant to stop therapies that contribute to their pet's recovery. The amount of frequency of dosing una de gato or other supplements might be lowered once the pet recovers, but it is unlikely that you would want to stop the supplements completely.

   Dismutase, the other supplement I often recommend, strengthens an animal against cancer. It is an antioxidant made from wheat and soy sprouts. The product is available in tablet form, and dogs usually eat it readily. (For more information on this product, see Van Cise's entry under arthritis.)

DOSAGE

- **Benefin:** 1 gram in either caplet or powder form per fifteen pounds of body weight, preferably on an empty stomach.

- **Uña de gato:** Small dogs, 10 drops of liquid formula twice daily; medium and large dogs, one 500-milligram capsule twice daily; giant breeds, 2 capsules twice daily. The herb works better on an empty stomach.

- **Dismutase:** Small to medium dogs, up to 6 tablets daily; large and giant breeds, 8 to 10 tablets. Give on an empty stomach.

Essiac Tea—Nino Aloro, DVM

My approach to cancer involves a combination of herbs, amino acids, vitamins, and coenzyme Q_{10}. Each case is individualized, but results are generally good.

One of the herbs I use is Essiac, in capsule form, to help promote recovery and for the long term as a preventive against recurrent tumors. Essiac is an herbal combination developed by a Canadian nurse, Rene Caisse, who for a period of more than fifty years treated many hundreds of patients with cancer. Essiac is Caisse spelled backward. Caisse never made her formula public in her lifetime. She said the formula had been given to her by a patient who had been cured from breast cancer by an Indian herbalist. The four main ingredients in Essiac are burdock, Indian rhubarb, sorrel, and slippery elm. In the 1970s Essiac was tested at two U.S. cancer institutions and said to offer no anticancer activity. According to Ralph Moss, Ph.D., in *Cancer Therapy: The Independent Consumer's Guide to Non-Toxic Treatment & Prevention* (Equinox Press, Brooklyn, N.Y., 1992), "the mixture remains worth investigating, not just because of persistent anecdotal reports, but because most of its identifiable components have individually shown anticancer properties in independent tests."

More on Essiac—Michele Yasson, DVM

For any animal being treated for cancer either conventionally or holistically, Essiac tea is an excellent natural remedy. It acts basically as a blood cleanser. It tends to increase elimination—you may see more voluminous stool. It also stimulates the appetite, which is desirable in cancer cases, and increases the immune system's effectiveness against cancer cells.

I recommend a tea called Whisker's Own Rednop Essiac, a blend of Essiac plus pau d'arco and red clover blossom, developed by Whisker's Holistic Pet Products at 800-944-7537. It comes in a powder form that you make into a tea and then administer by dropper down the animal's throat. Essiac tea is mildly bitter. When an animal is fighting a serious illness such as cancer, some people are reluctant to force a liquid medication on animals. Although I prefer the tea, there is an alternative—a freeze-dried crystal form of Essiac that can be put right into an animal's food. It is called E Tea and is made by Nature's Sunshine (800-223-8225).

DOSAGE
- **Whisker's Essiac:** Follow label instructions.

- **E Tea:** Small dogs, one-quarter of the human dose on the label; dogs up to fifty pounds, one-half the label dose; dogs more than fifty pounds, full amount.

NUX VOMICA FOR CHEMOTHERAPY

For animals receiving chemotherapy treatments, I recommend the homeopathic remedy Nux vomica to help the body cope more effectively against the toxicity of the drugs. Chemotherapy often generates adverse side effects. As the treatment progresses, animals are more likely to become sick and develop vomiting or diarrhea. Nux vomica can make a big difference. It can be given at any time during the treatment program.

DOSAGE
- If the side effects are not severe, give a single dose of Nux vomica 30C immediately after the chemo treatment. If side effects are severe, give twice a day for two days.

⚜ Dental Health ⚜

Gum disease among humans is epidemic. More than 95 percent of Americans, for instance, suffer from bad gums during their lifetime. Among dogs, the situation is nearly as bad. Eighty-five percent of canines over four years of age develop gingivitis—that is, infection and inflammation of the gums. Bad breath is a telltale sign.

Gum disease—also called "periodontal disease"—begins with the formation of plaque, a transparent, adhesive fluid composed of bacteria. The bacterial action eats away the supportive gum tissue of the teeth. When plaque is not removed by brushing, cleaning, or an animal eating the right food, mineral salts in the saliva form hard crusts—called "calculus" or "tartar"—over the plaque, which then irritates gum tissue. You see redness and then swelling, the start of gingivitis.

"If neglected, gingivitis turns to periodontitis, a much more serious condition," says Jan Bellows, DVM, a holistic practitioner in Florida, who is one of a handful of certified veterinary dentists. "Animals then develop progressive infection, inflammation, loss of the tiny ligaments that bind the gums to the teeth, bone recession, and loose teeth. Untreated gum disease may also contribute to health problems elsewhere in the body."

Some experts believe that proper dental care can actually prolong a pet's life by 20 percent, so this is a subject to take seriously. How can you prevent gum disease and veterinary dental bills and extend your dog's life? Here is what Bellows and other holistic veterinarians recommend.

Dental Care Dos and Don'ts—Jan Bellows, DVM

(Note: If you have Internet access and desire more information on dental health care for animals, see Dr. Bellows's informative Web site at www.dentalvet.com.)

- **Diet**. In the act of eating prey in the wilds, dogs and cats devour fur, hair, and tough elastic tissue that provides a natural brushing effect on their teeth. But our domesticated animals don't eat food with such "built-in" toothbrushes. Often the food is soft. Despite all the benefits of a good home-prepared meal, with raw or cooked meat added, the consistency of the food is overall soft. Dogs need something harder included in their diets, something that offers some abrasiveness but doesn't damage gum tissue. Some people boil oxtails and feed that as a natural brushing additive to food.

  We often resort to kibble for our animals out of convenience. Ideally the kibble you are feeding your animal should be high quality. Besides convenience, kibble also has a hard consistency that offers a brushing benefit to the teeth before it is mashed into mush. The quality kibble brand I recommend is Cornucopia. It is not a treatment for periodontal disease, but it helps as part of a prevention strategy.

  For tartar control and plaque buildup, I recommend a food

called TD—a prescription diet made by Hills and available through veterinarians. The food is designed to provide a brushing effect on the teeth. Nevertheless it does not take the place of daily brushing.

- **Brushing a must.** Whatever your food choices, you should still brush your animal's teeth if you want to prevent periodontal disease. Brushing is the most important thing you can do for your animal's dental health, and either you do it or face veterinary dental bills later on. If your animal already has gum disease, brushing is critical. Brush every day, just as you do for yourself. Do it twice if possible. Researchers have shown in dogs that if the teeth are cleaned every other day, the preventive effect still works. If you do it less often, forget it. You might as well not bother. It involves an effort, and many of my clients accept the daily brushing because I make a major issue of it.

  Small-breed dogs, such as Yorkshire Terriers and Maltese, are prone to more gum problems because their teeth are closer together. Regular brushing is particularly important for these animals.

- **Use a natural, soft-bristled brush.** Veterinarians and pet stores sell special oral care products. St. Jon's makes a number of good products. You can also purchase "natural" toothpaste at the health food store. Some of the brands I like are Nature's Gate (cherry gel), Peelu, and Dessert Essence.

- **How to brush.** When you do this for the first time, approach your dog gently. If you can start the brushing habit when your dog is young, it's quite easy, but even older pets will accept the process. Try to work the bristles of the brush under the gums. Place the bristles at the gum margin of the teeth. Move the brush in a circular or back-and-forth motion. Gently press the bristle ends into the area around the base of the tooth as well as into the space between the teeth. You can generally cover three or four teeth at a time. Ten strokes should be completed at each location. This is what it takes to clear out the daily accumulation of plaque. If not cleared, it builds up underneath the gums and leads to inflammation, gingivitis, and eventually periodontal disease. The upper teeth attract the most plaque, so spend the most time there.

- **For noncooperative animals.** If your animal isn't receptive to brushing, use a washcloth or piece of gauze to wipe the teeth, front and back. Gently rub the teeth clean around the gum line. Hopefully, you can graduate to a toothbrush, which is preferable. That's what it takes to get under the gum line.

- **If the gums bleed when brushed.** See your veterinarian.

- **Examine your animal's teeth and gums monthly.** Most dogs don't mind if you peek inside their mouths. Look for inflammation (redness), swelling, and broken teeth. A good place to search for inflammation is in the back of the mouth, where the upper fourth premolar teeth meet the gum tissue. This site is where the salivary glands secrete into the mouth. The fourth premolars are the fourth tooth back on each side from the canine, the so-called fang or eyetooth. Your examination should include the entire face. One side should look the same as the other, with no abnormal swellings. When looking at the head, feel the glands under your pet's neck. Both should be the same size. If one is swollen, that could indicate an abscess or infection in the mouth. Be alert for any swelling under the eyes. That may be another sign of an abscess.

- **Smell your pet's breath.** If it smells bad, that's a sign of gum disease or digestive problems, and a trip to the veterinarian is in order.

- **A regular dental checkup by your veterinarian is advisable.** Gingivitis can usually be reversed with a thorough cleaning by a veterinarian while the animal is anesthetized. If treated early, the gums can return to normal appearance and function. If left untreated, periodontitis results. If you need a specialist, contact the American Veterinary Dental Society (800-332-AVDS).

- **Tooth pain.** Cloves are a good stopgap measure for relief until you can see a veterinarian. Cloves contain analgesic properties. Apply the ground clove directly to the affected area.

- **Fractured teeth from chewing cow's hooves.** Many dog owners like to give their animals cow's hooves to chew on. The problem is this: The pressure that dogs apply on the hoof as they chew often breaks the fourth premolar tooth. Bacteria then work their way up the fractured tooth into the root, resulting in abscess. Cow's hooves are not a good idea. Don't give your dogs anything harder than the tooth surface to chew on. I suggest Gumma bones, made by Nylabone, available in most pet stores. If your animal fractures a tooth and is in obvious pain, you can help alleviate the situation by applying arnica ointment to the gum area twice a day for a day. You can also use the homeopathic remedy Arnica in the pellet or liquid form to speed the healing process (see the section on surgery where arnica is mentioned). Arnica works well. But be sure to see a veterinarian. If the tooth is fractured, and the nerve is exposed, the situation will require either root canal therapy or extraction.

- **Ease the stress of puppy teething.** For the discomfort of teething, chamomile works very well to decrease swelling and soothe disturbed gum tissue. A sign of discomfort is an animal pawing at its mouth. Simply apply a chamomile teabag to the gums. First boil the teabag, then put it in the refrigerator. Apply cold. Do this two or three times a day for a few moments until the teeth come in.

- **Vitamin C and coenzyme Q_{10} to fight gum disease.** In humans, a low level of vitamin C in the tissues is associated with a predisposition to periodontal disease. I prefer vitamin C in the form of sodium ascorbate crystals mixed in the food. The vitamin decreases pain, builds up the immune system against infections, and helps to fortify connective tissue and the tiny ligaments binding tooth to gum. Coenzyme Q_{10} is a fat-soluble vitamin and antioxidant that decreases inflammation, swelling, and pocket depths. The mouth must be cleaned first professionally in order for this nutrient to have a pronounced impact.

DOSAGE
- **Vitamin C:** Start with 250 milligrams twice daily. Increase daily dose by 250 milligrams each week until bowel tolerance is reached (see note to the reader at the beginning of part 2 for an explanation of bowel tolerance).

- **Coenzyme Q$_{10}$:** Small dogs, 10 milligrams twice daily; medium dogs, 50 milligrams once daily; larger dogs, 50 milligrams twice daily.

Raw Bones—Michele Yasson, DVM

I recommend raw, meaty bones at least once a week, more often if you can. Give knuckle bones and marrow bones to the big guys and chicken necks to the small dogs. Neck bones don't splinter into long pieces and so are much less risky. Bones help scrape the teeth clean.

I have had many animals facing dental treatment who avoided it just by going on a simple bone program like this. After three or four weeks their teeth are clean.

Most butchers know what you want when you ask for bones for pets. By keeping the teeth clean this way, you don't have the constant tartar and infection in the mouth.

Dentifrice to Counteract Plaque—Alfred Plechner, DVM

Polish your dog's teeth and gums regularly with Pearl Drops, a dentifrice available in drugstores. This does a good job to clean the mouth and counteract plaque formation. Apply the drops with gauze or a washcloth.

If you are interested in performing a more rigorous form of oral housekeeping, ask your veterinarian to show you how to use a dental scaler on your animal. Scaling the teeth once a month is a good way to prevent plaque buildup.

Calendula for General Gum Care—Thomas Van Cise, DVM

To help prevent gum disease, apply calendula, a homeopathic remedy. Purchase a bottle of the mother tincture of Calendula and put 6 drops in 1 ounce of distilled water. Brush with this solution on a daily basis. If there is inflammation, you may want to take a cotton swab and add some additional cotton (from a cotton ball) so that it soaks up the liquid. Use that to cover both the outside and inside of the gums with the Calendula.

Supplement for Better Oral Health—Ron Carsten, DVM

If you have a dog with gum and tooth problems, a good general nutritional supplement to benefit the mouth specifically is Biodent. This human product, made by Standard Process (800-848-5061), can be ordered for you through your veterinarian. It contains bone meal, carrot powder, spleen, and other nutrients that will create a healthier chemistry in the tissue of the mouth and help contain inflammation, while supporting any veterinary treatment that is being given. The product can help reverse deficiencies that have often existed for years.

The supplement takes time to work, so be patient. Keep the mouth clean. Brush the teeth on a daily basis if possible and keep building up the tissue with these nutrients. Also, by feeding animals better food, including some raw meat and vegetables, they tend not to develop a lot of the typical oral conditions.

DOSAGE
• Give twice daily. Small dogs, 1 tablet each time; medium dogs, 2 tablets; larger dogs, 3 tablets.

⚜ Diarrhea ⚜

See Digestive Disorders

⬇ Digestive Disorders ⬇

The section is divided into the following conditions, some of which have similar causes: constipation, diarrhea and vomiting, digestive enzyme deficiency, gas, irritable bowel syndrome, and stool eating.

CONSTIPATION

Too Many Bones—Lynne Friday, DVM

I don't see constipation much in dogs, unless they are overfed with bones. Particularly troublesome are pork bones, which are brittle and break up easily. They can create a cementlike impaction in the colon and actually rip the intestinal walls as they come out. I have had to knock out some animals and pull out the pieces. By then the rectum is bleeding badly.

Metamucil works great. Green beans baby food or cow's milk will help keep dogs loose if they have a tendency to constipation.

If you need to take bolder action, a coffee enema is very effective. This method promotes detoxification of tissues and blood, and the elimination of toxic bile, by stimulating enzyme systems in the gut wall and liver. Use 1 tablespoon of instant coffee for each cup of warm water. You'll need 1 pint of liquid for a small dog and 1 quart for a large dog.

Suck up the mix in a rubber ear bulb syringe that you would use to flush out the ears. For large dogs you can use a turkey baster. Put some Vaseline or vegetable oil on the stem of the syringe or baster to help it go in smoothly. Insert it into the animal's rectum and gently flush out the colon. Don't instill all the liquid at one time. Instill a portion of the liquid, then let the animal walk around. Then repeat. The enema process can be done in a half hour.

Once I treated a 150-pound St. Bernard who hadn't had a bowel movement in five days. The owner liked to feed him pork chops. A coffee enema produced some mighty salvos that did more than hit the fan. Try being on the business end of that. I wore high boots for that operation.

DIARRHEA AND VOMITING

THE ANTIBIOTIC AND DIARRHEA CONNECTION

Many holistic veterinarians recommend probiotics for diarrhea. Probiotics are nutritional supplements, available at all health food stores, that contain billions of beneficial bacteria, such as *Lactobacillus acidophilus* and *Bifidobacterium bifidum*. Many strains of beneficial bacteria are normally present in the gut and perform numerous functions critical to health, including the production of important enzymes, containment of pathological microorganisms, and protection against the formation of cancerous substances. Frequently animals become depleted as a result of taking medications and antibiotics. Antibiotics not only destroy pathogenic bacteria, but also devastate the population of good bacteria. The loss of these beneficial microorganisms can cause vomiting, diarrhea, liver problems, immune imbalances, and allergies.

In any case of persistent diarrhea or vomiting, whatever the cause, see a veterinarian.

Using Probiotics—Ron Carsten, DVM

Antibiotics are infamous for disrupting the normal, essential digestive tract bacteria. Dogs seem to develop more problems from antibiotics than do cats.

To avoid the problems frequently associated with antibiotics and to either maintain or restore the beneficial bacteria population in the gut, start giving the probiotic concurrently with any antibiotic treatment your veterinarian has prescribed. Continue for at least two weeks or more after the antibiotics are completed.

When I treat an animal with a history of multiple antibiotic treatments and digestive problems, I routinely prescribe a probiotic supplement. Quite often I see a major improvement that I relate to the restoration of a bacterial balance. These cases frequently involve dogs who had antibiotic courses as puppies and subsequently suffered from digestive problems. I recommend using the probiotic for at least one month in such cases and ideally for two or three months to fully reestablish the beneficial bacterial colony in the gut.

Probiotics come in different forms—usually as liquids or capsules.

DOSAGE
- There is no exact science for dosing. In general, give your dog each day the equivalent of 5 to 8 billion microorganisms twice a day regardless of size. Monitor your animal closely, and reduce the dose or discontinue the product if problems arise. There may be some individual variation in response. Some patients may be unable to accept a higher dose. This is likely owing to the overall health and condition of the digestive tract. A problem could indicate the presence of other digestive disorders that need to be identified by a veterinarian. It is a good idea to obtain a stool evaluation to determine bacterial status. A reevaluation of the stool after the probiotic has been given for some time is also useful to assess whether bacterial balance has improved.

Fasting—Charles Loops, DVM
Most diarrhea and vomiting situations resolve in twenty-four hours if you fast the animal. If the problem is diarrhea, provide only liquid for the twenty-four-hour period. If the animal is vomiting, do not give any food or liquid.

Be observant. If the diarrhea or vomiting are severe and continuing, see a veterinarian.

Fasting Plus Clay Plus Probiotics—Donna Starita Mehan, DVM
As a general rule, fast the animal for a day. Water is okay, but let the digestive tract have a rest. Provide your animal with a probiotic supplement. Find a good bentonite clay product, usually available in health food stores. Mix the powder into a little yogurt or broth and give to your animal. The mineral powder swells up, slows down the bowels, and acts as an intestinal broom, sweeping away toxins.

DOSAGE
- 1/2 to 2 teaspoons of bentonite clay, depending on the size of the animal. Give up to three times.

Homeopathics Plus Probiotics—Carvel Tiekert, DVM
For the uncomplicated, now-and-then variety of diarrhea, I recommend any of the widely available homeopathic combination remedies for diarrhea along with a probiotic supplement.

Keep in mind also that dogs like to eat junk and can develop diarrhea for that reason alone. Usually it will go away even if you don't do anything. But any time diarrhea continues for some time with an animal, consult with a veterinarian to determine the problem.

Slippery Elm, Nux Vomica, and Clay—Roger DeHaan, DVM

Slippery elm is a wonderful herb that heals, soothes, and nourishes the inflamed digestive tract. I usually recommend Nux vomica, a homeopathic remedy, along with it. Nux vomica counteracts nausea, irritation, and chemical upset in the stomach and upper intestine, while the natural compounds in slippery elm heal the gut.

The combination works quickly together to improve animals who vomit daily or several times a week. Within a day or two many are substantially improved.

An alternative approach is using a third each of slippery elm, aloe vera gel, and powdered bentonite clay, all available in health food stores. The clay has the unique property of pulling out toxins from the intestinal tract. Usually where there is inflammation there are poisons. Bentonite is also a rich source of trace minerals.

Often the problems of diarrhea and vomiting are caused by wrong diet, chemical sensitivities, or reactions to vaccinations. If the remedies don't work, consult with a holistic veterinarian.

DOSAGE

- **Slippery elm:** 1 teaspoon of powder two or three times a day for each twenty-five pounds of body weight. Mix in warm water or chicken broth. Give at time of feeding.

- **Nux vomica 30X:** Twice daily. If a severe episode is occurring, give hourly for four hours, and then three or four times a day as needed. Don't give with food.

- **Bentonite clay:** Small dogs, 1/2 teaspoon of powder mixed in food; medium dogs, 1 teaspoon; large dogs, 2 teaspoons; giant breeds, 1 tablespoon.

Nux Vomica for On-and-Off Diarrhea—Maria Glinski, DVM

Nux vomica is a useful homeopathic remedy for any gastrointestinal tract imbalance, particularly for dogs who have on-and-off diarrhea or constipation. If you have such an animal, keep this remedy on hand. It works quickly, restoring balance and normal motility to the gut.

DOSAGE

- **Nux vomica 30C:** 2 or 3 drops twice a day for three days. If diarrhea is acute or persists, see your veterinarian.

Chinese Curing Pills Plus Pepto-Bismol—Jody Kincaid, DVM

A Chinese herbal formula appropriately called Curing Pills is a useful natural remedy for an uncomplicated upset stomach or vomiting. I recommend it along with Pepto-Bismol, which will coat and soothe the stomach lining. Curing Pills is a human product and comes in the form of tiny, BB-size pills. It is available in health food stores or Chinese pharmacies.

DOSAGE

- **Curing Pills:** Adjust the dosage according to the size of the animal.

- **Pepto-Bismol:** 1 teaspoon to 1 tablespoon, depending on the animal's size. If the upset appears severe, administer every two hours. If the problem persists for more than a day, or a more serious condition is involved, see a veterinarian.

Pectin for Diarrhea—Nancy Scanlan, DVM

For both acute and chronic diarrhea, mix pectin into an animal's food. Pectin is a natural form of fiber found in all plant cell walls and the skin and rind of fruits and vegetables. It has a gel-forming property that acts effectively to bind a loose bowel. It is important to mix it into the food *before feeding* so it absorbs moisture. If you merely sprinkle it on top, it will form a hard rock in the stomach and animals will throw it up. You can purchase pectin at health food stores.

DOSAGE

- Small dogs, 1/8 teaspoon; medium and large dogs, 1/4 teaspoon; giant breeds, 1/2 teaspoon.

Applesauce for Diarrhea—Alfred Plechner, DVM

For mild cases of diarrhea, add applesauce to the food or feed it by itself. Applesauce contains pectin, a natural fibrous substance, and acts to tighten the bowels. You can expect a less frequent loose stool, a controlled stool, and then a solidified stool. Many people feed their animals rice as a binder when diarrhea occurs. Add the applesauce to it for an even better effect.

Kaopectate for Diarrhea—Lynne Friday, DVM

Kaopectate is a reliable preparation. Follow label instructions. If in doubt, use the pediatric dose.

DIGESTIVE ENZYME DEFICIENCY

You are what you digest. The same is true for your pets. That's why many veterinarians and pet nutrition experts increasingly recommend digestive enzyme supplements. Digestive enzymes are produced in the pancreas and salivary glands and help break down the protein, carbohydrate, and fat components of food for use by the body. As animals age, the production of these enzymes often slows down. Supplements are particularly beneficial to aging animals with slumping enzyme production. Deficiencies can also be genetically related, and symptoms will show up among puppies.

Research shows a strong connection between deficiencies and diseases—both acute and chronic. Common signs of deficiencies are voluminous stool, often with undigested fat clearly visible; animals who eat their own feces; and animals who are overtly underweight despite big appetites.

Many holistic veterinarians use enzyme supplements as a primary tool in dealing with many different problems. In some cases they recommend enzymes alone, while in many others it is one part of a multiple-remedy approach. Improved hair coat and skin, increased vigor, a reduction in allergic problems, and maintenance of good body weight are typical benefits of supplementation. Many animals also become more resistant to disease and infections when supplemented. Veterinarians say that enzymes may also aid older animals suffering from joint ailments. By enhancing digestion and absorption of nutrients, including antioxidants and the mineral magnesium, the body is better able to counteract harmful degenerative processes.

Digestive enzyme formulas contain the individual enzyme components that break down different kinds of food. Protease is the enzyme that breaks down protein. Amylase works on carbohydrates, and lipase is the fat-breaking enzyme. Veterinarians advise that it is important to use supplements with a balanced formula of enzymes.

Over the years, highly effective plant-based enzyme supplements for pets have been developed from *Aspergillis oryzae* (a fungus) that are much less expensive than prescription products derived from animals. These supplements are widely available in health food stores and pet stores.

Enzymes for Better Health—Nancy Scanlan, DVM

No matter what you feed your animal, I recommend regularly adding one of the good pet digestive enzyme products right into the food. Prozyme (800-522-5537) is one such product. When animals eat cooked food, many of the enzymes are destroyed. Today there are so many animals with allergies. Enzymes help in the absorption not only of major nutrients that keep the body healthy, but also of the micronutrients that will decrease skin inflammation. People often ask whether it is okay for all the creatures in a multianimal household to have the enzymes, not just the one with problems. Or how do they divide the enzymes when all the animals eat out of the same bowl. No problem. They all benefit from the enzymes. After starting animals on digestive enzymes, people tell me how much better the coat is on all the animals.

Deficiency and Malabsorption—Alfred Plechner, DVM

Malabsorption, the inability to properly absorb nutrients from food, is a major problem that isn't talked about much. I find that about 70 percent of my patients cannot digest food properly. Often an animal has plenty of enzymes, but our modern foods are so concentrated and have so many unnatural combinations that they appear to outstrip the ability to break them down.

Splayed toes and cow-hocked legs are signs that animals aren't absorbing their calcium correctly. I see this all the time. This is a reflection of malnourishment in general. The whole system is being shortchanged.

The classic sign of a trypsin deficiency is an animal eating its own stool. Trypsin is a major pancreatic digestive enzyme that contributes to the breakdown of protein, fats, and carbohydrates. In my practice I routinely test animals for trypsin. Over the years I have determined that nearly a quarter of them have small or moderate trypsin deficiencies.

The impact of deficiency can show up early in puppies, as soon as they start eating solid food. They may grow at a slower pace or not reach full size. The signs could also possibly take several years to show. Often there is an allergiclike dermatitis, hair loss, and red, scaly itchy skin that an animal gnaws on constantly. You may see large stools, often with undigested fat clearly visible. In some rapidly growing puppies and hunting and working dogs, the malabsorption may cause a weakness and lameness.

Dogs with an enzyme deficiency are often thought to be thin despite a ravenous appetite. This is not so in every case. Sometimes the deficiency may contribute to obesity. Many commercial foods have poor-quality, adulterated sources of protein that are hard to break down. The carbohydrates may be easier to break down. So an animal eating voluminous amounts of food in order to get more nutrition will take in more—and absorb more—carbohydrates. This translates to more calories and may result in weight gain.

The causes of trypsin deficiency are basically twofold:

1. **Genetic.** When I first became interested in this problem, I traced a deficiency problem through generations of German Shepherds, Dobermans, and Irish Setters. Now I find it in virtually all breeds, including mixed breeds. The problem is a hormonal-immune disorder due to contemporary breeding practices (see Plechner's explanation of this disorder in chapter 16).

2. **Acquired.** Viral and bacterial infection, or any insult to the pancreas, can affect trypsin production. The aging process also slows down the pancreas and often interferes with enzyme activity. I find this problem present now in practically all breeds, pure or mixed, regardless of age. It shows up earlier in life if the genetic hormonal-immune imbalance is more severe.

With or without such deficiencies, many dogs simply do not have the digestive juices to break down the highly concentrated and processed foods they are fed. The result is malabsorption of food and often food allergies (see section on food allergies). If not enough nutrition is extracted from the food, dogs may be attracted to stool that is loaded with undigested food. Dogs love cat stool because protein levels are way too high in cat food and cats cannot digest the food totally (see stool eating later in this section).

Another aspect of malabsorption is when dogs eat nonfood items. You would be surprised at some of the things they eat. Plastic. Socks. Panty hose. Thread. String. Paper. This unnatural craving is called "pica." In my opinion it is caused by a number of things, such as an enzyme deficiency in which the animal can't fulfill its nutritional needs; a mineral deficiency—that is, not enough trace minerals in the diet; and food sensitivities that aggravate the gut and interfere with proper absorption.

The solution for these kind of problems is often fairly simple— the addition of a good nutritional supplement. The product I use is Power for Life, made by Terra Oceana (805-563-2634). With a wide range of trace minerals, enzymes, and whole-food factors, it covers the malabsorption problem very well.

DOSAGE
• Follow label instructions.

Deficiency in Older Dogs—Carolyn Blakey, DVM

Digestive enzyme supplementation is beneficial for older animals, particularly if they are showing signs of frailty or when there is a chronic digestive disorder. Such disorders often stem from the pancreas not producing enough digestive enzymes. I recommend enzymes whenever I feel an animal is not digesting its food well. Signs of such a deficiency are when there are huge volumes of stool, the animal is eating a lot but can't gain weight, or the animal is eating stool. These are times to bring on the enzymes. Digestive enzymes can be used both for treatment and, on a prevention basis, for the long term. There are many good digestive enzyme products for pets.

GAS

Homeopathic for Occasional Gas—Charles Loops, DVM

Carbo vegetabilis 6C or 12C is a useful homeopathic remedy for the occasionally gassy dog.

DOSAGE
- Once a day as needed.

Better Diet Plus Enzymes—Carvel Tiekert, DVM

Experiment with the diet. Animals respond differently to different foods. Often I find the problem disappears when you introduce a higher-quality diet.

Plant-based digestive enzymes, which are sold widely over-the-counter, resolve the problem in most cases, particularly where a better diet is being fed in the first place, but also for animals eating some of the cheaper foods that cause considerable gas.

In older dogs that suddenly start having gas problems, plant-based enzymes may not work. You may need pancreatic (animal-based) enzymes, as well as a hydrochloric acid supplement.

The Ginger Snap Solution—Lynne Friday, DVM

Feed the animal a ginger snap with meals. Ginger aids in digestion, and I have found that this simple approach helps in many cases.

IRRITABLE BOWEL SYNDROME

This common problem is usually caused by food, allergies, bacteria, or parasites. Irritable bowel shows up typically as diarrhea in dogs, although some animals can also experience vomiting.

A medication called metronidazole is highly effective in rapidly clearing up the condition if it is due to a bacterial overload. When bacteria or parasites are not involved, the cause is probably allergic in nature, creating irritation, inflammation, and turmoil in the intestines and frequently skin allergies as well.

Ayurvedic Herbal Approach—Tejinder Sodhi, DVM

A combination of two Ayurvedic herbs—triphala and boswellia—work very well to provide symptomatic relief of the diarrhea, constipation, and allergic reactions associated with this condition. These products can be purchased at health food stores, Indian stores, or through Ayush Herbs (800-925-1371). Many of the animals I see have been prescribed medication by other veterinarians, and frequently with this combination of herbs I can wean dogs off drugs within a few weeks.

Triphala is a traditional Indian herbal formula made from three fruits—haritaki, bahera, and amla. This is an intestinal cleanser and digestive aid par excellence that promotes regularity and helps eliminate toxins from the body. It also has a great tradition as a *rasayana*, an Ayurvedic term for herbal compounds that rejuvenate and balance the body.

Boswellia is a well-established anti-inflammatory herb prepared from the gummy extract of the Indian frankincense tree.

DOSAGE

- **Triphala:** For store-bought triphala, available in powder or capsules, calculate dosage according to dog's size compared with a human's. For triphala supplement from Ayush Herbs, give dogs up to thirty pounds 1/2 to 1 tablet twice daily; dogs up to sixty pounds, 1 tablet twice daily; larger dogs, 1 1/2 tablets twice daily.

- **Boswellia:** Dogs up to thirty pounds, one 500-milligram capsule twice daily; dogs up to sixty pounds, 1 capsule three times daily; larger dogs, 2 capsules twice daily.

The Antioxidant Approach—Wendell Belfield, DVM

I have had nearly 100 percent success—when no bacteria or parasites are involved—with an antioxidant formula I developed called Vital Tabs, available through Orthomolecular Specialties at 408-227-9334. The formula contains vitamins A and E and selenium and helps keep oxidative damage under control in the bowel. Dogs usually respond to this supplement within a week. Diarrhea and vomiting stop.

Some animals need to be maintained permanently on the supplement. Others can come off of it and are fine. Stress and allergies can trigger recurrences. Should that occur, return to the initial therapeutic dosage.

I don't recommend vitamin C for irritable bowel patients because they tend to have a low threshold or tolerance for the vitamin. Always feed your animal high-quality food, particularly with this condition.

DOSAGE
- Follow label instructions.

The Food Allergy Connection—Alfred Plechner, DVM

This problem often has to do with food allergies and abnormal activity of antibodies in the mucous membrane of the intestinal tract, a result of imbalances in the endocrine-immune systems. (For more details on this widespread imbalance, see Plechner's discussion in the food allergy section and in chapter 16.)

STOOL EATING

This problem is often caused by a lack of digestive enzymes or hydrochloric acid, genetic flaws, or poor diet.

Three Simple Solutions—Nancy Scanlan, DVM

Here are some simple remedies that often work:

- **Digestive enzymes.** Mix into a dog's food. They help break down the food so that the animal obtains more nutrients.

- **Add meat tenderizer to the food.** It also helps to digest the food.

- **Raw zucchini.** I have no idea why it works, but it frequently helps.

Improve the Diet—Roger DeHaan, DVM

A poor-quality diet means that a dog doesn't get enough of the good nutrition it needs. Whatever the cause, improving the diet with high-quality food is always the first place to start the healing process.

Older animals, just like older humans, may have a deficiency in hydrochloric acid, the digestive juice produced in the stomach that breaks down protein. A deficiency can also be caused by a poor diet. You may be able to compensate for a deficiency by using apple cider vinegar, which contains acetic acid. This acid is almost identical in chemical structure to hydrochloric acid. The body is able to provide the added chemicals that enable the vinegar to compensate for hydrochloric deficiency, thus helping in the digestion of protein as well as minerals. For deficient animals, add 1 teaspoon of vinegar directly into the food per twenty-five pounds of body weight. Most dogs like the taste.

An animal with poor digestion isn't assimilating food well and will look to other sources—such as stool—for additional nutrients. Supplementing with a digestive enzyme is another good idea.

Enzymes and Trace Minerals—Joseph Demers, DVM

Young dogs often eat stool as part of their experimentation with life. The habit is usually temporary. When older dogs do it regularly, it's a sign of some deficiency, such as certain digestive enzymes. I recommend a digestive enzyme supplement.

Stool eating, or eating of any unnatural objects such as dirt or plastics, may also be a sign of trace mineral deficiency. So I also recommend a good trace mineral. Kelp and bentonite are good providers of trace minerals. One particular supplement I often use is Trace AniMinerals, from Pet's Friend (800-868-1009).

⅍ Drug Side Effects ⅍

See Toxicity and Drug Side Effects

⅍ Ear Problems ⅍

Chronic ear problems, when both ears are involved, indicate allergies, an ailing liver or kidneys, or some other internal disorder. This is definitely a scenario that calls for a holistic approach and digging down into the cause.

Many alternative veterinarians regard allergies as a common trigger of ear infections. There is often a secondary yeast infection present, the result of moist ears created by the underlying allergy process. The yeast infection requires treatment, frequently on a fairly regular basis, unless the underlying allergic response is handled.

Conventional medicines tend to suppress the normal immune response in the area of the ear and perhaps systemically as well. Strong antibiotics are often used. There's a danger in this type of treatment, says Joseph Demers, DVM: "The ear infection may go away, but in six months the dog develops another one, or maybe bronchitis. The animal is then put on more antibiotics. The condition clears up temporarily. Then sometime later it returns again, or the animal this time develops gastrointestinal symptoms with diarrhea and vomiting. Again antibiotics are used, along with perhaps other suppressive drugs. Has the condition gotten better? No. The dog may have been on drugs for years before a frustrated owner tries an alternative treatment to deal with the chronic ear infections or a more serious problem such as colitis. Situations like this demonstrate the shortcomings of a purely drug approach to illness. The disease was originally at the surface level—in the ears—but became

---

MITES? REAL OR IMAGINED?—CARVEL TIEKERT, DVM

The most common misdiagnosis made by pet owners is that their dogs have mites. "My dog has mites," they will tell me. "The ears are red. The dog is shaking his head."

Some dogs will shake their heads so much that they actually do circulatory damage to the tips of their ears. And it probably isn't a mite problem. Frequently when we look in the ears and see inflammation, but no sign of mites, the problem is usually an allergy. The itchy ears are part of a generalized allergy problem.

I don't believe that mites are that common. If they are present, just put a few drops of mineral oil in the ears with a dropper. That will drown the mites, but the presence of mites may require treating for a length of time.

In general, see a veterinarian when an ear problem develops. The animal could have a damaged eardrum and you would never know it. The veterinarian needs to look in the ears with a otoscope. If you put the wrong thing in the ears on your own, you may cause problems. For instance, if the ears are inflamed and you think there are mites involved when in reality there are none, using a strong mite medicine may make the condition worse.

suppressed and went internal, became suppressed again, and went deeper."

Stress is an overlooked cause of recurrent infections and dogs continually scratching their ears. "You need also to look at potential stress factors in addition to considering offending substances in the pet's diet or environment," says Paul McCutcheon, DVM. "Look for the reasons, and do not just treat the symptoms. You can use as much medication as you can stick down the ear canal, but that won't resolve the initiating reason."

HERBS

The Neem Solution for Mites—Tejinder Sodhi, DVM

Neem oil is a powerful antifungal and antiparasitic herbal agent derived from the Neem tree (*Azaradichta indica*) in India. It generally eliminates the problem without the need to use any toxic insecticide. It is available through Ayush Herbs at 800-925-1371.

DOSAGE
- 5 to 10 drops twice daily in the affected ears for one week. Skip a week and repeat treatment. Skip another week and repeat.

NUTRITIONAL SUPPLEMENTS

Colloidal Silver—Joseph Demers, DVM

The combination of acupuncture and eardrops is often helpful. You may want to try colloidal silver for an uncomplicated ear infection. If there is a smelly discharge, and the dog is shaking its head, use the classic combination of garlic and oil of mullein. These products are available in health food stores. If neither of these preparations work, see a holistic veterinarian.

DOSAGE
- **Colloidal silver:** 5 to 6 drops in the ear daily for up to ten days.

- **Oil of mullein:** Follow label instructions.

The Acidophilus Treatment—Nancy Scanlan, DVM

For either bacterial or yeast infections of the ears, use an acidophilus supplement containing this friendly strain of bacteria that normally resides in the body and provides many essential functions. Here's how to do it:

1. Buy a container of acidophilus in capsule or powder form at the health food store.

2. Clean out the ear of your animal using any of the good natural pet ear cleaning products. Or put 1 ounce of vinegar in a cup of water and flush out the ears. Animals will shake their heads afterward. That's normal any time you put something in their ears. Make sure you get all the water out.

3. Put the equivalent of 1/4 of a capsule of acidophilus into 1 ounce of water. Take an eyedropper and squirt the liquid into the ear to get it deep down. The animal will again shake its head.

4. The acidophilus helps chase harmful bacteria and yeast out of the ear. Leave the acidophilus residue in the ears. The acidophilus will die in there—the ear canal is not a normal habitat for them. Simply repeat this procedure periodically to replace the acidophilus that die.

Bacteria infections are usually gooey looking and may have some pus. Yeast infections are identified by their strong odor—like smelly feet—and an abundance of sticky, dark brown wax. Sometimes there may be a combination of yeast and bacterial infections. Mite infestations are also associated with copious wax; however, the discharge is black in color and crumbly.

The longer that ear infections have gone on, the more debris there will be in the ear canal and the longer the condition will take to resolve. If the infection is of recent origin, you can expect to see improvement within a few days. If the ears stink, you should notice an improvement in the smell. If the ears are full of gunk, you should see less debris. If there is a discharge, you will see a change from color to clear.

DOSAGE
- Twice a day for therapy, once a week preventively for dogs such as Cockers, who tend to get ear infections often. For dogs such as German Shepherds, who have a drier ear, repeat once a month.

FOOD AND SPECIAL DIETS

Feed a Better Diet—Roger DeHaan, DVM

Change your animal's diet to more wholesome, natural food. Years ago I had a case of a dog with cruddy skin and constantly infected ears. The owners were feeding the dog a very poor diet. I advised them to switch to a natural food. In a short time the dog was transformed. Poor diet is often the reason for poor health.

Repeat: Feed a Better Diet—Nino Aloro, DVM

I see many dogs, and particularly Cockers, with otitis, an inflammation of the ear canal. Often these animals have been referred after being "through the mill" of steroids and antibiotics. Their problems haven't cleared up.

Typically you will see a nonpurulent buildup of brownish or yellowish wax along with red ears. Animals are scratching their ears and shaking their heads. I regard this in large part as an allergic reaction to poor-quality food and things like pizza, french fries, and cheese that animals shouldn't be eating. My recommendation is to change the diet to the most wholesome food you can buy. Better yet, if you have the time, prepare home-cooked meals with vegetables, rice (long grain, not instant, and cooked until it is mushy), chicken, and healthy items that are not allergic to the animal.

I also suggest putting the animal on a good vitamin/mineral supplement. I use K-9 Forte from Vetri-Science (800-882-9993), a product sold through veterinarians.

MIXED AND MISCELLANEOUS APPROACHES

Olive Oil and Yellow Dock for Mites—William Pollak, DVM

Step 1: Mix 1/2 ounce of olive oil and 400 IU of vitamin E in a dropper bottle. Warm to body temperature and apply a half dropperful into the ear. Massage the ear canal for a minute or so. Let your pet shake its head and then gently clean out the canal with cotton swabs. Apply the oil every other day for six days. Then let the ears rest for three days. The oil mixture smothers mites and initiates a healing process.

Step 2: Dilute a tincture of the herb yellow dock by putting 9 drops in 1 tablespoon of water. Treat the ears with this mixture, as done in step 1, once every three days for six weeks. Ear mite eggs are quite resistant after they have hardened. For this reason it is necessary to undertake this step. The eggs will hatch out in cycles. If the medicine is present for six continuous weeks, the mites will be eliminated.

Step 3: Thoroughly shampoo the head and ears every two days for at least two to three times to eliminate any mites that may have ventured out from the ears. Also shampoo the tip of the tail, which may have acquired mites when it is curled near the head. Make a tea infusion of yellow dock, cool it down, and use it as a final rinse.

Generally, healthy animals have less problems with ear mites.

Vinegar for Waxy, Irritated Ears—Carvel Tiekert, DVM

If the ears are somewhat waxy, irritated, and inflamed, use diluted vinegar to wash the ears. Use two parts water and one part vinegar to flush out the ears every day or two. This will keep up the acid level and produce an unfriendly environment for any yeast organisms populating the ears. If the ears are soupy with pus, see a veterinarian. This may indicate a serious bacterial infection.

Oxygen for Chronic Ear Infections—Thomas Van Cise, DVM

For chronic infections, such as Cocker ear, I recommend the following combination:

- Earth Bounty Oxy-Max, a liquid oxygen product that neutralizes hostile microbes, from Matrix Health Products (800-736-5609), available in health food stores.

- R-7, an ear wash made by Rich Health, a product you can buy in pet stores.

The combination mechanically cleans out the ear, which most ear products don't do. Most tell you to put in a few drops, but you can't clean an ear with a few drops. The infusion of liquid oxygen stops the bacterial growth. The main reason for the infection is that there is little or no oxygen in the ear, and the bacteria thrive in that kind of a situation. By adding the oxygen, you eliminate that. Most of the time this approach seems to eliminate mites as well.

Put 6 drops of Oxy-Max in 1 ounce of R-7. Stir together. Fill the ear canal with liquid, then massage the ear at the base. Gently wipe out the material with cotton balls on your fingertips, not with cotton swabs. Use this technique preventively once or twice a week or as needed. For some dogs you will need to do it every couple of days and for others maybe once a year.

DOSAGE
- Twice daily until no more debris comes out of the ear, and then to make sure, repeat for another two days.

⚜ Epilepsy (Seizures) ⚜

Epileptic seizures, also known as convulsions, are fairly common in dogs. They are caused by an abnormal functioning in the brain—a kind of short circuit—where electrical impulses go haywire. This results in two types of seizures. One is called a "petit mal," characterized by spasm in a leg or one or more groups of muscles without a loss of consciousness. "Grand mal," the more severe type, causes loss of consciousness along with more generalized spasms. During an episode, which can last up to five minutes, there may be jerking, salivating, and loss of bladder control. A dog may appear confused and exhausted afterward.

Epilepsy is a complex issue, and there is usually not just one simple answer to it. Genetics, toxic exposures, allergies, and trauma may all play a role.

The conventional approach is to administer central nervous depressants—such as phenobarbital—for the remainder of a patient's life. Many holistic veterinarians use combinations of acupuncture, diet, herbs, flower essences, and nutritional supplements to counteract epilepsy. Depending on the severity of the condition, they may be able to lessen or even eliminate the need for medication with these methods. Frequently it requires an integrated approach—using holistic measures and drugs—to control the seizures.

"I have successfully weaned dogs off medication after a number of weeks and been able to maintain them without drugs on good diet and supplements alone," says Wendell Belfield, DVM. "You should work with a holistic veterinarian. Do not stop medication on your own."

One area to pursue with your veterinarian is the allergy connection, especially if the animal has no history of trauma to the head, a prolonged whelping and presence in the birth canal, or exposure to toxins. Research has shown that seizures in some dogs may be caused by food sensitivities (see section on food allergies). "I have found underlying food allergies involved with epilepsy many times," says Maria Glinski, DVM. "Avoid foods with preservatives, coloring, or chemical additives. Serve your animals top-quality food or homemade meals to help reduce the severity of this condition."

FLOWER ESSENCES
(See chapter 11 for general information on essences.)

Rescue Remedy for Seizures—Carolyn Blakey, DVM

Rescue Remedy, or Five Flower Remedy, as it is also called, is an effective and safe tool that pet owners can use to stop seizures. This well-known flower essence often works immediately. Keep the liquid remedy handy if you have an animal with a history of seizures. Give it when a seizure develops. Better yet, give it when you see the telltale signs of an episode. Such signs are variable: animals may become wobbly, clingy, or "spacey"; they may be wanting to hide; or they may suddenly develop the seizure.

Often, with this remedy, a seizure can be aborted before it starts. Many of my clients tell me they are able to cut the number of seizures in half, or by a quarter, and minimize the intensity and duration of episodes. Animals are back to normal much quicker.

Rescue Remedy is not a cure. It buys time while you seek a more permanent solution with your veterinarian, whether it is controlling the problem with drugs or individualized holistic treatments such as acupuncture, herbs, and homeopathic medicines. There are generally no quick and easy answers. Seizures are a deep problem.

DOSAGE
- A few drops in an animal's mouth or lift the lip away from the teeth and squirt a few drops onto the gums.

HERBS

Valerian Root—Maria Glinski, DVM

If your animal still has seizures after you make dietary changes in an attempt to eliminate possible food allergies, I recommend the herb valerian root. Valerian is well-known for its activity on nervous disorders. In mild cases I can usually control seizures with valerian alone.

I use either a liquid or capsule form depending on the size of the dog. The glycerin-based liquid drops are made by Gaia (800-831-7780), available in health food stores. The valerian root capsules I use are 530 milligrams per capsule, made by MMS Pro (available through Emerson Ecologics at 800-654-4432).

Dogs are not being tranquilized by valerian, but they may get a little sleepy if you give too much. Go slow if you increase the dose, and stop if an animal seems to be getting drowsy.

For more severe cases, or if the valerian is not enough, I will add acupuncture and individualized Chinese herbs. If I have to use phenobarbital, the natural approach along with it is powerful enough so that only a minimum dose of the medication is needed.

DOSAGE
- **Drops:** Small dogs, start with 5 drops and increase to 10 if needed; dogs up to fifty pounds, the range is 10 to 20 drops. Give twice a day.

- **Capsules:** Large dogs, 1 capsule up to three times daily depending on need; giant breeds, 2 capsules one to three times daily.

Chinese Herbs—Stan Gorlitsky, DVM

Many years ago I found a traditional Chinese multiherb formula that features bupleurum, a root with a long reputation for healing the liver. Working with an herbalist, I made a few modifications to the formula. The result is a formula I call Bupleurum 12 Combination, available through my clinic (803-881-9915). The product comes in powder form and is mixed into an animal's food.

The combination has a strong calming effect on the nervous system and can often on its own dramatically reduce the intensity and frequency of seizures. In addition, it protects the liver against toxicity and, in particular, against the buildup of drug toxicity from long-term use of phenobarbital for seizures. Animals frequently develop a tolerance to medication and require higher dosages for control. As a result they may become lethargic. With this formula I can usually reduce the amount of medication needed to control seizures. Sometimes I can eliminate medication totally.

If you want to try this formula, work with your veterinarian. Do not reduce medication on your own.

DOSAGE
• Follow label instructions.

NUTRITIONAL SUPPLEMENTS

Taurine for Early Cases—Karen Bentley, DVM

I use a variety of natural remedies for seizures depending on the individual condition. For an animal who has just started developing seizures and has not been on too much medication, the amino acid taurine by itself can often abort epileptic episodes or help diminish the intensity of seizures. You can give it long term. Seizures are usually complicated matters, and by the time I see animals they have generally been on phenobarbital or some other heavy-duty medication prescribed by another veterinarian.

DOSAGE
• Small dogs, 500 milligrams two to three times daily; for larger dogs with severe seizures, up to 3,000 milligrams total a day. Open capsule, mix into food.

MIXED AND MISCELLANEOUS APPROACHES

Is Your Dog Overdosing on Light?—Lynne Friday, DVM

Be aware of the light source around animals with neurological problems, particularly epilepsy. Too much or too little light can exacerbate their problem.

An example of too much is constant exposure to the television screen. Animals are much better off without TV. Keep them away from Nintendo games as well. Intense rapid-eye images and furiously flickering screens generate too much stimulation for the brain and lower the ability of a dog's nervous system to counteract seizures, whatever the actual cause may be. In short, TV simply lowers your pet's neurological threshold. This is a serious consideration if you have an affected animal.

Install full-spectrum lighting where your animal spends much time. Dogs with epilepsy may be light-sensitive. Their condition may become aggravated during the shorter days of winter. If your animal experiences more seizures between October and March, the problem may very well be due to shorter light days. You may be leaving lights on in the house, but the lights are generally of the incandescent and fluorescent types. Full-spectrum lights are more natural. They stimulate the body's production of melatonin, the hormone that governs the internal biological clock overseeing hormonal secretions, the sleep cycle, and repair and rejuvenation activities. Use the same full-spectrum lights you get for growing plants. Make sure the animal has access to it. You will find that animals will spend considerable time under the light if they have a light deficiency. You will also find they have fewer seizures.

⚜ Eye Problems ⚜

Regular physical examinations are a must for animals, and if any problem is developing in the eyes, the veterinarian should be able to pick it up. If you detect something going on in one or both eyes, point it out to your veterinarian. Don't take chances with the eyes.

A severely red eye or an eye closed shut should be examined. It may not appear to be serious, but veterinarians say they have seen eyes lost because people waited twelve hours too long.

HOMEOPATHIC MEDICINES

Euphrasia for Infections—A. Greig Howie, DVM

I recommend eyebright (*Euphrasia*) in the form of a homeopathic tincture, available in health food stores. It helps soothe the eye and acts against conjunctivitis, inflammations, and infections.

DOSAGE
- Dilute 1:15 with distilled water. Use it as an eyedrop. Put 2 to 3 drops in the affected eye three or four times daily as long as the eye is red and inflamed.

NUTRITIONAL SUPPLEMENTS

Coenzyme Q_{10} for the Eyes—Paul McCutcheon, DVM

Frequently I am able to arrest, and occasionally even reverse, the typical opacities that develop in aging dogs with coenzyme Q_{10}, a potent antioxidant. Such opacities may or may not involve cataracts. The surface sign of a clouding lens is a decent indicator of tissue degeneration occurring throughout the animal's body. I have had good experiences with coenzyme Q_{10}, sometimes by itself and other times in conjunction with other antioxidants. This is a good supplement to start with. It helps to energize cells and counteracts free-radical oxidative activity in the body.

DOSAGE
- Small dogs, 15 milligrams daily; large dogs, 30 milligrams.

MIXED AND MISCELLANEOUS APPROACHES

Nourish the Liver to Help the Eyes—Ron Carsten, DVM

Cleansing and nourishing the liver usually helps most chronic eye conditions that have not responded well to drug therapies. The basis for this approach stems from Chinese medicine, which describes a strong connection between the liver and the eyes.

I consistently see better results by adding a simple program with milk thistle, the herb that detoxifies the liver, and glutamine, an amino acid that nourishes the intestinal tract, which in turn eases the burden on the liver. Give supplements with meals.

DOSAGE
- **Milk thistle:** 250 to 500 milligrams twice a day for dogs, depending on size and severity of the condition.

- **Glutamine:** 500 milligrams twice a day for all animals.

Beat the "Blues" with Zinc and C Drops—Mark Haverkos, DVM

Older dogs often get a "bluing," or grayishlike opacity, of the eyes that affects their vision. I have had good results with Eye-C, a liquid remedy from Dr. Goodpet (800-222-9932) that contains zinc and vitamin C. The product, if used regularly, often clears up such opacities. Within six to eight weeks you often notice improvement. Dog owners say their animals are seeing better. Sometimes the product appears to reduce cataracts. It will also help with conjunctivitis, sometimes by itself or as a topical enhancement to antibiotic treatment.

DOSAGE
- 2 drops in a dog's eye once or twice daily.

⚜ First Aid ⚜

FLOWER ESSENCES
(See chapter 11 for general information on essences.)

Rescue Remedy to the Rescue—Jean Hofve, DVM

Always have Rescue Remedy on hand—just in case of an emergency. This is a marvelous Bach flower remedy for any emotional or physical trauma. You can buy Rescue Remedy at any health food store. It reduces pain, removes the edge of panic, and enhances the body's own coping mechanisms.

DOSAGE
- A few drops into the mouth or rubbed onto the head of the animal. Can be given frequently.

HOMEOPATHIC MEDICINES
(See chapter 10 for general information on homeopathics.)

Arnica for Trauma—Charles Loops, DVM
The amazing results consistently experienced with the use of Arnica after trauma gets more people interested in homeopathy than in any other remedy. Arnica is a magnificent remedy for pain, shock, bruising, contusion, animal fights, or bites. It should be the first remedy you reach for. It will stop bleeding, arrest shock, reduce pain, and remove anxiety associated with injury and surgery (see section on surgery). The sooner it can be given after injury, the better the response. Keep a supply in your first-aid kit, car, workshop, kitchen, and bathroom.

Arnica 30C will work for just about every situation. For life-threatening, major shock situations, higher potencies of 200C or 1M have amazing results. I have seen Arnica at such high potencies literally keep animals alive who were severely injured by automobiles. If they do succumb to their injuries, they do so much more peacefully.

DOSAGE
- Repeat doses as needed. Immediately after trauma, a dose can be given every few minutes. The farther in time from the trauma, the less frequently the remedy is given.

Arnica Gel—Robert Goldstein, VMD
If you want double the healing help, use an arnica gel topically along with the homeopathic remedy orally. Arnica gel contains *Arnica montana*, a plant with a great healing history against bruises, aches, and pains. The brand I use is ArniFlora, made by Boricke and Tafel, available at health food stores and even some pharmacies.

Apply the gel up to four times daily (externally only) for bumps, bruises, swelling, or joints that are stiff from overexertion or arthritis. Part the hair and gently rub the gel directly on the skin. Avoid getting it into the eyes, and do not use the product if there is any break in the skin. If pain or swelling appears to worsen or persist for more than two or three days, see your veterinarian.

Calendula for Cuts and Raw Skin—A. Greig Howie, DVM

Calendula (marigold) is a remarkable healing agent. I am amazed at how fast it works for scratches, cuts, and raw skin. Calendula ointments, or liquid mother tinctures, are readily available in health food stores. If you use the liquid form, put a dropperful in a cup of water with a pinch of salt to clean out a wound. Don't use it for puncture wounds, because it may heal the top of the wound too fast and leave the infection below. There is no problem if an animal licks it off after you apply it.

MIXED AND MISCELLANEOUS APPROACHES

Stop Bleeding with Pepper—Stan Gorlitsky, DVM

If an animal incurs a minor bleeding wound or cut, sprinkle on some common cayenne pepper from your kitchen spice rack. Pepper enhances the clotting process and helps to stop the bleeding.

Activated Charcoal for Poisoning—Roger DeHaan, DVM

For emergency situations over weekends or where you can't get to a veterinarian, activated charcoal is a great remedy. This is for the quick response, where your animal has gotten into a bottle of medicine and downed quantities of pills, or raided the neighbor's garbage can, or eaten a poisonous plant or rotting fish on the beach. You can purchase it at health food stores or through Holistic Veterinary Services (218-846-9112).

Activated charcoal is a time-tested, primary remedy that is always safe and never contraindicated. You almost can't give too much of it in situations like these. The secret of activated charcoal is its adsorption power—that is, its ability to draw poison to itself, form a permanent bond with the poison, and escort it out of the body.

Charcoal is the black part of partially burned wood. In folk medicine it has long been used as a remedy for many poisons and is referred to as "the universal antidote." Activated charcoal means the wood has gone through a special process of slow burning in a pit under oxygen deprivation, which gives it several times the "binding power" of normal charcoal. The substance can hold many times its own weight in toxic substances.

If an animal ingests a toxic substance and vomiting occurs immediately, then there is really no crisis. The concern is if the poison is not vomited from the system. The charcoal benefits the animal by adsorbing whatever poison is present in the system and eliminating it through the bowel. But in any case, see your veterinarian or nearest emergency clinic as soon as possible.

The charcoal can be given as a capsule to the animal, but it can also be opened and syringed or force-fed in any food the pet likes, such as yogurt, applesauce, or chicken broth. The powder is black and messy, but it can make a difference in time of crisis.

The U.S. Food and Drug Administration rates activated charcoal as effective in adsorbing many drugs, poisons, and gases. Today you will find this substance in most hospital emergency rooms, where it is used for drug overdoses and accidental poisonings.

Call your veterinarian or veterinary emergency clinic any time a poisoning occurs.

POISONING BY MEDICATION

According to the American Veterinary Medical Association, drugs are by far the most common type of canine poison exposure. The association strongly advises keeping all medications "out of the reach of inquisitive noses, which are too often attached to undiscriminating mouths!" Similar to children, dogs can be poisoned by human or veterinary drugs as a result of accidental ingestion or overdose.

Human over-the-counter pain relievers are occasionally used in veterinary medicine but should be given only if a veterinarian specifically directs you to do so. Dogs, and cats, do not respond in the same way to human medications as people do. A minimal human dose can poison an animal. As little as 2 regular-strength tablets (325 milligrams) of acetaminophen (Tylenol), for instance, can cause signs of poisoning—salivation, vomiting, weakness, and abdominal pain—in dogs, particularly small animals.

For an excellent overview of common poison dangers, refer to the American Veterinary Medical Association's "Pet Poison Guide" on the organization's Web site. The Internet address is http://www.avma.org/pubhlth/poisgde.html.

DOSAGE
- 2 to 16 capsules, or 1 to 6 teaspoons of powder, depending on size of animal and potential severity of poisoning. Treatment may be repeated in ten to thirty minutes.

Comfrey for Fractures—Norman C. Ralston, DVM

Use comfrey to help speed bone healing. It is available in different forms: homeopathic remedies, herbal tinctures, and powders and capsules. Comfrey can be used internally or as a poultice applied directly to an affected area. It can make a dramatic difference for slow healing breaks.

Weeds for Wounds—Carolyn Blakey, DVM

Plantain, a common weed found in many backyards, has numerous healing and antiseptic benefits. It can be applied to superficial wounds, infections, stings, bites, or localized itchiness (such as poison oak or ivy) or used to help draw toxins or splinters to the surface of the skin. Boil plantain leaves in water. Dip a washcloth and apply as a warm poultice over the affected site. Use it several times a day for a few minutes each time or as often as you can while there is a problem. If the wound worsens, see a veterinarian.

⚕ Fleas, Ticks, and Insect Pests ⚕

Even though flea allergies are the most common allergies, holistic veterinarians often comment that healthy animals are less likely to be "flea magnets." The key to resistance, they emphasize, is feeding a superior diet.

As William Pollak, DVM, says: "The best flea control is a vital animal that radiates health and fitness, an animal consuming fresh, wholesome food and living in a good, natural balance with its environment. The presence of fleas is an indication that you need to create greater life energy in your pet."

Florida, with its heat, moisture, and sandy soil, is a paradise for fleas. Yet Florida veterinarian Joseph Demers, DVM, says that dogs who are healthy just don't attract the fleas, or if they do, it is minimal. The same holds true with the wild animals who are brought in. The weak ones are full of fleas, ticks, and parasites, he says. The stronger ones are much less affected.

FLEAS

Natural Vs. Advantage—Robert Goldstein, VMD

I have spoken to both holistic and conventional veterinarians about Advantage and similar products. The consensus is that these are relatively safe and a vast improvement over the older generation of products derived from nerve gas (organic phosphate poisons) that had overt, proven negative health effects.

My advice is to use natural approaches first, and if they work, fine. But if you have a continuing problem, use Advantage, which appears to be the best of these products according to my research. However, it is not for every animal. If your animal is older, debilitated, or battling an acute or chronic disease, such as cancer, don't use it.

With any chemically based product, there may be some side effects in a small number of cases. A local, transient rash or irritation is the most common. Rarely, an animal might go off feed, vomit, or show increased thirst, urination, or diarrhea. If these signs occur, stop using the product and consult your veterinarian at once.

First, though, give natural methods a fair chance. I recommend Internal Powder, available through Earth Animal at 800-711-2292. This product is a formula I developed nearly twenty years ago that contains unprocessed brewer's yeast and mineral-rich ingredients. Follow the label instructions. It can be mixed with yogurt and then blended into your dog's food. You can safely double the dose on the label to gear up for flea season.

Garlic is another useful flea deterrent, as well as an all-around immune system and cardiovascular "tonic." If you don't like the odor it produces, add some chopped parsley.

To boost the natural program from the outside, I am a longtime fan of a product called 100% Natural Flea and Tick Repellent, made by Quantum Herbal Products and available through the manufacturer (800-348-0398) or Earth Animal.

I also recommend Cloud Nine Herbal Dip by Halo (800-426-4256). It is safe and easy to use and contains powerful aromatic herbs (pine needle, peppermint, tea tree oil, rosemary, sage, and eucalyptus) that will last a good month on your animal's body. It can be used as a dip or spray or added for antiflea power to your favorite shampoo.

If your animal is still plagued by fleas after using these kinds of natural approaches, I suggest turning to Advantage. Use it only as often as necessary. Many of my clients stretch the dose to every six weeks and find no falloff in effectiveness.

When to Use the New Flea Products—Carvel Tiekert, DVM

Over the years I haven't found that natural products work well in the face of a severe flea problem. I have a huge number of satisfied clients using Advantage, Program, or Frontline, the new pharmaceutical antiflea medications. Many of these pet owners previously tried natural products and suffered through the constant warfare. The new products appear safe and effective. I have encountered only one animal who had a skin reaction.

I don't push the pharmaceutical products because I don't think they are necessary in most cases. I suggest waiting until there is a problem before starting them. If a problem develops, first try brewer's yeast, which works for some animals, or garlic, or some other natural flea control product available at pet and health food stores.

One case where I found the pharmaceutical approach necessary involved a Golden Retriever with a chronic, unremitting, severe flea allergy. He was ultrasensitive to fleas. After one or two bites, he itched for days. We tried all the natural weapons at my disposal on this dog. Frontline came along, and we started him on that. Within two weeks he was no longer scratching. Within a month the sores disappeared and the dog had a flea-free summer and a good coat for the first time in five years. Sure, it may be more toxic, but I had a happy dog and a happy owner.

Frontline and Advantage kill the fleas on the animal. Program sterilizes the fleas. If you have an animal sensitive to flea bites, Program won't provide immediate relief because the fleas are still aboard. Eventually it will help, since you won't have hatching eggs to renew the cycle, and the number of symptom-producing flea bites will be significantly reduced. However, if the animal ranges over any territory of consequence where it can attract a new crop of fleas, then Program is virtually useless.

As for collars, herbal or otherwise, they aren't effective in my experience. Don't forget regular combing of the hair coat. The flea comb is the most important thing an owner can use to determine whether the flea battle is being won or lost.

Natural Remedies for Fleas—Joseph Demers, DVM

A combination of brewer's yeast and garlic may be helpful, as long as the animal isn't sensitive to the yeast. If scratching intensifies after you start brewer's yeast, then you know it's not the right thing for your pet.

You can help control fleas inside your house by using boric acid products on your carpets and floors and outside with nematodes and diatomaceous earth. These products are widely available in health food and pet stores. Follow label instructions.

Make it your routine to regularly bathe, brush, and comb your animal. If your animal is healthy, these simple measures can go a long way to minimize the presence of fleas.

For flea and other insect bites, the homeopathic remedies Apis mellifica and Rhus tox often provide relief within twenty-four hours from the usual scratching.

Dosage
- **Apis mellifica 6C:** Give up to five times daily if there is a raised red bump at the site of the bite.

- **Rhus tox 6C:** Give up to five times daily if there is less sign of inflammation.

Fleas Flee from Flowers—Carolyn Blakey, DVM

For situations where your animal is bothered by a few fleas and there is no major infestation, and you don't want to use a poison, try Flee Free, a liquid flower essence remedy from Molly Sheehan's Green Hope Farms (603-469-3662). You can use it as a spray or give directly to the animal.

Dosage
- Follow label instructions.

Nontoxic Dip—Lynne Friday, DVM

If you need to resort to a dip, I have found an excellent nontoxic product that works well for virtually all patients, whether they are very young or very old. It is called LymDyp S and is a ready-to-use solution of sulfurated lime that leaves a nice scent on the animal. It is available through DVM Pharmaceuticals, Inc. (305-575-6200), but needs to be ordered for you by your veterinarian.

DOSAGE
- Follow label instructions.

TICKS

Homeopathic Ledum for Ticks—Charles Loops, DVM

The homeopathic remedy Ledum works well for puncture wounds and in particular to counteract tick-borne diseases such as Rocky Mountain spotted fever or Lyme disease.

Use Ledum if you see any swelling or sensitivity at the site where a tick has been removed. Most of the time there is no reaction. However, if you live in an area where there is a known prevalence of tick disease, Ledum is an effective preventive measure that can be used during the height of the tick season.

DOSAGE
- Give Ledum 30C once after removal of tick. For general prevention, give every five to seven days during tick season.

LEDUM FOR SPIDER BITES

Spider bites usually produce a local hard swelling without heat. If you suspect a bite of this nature, Ledum is a good remedy.

DOSAGE
- Ledum 30C twice daily for two or three days or until the swelling disappears.

More on Ledum Vs. Ticks—Michele Yasson, DVM

I have seen more dogs develop the fever and arthritic symptoms of Lyme disease after being vaccinated for the disease rather than after being bitten by a tick. I have treated many animals who have become lame after vaccination—some within a matter of days, others in two months or more. Some medical experts have mentioned the connection between the vaccine and symptoms.

The homeopathic remedy Ledum is excellent for any kind of puncture wound in general, and for Lyme disease in particular, it is one of the best natural medicines available. A tick bite is like a puncture wound. If your animal gets a tick, remove the insect and then use the Ledum.

Echinacea is also useful as a natural immune booster, and I recommend it for cases of tick bite. I prefer the capsule form, which is tasteless and can be mixed right into the food.

DOSAGE
- **Ledum 30C:** Once within twenty-four hours of removing the tick. If the tick is engorged with blood, this is an indication that the insect has been present longer. In such cases, give Ledum once a day for two days.

- **Echinacea:** Dogs under twenty pounds, one-quarter the human dose; dog up to fifty pounds, one-half the human dose; dogs over fifty pounds, full human dose. Give for five days.

FOR OTHER INSECTS
For insect bites and sudden swelling, the homeopathic remedy Apis is most effective. Apis is good for situations involving swelling. Many times you see the swelling go down after the first dose.

DOSAGE
- **Apis 30C:** Once may be enough, but the dose can be repeated as often as every ten minutes, for a total of four doses a day if needed.

MANGE

These minuscule mites, normally present in the hair follicles of dogs, often multiply in young dogs with weak immunity or who are under considerable stress. The sign of mange is the development of skin irritation, sores and scratching, and hairless patches on the face, undersides, elbows, and paws. Often veterinarians see the problem in puppies after vaccination, spaying, and neutering.

Ayurvedic Herbs—Tejinder Sodhi, DVM

I have used a three-part Ayurvedic herbal approach to this problem with excellent results. With only a few exceptions, this method eliminated the parasites within three to six weeks. The individual products—neem oil, ashwaganda, and triphala—are available through Ayush Herbs at 800-925-1371. Neem is well-known for its antiparasitic properties. Ashwaganda counteracts stress and enhances the immune system. Triphala is the classic Indian herbal formula to cleanse the intestinal tract.

DOSAGE AND USE

- **Neem oil:** If dog is chewing its paws because of mange, put 10 to 15 drops of oil in a basin of warm water. Soak paws twice a day for five to ten minutes each time. Afterward, gently rub oil into affected skin. If mange is present elsewhere on the body, use a washcloth that has been soaked in warm water to cleanse the affected area. Then gently rub oil into the skin morning and evening.

Caution: Do not use the oil around the eyes.

- **Ashwaganda:** Dogs under twenty pounds, give 10 drops of liquid ashwaganda twice daily for each ten pounds of body weight; dogs up to thirty pounds, one 500-milligram capsule or tablet twice daily; dogs up to sixty pounds, 500 milligrams three times daily; larger dogs, 1,000 milligrams twice. Give after feeding.

- **Triphala:** For store-bought triphala, available in powder or capsules, calculate dosage according to dog's size compared with a human's. For triphala supplement from Ayush Herbs, give dogs up to thirty pounds 1/2 to 1 tablet twice daily; dogs up to sixty pounds, 1 tablet twice daily; larger dogs, 1 1/2 tablets twice daily.

Supplements Plus Homeopathy—Joseph Demers, DVM

I recommend a broadside of reliable supplements along with a homeopathic approach, depending on the individual animal. Some of the products that help fortify the immune system and give relief include colloidal silver drops, vitamin E, or aloe vera applied directly on the sores. These products are available in health food stores.

Animals with mange frequently have a marginally functioning thyroid gland. For such cases, kelp is useful to stimulate the gland, which governs the skin. An excellent kelp product is Sea Meal, made by Solid Gold (1-800-DOG-HUND). Follow label instructions.

⚜ Food Allergies ⚜

See also Digestive Disorders

A healthy animal may not have trouble eating most foods. However, if you feed the same food daily for years, there is potential for intolerance to develop—particularly if you are feeding a cheap, poor-quality commercial pet food. Any individual animal can become allergic to any food—a protein source, a fruit, a vegetable. Just a small amount of an offending food could be enough to trigger reactions in some animals. In others, reactions occur from constant feeding of the same food.

Food allergies may manifest as intestinal upset, poor absorption of nutrients, or a variety of other problems. Remember that each animal is individual. Two hypersensitive dogs will probably react differently to the same food depending on their individual weaknesses and strengths.

"The HIT List" of Troublesome Foods—Alfred Plechner, DVM
(Note: Food allergy expert Alfred Plechner, DVM, was a co-creator of the first lamb and rice diet, marketed by Nature's Recipe, and also helped design the company's line of special diets for food-sensitive animals.)

Based on years of treating animals for food allergy-related disorders, I created an allergic "HIT list" of major food offenders. These are the foods that set off the alarm most frequently—that is, that cause the most trouble in sensitive animals. You may have a dog who is sensitive to any one or several of them. In past years animals may have been able to tolerate these foods, but because of hormonal-immune system imbalances caused by improper breeding practices, increasing numbers of animals are intolerant and can develop both acute and chronic conditions as a result.

THE HIT LIST

1. Beef and beef by-products.
2. Milk. In my experience, perhaps as many as 80 percent of animals, no matter what age, cannot tolerate cow's milk. After drinking it, they usually have gassy stomachs, vomiting, loose stool, or diarrhea. Raw, low-fat, or nonfat—it doesn't matter. There is a much greater tolerance to cottage cheese, other cheeses, and yogurt.
3. Yeast, yeast-containing foods, brewer's yeast (as given to animals for supposed flea protection). Unfortunately, quite a few animals are sensitive to yeast.
4. Corn and corn oil.
5. Pork.
6. Turkey.
7. Eggs. They can be allergenic, particularly the whites. If you want to test your animal, cook the eggs. Don't give them raw. Years ago eggs were used in preparing distemper vaccines for dogs, but they were dropped from the formulations when it was found that they caused allergic reactions in many animals.
8. Fish and fish oils. If you want to provide omega-3 fatty acids to your animal, use plant oils instead, such as flaxseed oil.
9. Wheat and wheat by-products (when in combination with other allergens).
10. Soybeans. This used to be a fine source of protein, but now many animals can't handle it. Tofu, the fermented soybean product, is less allergenic, but nevertheless some animals are sensitive to it.
11. Chicken.
12. Lamb *and* rice!!!! Surprise. See following text.

The HIT list may shock you. You may be thinking, There is nothing left to feed my animal. Lamb and rice, too. Isn't that supposed to be a hypoallergenic combination—that is, food that is safe for sensitive animals? Please read on. There is hope: there are solutions for highly sensitive animals.

When I first participated with Nature's Recipe to develop a commercial lamb and rice diet, the intention was to produce a cleaner food that would be palatable and tolerated by the many animals sensitive to the adulterated beef by-products widely used in the pet food industry. The thinking was that if you fed a food—such as lamb and rice—that animals weren't used to eating, you could avoid or minimize food allergies. That was in the mid-1980s—and the idea worked.

Today, however, there are something like sixty versions of lamb and rice on the market. Diets are inundated with lamb and rice, and increasingly animals are developing an intolerance to lamb and rice recipes. The sensitivity can possibly be explained in part as a result of the constant exposure to lamb and rice, or it could be due to some individually offensive ingredient used in a particular formulation. I have found that often an animal can tolerate one brand of lamb and rice but not another, so you have to wonder what else is in the other brand. Pet foods are highly processed with many chemicals and multiple ingredients, often of questionable purity, and any one of them could be the triggering agent.

Interestingly, I have found recently that some animals who now appear to be sensitive to lamb and rice can handle beef-based diets better, at least for a while. This may possibly be because they haven't been exposed much to beef. If you decide to try your animal on beef, it should be a healthy form, not adulterated and shot up with hormones.

Many health-oriented pet owners like to feed rice to their animals, and particularly brown rice, which is more nutritious. Just be aware of the possibility that some animals may react to the rice whether it is white, brown, or basmati.

In order to help affected animals who seemingly have fewer food options open to them, I worked with Nature's Recipe eight years ago to develop "limited antigen diets." The idea was to combine potatoes with duck, venison, and rabbit—foods that animals had little exposure to and that were thus less likely to cause problems. Testing validated the concept, leading to the production of a number of dry and canned foods for dogs and cats. Each item has just two ingredients so as to limit the potential for allergic reaction.

The recommendation is to use a particular food for four to six months and then switch to another. For example, you feed duck and potatoes for four months, then switch to rabbit and potatoes. These foods, sold under the label of Innovative Veterinary Diets, are widely available on a prescription basis from veterinarians for animals with food disorders. For additional vitamins, minerals, and enzymes, I recommend adding to the base food fresh vegetables and fruits that your animal can tolerate, plus a good nutritional supplement. The supplement I recommend is Power for Life, made by Terra Oceana (805-563-2634). It contains a health-boosting range of vitamins, trace minerals, enzymes, and whole-food factors. Follow label instructions.

Outside of the food itself, there is another extremely important aspect to the issue of food allergies. Many of our companion animals suffer from a widely unrecognized endocrine-immune dysfunction, a genetic fallout from years of inbreeding and line breeding. Among other things, this can create an erratic metabolism, intolerance to many foods, and abnormal immune reactions.

When certain hormones go awry, they fail to properly regulate the immune system. In the digestive tract, uncontrolled immune cells challenge food components as foreign invaders, setting off a whole scenario of upset, intolerance, and malabsorption, resulting in animals not being able to extract adequate nutrition from the food.

As genetic defects become perpetuated in the gene pool of breeding stock, it appears that more and more animals are able to tolerate fewer and fewer foods. With severely affected animals, unless you correct their deep-seated hormone-antibody levels with replacement therapy, there is hardly anything left they can eat. This may sound overly dramatic, but the reality in my practice is that I see more pets in this sad shape now than before—and I have been studying this problem for many years. The situation has become worse, and many animals are dying early in life because of it. In my opinion we have entered into a genetic ice age! See chapter 16 for information about a blood test that can determine such genetic imbalances and what can be done to address them.

TIPS FOR FEEDING SAFER FOODS
If you have a food-intolerant animal, the following suggestions can help minimize problems:

- Always read the list of ingredients on the label. The shorter the list, the better. The longer the list, the higher the odds of encountering an ingredient the animal can't tolerate.

- The first three ingredients on the label usually make up 90 percent of the contents.

- Try to avoid ingredients on the HIT list, foods that often cause reactions in susceptible animals.

- Look out for, and avoid, products with chemical additives. This means the artificial colors, artificial flavors, artificial sweeteners, chemical preservatives, and stabilizers. All have the potential to intensify or wholly activate an allergic reaction.

- Fresh and wholesome foods are, of course, much better for your animal as they are for us. But they, too, have the potential to cause reactions because of hormonal-immune imbalances. This includes raw meat. The food may be great, but your animal just may not be able to tolerate it.

THE ADD-BACK PLAN

On your own you can try developing an individually safe diet for your pet. If you feel there is some problem with the food you are giving your animal, start feeding a simple diet of low-fat cottage cheese and potatoes. I have found that to be tolerable for most animals.

Do this for a week. Feed one part cottage cheese to four parts boiled white potatoes (don't use red potatoes, as they have a tendency to create diarrhea). If the stools are good, and there are no signs of food intolerance such as scratching, stomach upset, or diarrhea, then do a slow add-back of foods, one at a time, and each for a week before you add another.

I suggest starting add-back with a homemade food first, perhaps some vegetables or even chicken. If there are no reactions, you might find a commercial chicken product for pets and test it the same way the following week. Make sure the contents include no common allergenic items. See if your animal does as well as on the homemade chicken.

You can continue to add back any food to the regular diet after it has passed the seven-day test. You can then rotate, mix, and ad-lib within the boundaries of tolerated food. In this way you can soon develop an individualized hypoallergenic menu for your animal.

Another option is that after a week of cottage cheese and potatoes, you can also introduce a commercial pet food in this same add-back manner. Be alert for reactions. Remember that commercial food has multiple ingredients that increase the potential for reactions.

The key points of the add-back diet are these:

- Add back only one food per week.

- If your animal is on any program of medication, don't stop the medication unless your veterinarian says it's okay.

- Eliminate any chew sticks, vitamins, biscuits, or snacks when you are testing. Any one of these items can be the cause of allergic reactions. In this plan, all foods and even ingredients in nutritional supplements are guilty until proven innocent. Later, once you have a firm handle on a problem-free diet, you can slowly begin to reintroduce supplements again. But monitor them as you would the food.

- It's okay to feed from the table if you eat healthy. Unseasoned pastas, vegetables, and salad can be mixed into a base diet. But if your animal starts to scratch, vomits, has diarrhea, or becomes lethargic, than the light bulb should go on. You may have fed something that your animal cannot tolerate. Use common sense!

Observations on Lamb and Rice—Maria Glinski, DVM
I am seeing more food allergies to things we never saw animals allergic to ten years ago, such as lamb and rice.

More Observations on Lamb and Rice—Nancy Scanlan, DVM
Many companies are still selling lamb and rice diets as the answer to food allergies. It's not the answer anymore. Any dog can be allergic to any protein or grain. Lamb and rice was used for so long because previously nobody was feeding it. Now everybody feeds it. Today we are seeing duck and potato diets; this may work for a while, but eventually animals may become sensitive to that. Then we'll see octopus and quinoa, ad infinitum, until we run out of exotic meats and grains to feed hyperallergenic pets.

Too many of the commercial foods have multiple ingredients, which multiplies regular exposure and promotes the potential for multiple sensitivities. I prefer to try to limit the number of meats and grains present in the diet so you can more easily fall back on a different food source if a food allergy does develop. You may have to go to a mono diet, where you start with one food and then add others slowly to test for sensitivity.

Some people will feed a special hypoallergenic diet and then continue giving a treat that has ingredients their animals may be allergic to, such as dairy, wheat, or beef. Watch out for the "extras" you give your animals, including table scraps. They can cause problems just as much as the daily entrée.

Research the Food Tradition of Breed—Lynne Friday, DVM

Years ago I was able to help about half my skin cases on lamb and rice, and within two to three months their skin was fine. Now there is so much lamb in commercial foods that it isn't working anymore. If your animal has persistent problems, try to do some research. Learn about the background of your animal, where it came from, what foods it traditionally ate and evolved on. I recommend a book by William Cusick called *Canine Nutrition* (available through Doral Publishing at 800-633-5385), which covers this issue and offers breed-specific food ideas.

I attribute fully half of all the skin problems I see in my practice, and many cases of diarrhea in dogs, to inappropriate grain, protein, and other food sources for a particular breed or breed mix. We have food here available year-round that may be wholesome and healthy but just may not be appropriate for an individual pet.

Chow dogs originated in China, where they were fed indigenous grains such as rice and barley. You put them on beef-based products and wheat, on "our stuff," and they develop horrible skin conditions. Similarly, when you come to a veterinarian with a Shar-pei puppy, a breed that also originated in China, the veterinarian knows you are going to be making many visits to the clinic over the lifetime of the animal. They have many skin and allergy problems.

Try a Vegetarian Add-Back Diet—A. Greig Howie, DVM

Usually a combination of things relates to allergic skin conditions, such as pollen, food, and fleas. If you can eliminate just one of the offenders, you may be able to minimize or prevent symptoms.

Food is a practical place to start. Feed your animal something it is not used to. Years ago it was lamb. Lamb was something that pets normally didn't eat in this country. So we gave the animals lamb, thinking it would be great for skin problems. But now there is lamb in all the dog foods, so you can't use that anymore. Instead try feeding oatmeal, sweet potatoes, and some meats they never eat. You might have to go to a vegetarian diet. It not a balanced diet, but you can try it for a couple of weeks to see if this clears up the problem. If it does, then you start adding things back into the diet and look for any reactions.

Food Allergy or Quality Allergy?—William Pollak, DVM

Diets that contain poor and inappropriate ingredients—and unfortunately this represents a good deal of what is sold as commercial pet food—create animals who do not function properly. Their systems are continually besieged with toxicity. Under this constant burden, even otherwise harmless and beneficial nutrients become part of a cascade of events that unleashes an "attack" mode against the food inside the animal. The symptoms that arise from this we say are related to food allergies. We blame the individual ingredients.

Allergy in all its forms is a reflection of a system starving for higher nutrition and health. An appropriate diet for an individual animal is soothing, nourishing, and a source of wellness, orderliness, intelligence, and vital life energy for the body. A diet of fresh, varied, and wholesome food, along with vitamin and mineral supplementation, offers the nutrients that create health and vitality and eliminate allergy and disease. Rather than eliminating food and dealing with food allergies on the level of illness, feed a better diet and operate from the level of wellness. This approach works for a large majority of animals.

⊌ Gas ⊭

See Digestive Disorders

⚜ Gum Disease ⚜

See Dental Health

⚜ Heart Problems ⚜

The conditions veterinarians see most frequently are congestive heart failure and cardiomyopathy, a degeneration of the heart muscle. Typical clinical signs include the following:

- coughing, usually at night or upon arising.
- wheezing, shortness of breath.
- potbelly or swollen limbs.
- lack of energy and lethargy, with continual sleeping and depression.
- fainting, stumbling, or weakness.
- loss of appetite.

Such signs can result from many different causes. Your best bet, if you see any of these, is to get a veterinarian's diagnosis at once. If the heart is ailing, early detection and prompt correction improve the prognosis. An annual checkup is good insurance against heart disease.

Heart disease is not necessarily an "old dog" phenomenon. Many dogs grow old before their time with weakening hearts and impaired circulation. "The problem has become increasingly prevalent at younger ages," says Robert Goldstein, VMD. "Seven or eight is not uncommon. Unlike the situation with humans, the problem is not a result of clogged arteries. Some heart conditions are congenital, but I believe the trend involving younger animals is largely related to poor-quality nutrition, unnecessary vaccines, and exposure to environmental and chemical pollutants, which create inflammatory responses to a suppressed immune system."

For an existing heart condition, follow your veterinarian's therapeutic program, which generally includes a variety of medications. Alternative and conventional therapies used in concert can be quite effective.

Holistic veterinarians often recommend acupuncture for animals with heart problems. It helps rebalance the body and remove energy blockages. See chapter 12 for more on acupuncture.

The most popular nutritional supplement for heart conditions is coenzyme Q_{10}, called coQ_{10} for short. This fat-soluble vitamin has been widely studied and used clinically around the world for heart patients. It is a magnificent nutrient, recommended by many holistic veterinarians for their heart patients. You can purchase the product in health food stores.

CoQ_{10} directly contributes to the production of energy in all cells of the body, a highly therapeutic benefit for ailing hearts. The heart muscle, which pumps blood through the body nonstop around the clock, has a particularly high requirement for energy. CoQ_{10} also provides powerful antioxidant protection in the body. It is a very safe supplement and is most effective when given with food that contains some fat. Many veterinarians recommend CoQ_{10} along with other heart supportive supplements, such as vitamin E, the amino acid L-carnitine, and hawthorn, a cardioprotective herb. Holistic practitioners often suggest putting animals prone to heart problems, such as Shar-peis and Dobermans, on such a preventive program early on in life.

In this section you will see a variety of dosage recommendations. If you have any doubts about what is appropriate for your animal, always start low and increase the amount if necessary. Ideally, consult with a holistic veterinarian.

NUTRITIONAL SUPPLEMENTS

CoQ$_{10}$ for Any Heart Problem—Carolyn Blakey, DVM

For anything even faintly resembling a heart or circulatory problem, coQ_{10} is the nutritional supplement of choice to help the heart muscle and blood vessels. I regard it as an effective addition to any heart treatment. It won't interfere with anything your veterinarian is doing. It will only help.

I use it when animals have a chronic heart cough, a swollen

abdomen from fluid retention, a heart murmur, cardiomyopathy, and common heart insufficiency. It is a rare older dog who doesn't come in with some sign of this kind of insufficiency. The heart just can't move blood with enough pressure and force. The heart muscle is tired, and we need to feed it. CoQ_{10} is the perfect nutrient for these older hearts. It energizes the heart muscle, generating more go power. Animals cough less. They behave as if their blood is moving as it's supposed to, delivering oxygen and blood-borne nutrients in a more efficient manner. The heart murmur won't go away in the older dog, although I have occasionally seen that happen in younger animals.

DOSAGE
• Give twice daily. Small dogs, 10 milligrams each time; larger dogs, 30 milligrams.

CoQ_{10} for Valve Problems—Pamela Wood-Krzeminski, DVM

For valvular conditions in dogs, I have used coQ_{10}, and it works well. I wouldn't hesitate to recommend it for most cardiac conditions. Animals feel better with it. It works to improve circulation and oxygenation to the heart muscle. If the pump works better, the whole system is going to perk up. Usually you see improvement within a couple of weeks.

CoQ_{10}, Vitamin E, Carnitine, and Kelp—Robert Goldstein, VMD

Above all, feed the best possible diet. Then add to the food a number of excellent heart-specific nutrients—all readily available in health food stores. These nutrients can enhance your animal's prognosis and improve its quality of life.

My heart supplement program includes coQ_{10}, which, when given long-term, can lessen your animal's dependence on medication. It also encourages more exercise, improves circulation, and promotes weight loss in obese animals. Vitamin E is a potent antioxidant and anti-inflammatory vitamin that improves circulation and heart output. L-carnitine is an amino acid that improves the strength of the heart muscle, gives general support to the muscles, and helps burn fat. Finally, powdered kelp offers an excellent source of minerals that supplies the body's electrical system, which in turn keeps the heart pumping. Commercial pet foods are often deficient in minerals or contain minerals in a form that are poorly absorbed. Look for a deep, cold-water source of kelp at health food stores.

Just as it is with humans, regular exercise is important for animals. It improves general circulation. Ultimately the best answer for heart disease lies in prevention, where diet and exercise share the spotlight.

To create an individually tailored nutritional and remedy program for patients with heart disease and other serious, life-threatening conditions, I use a special test I developed years ago. The test is called the Bio-Nutritional Analysis and is available to veterinarians at 800 670-0830 (for more details see chapter 16).

DOSAGE

- **CoQ₁₀:** Dogs up to fourteen pounds, 10 milligrams daily; dogs up to thirty-four pounds, 20 milligrams; dogs up to eighty-four pounds, 30 milligrams; giant breeds, 40 to 50 milligrams.

- **Vitamin E:** Dogs up to fourteen pounds, 200 international units (IU) daily; dogs up to thirty-four pounds, 400 IU; dogs up to eighty-four pounds, 600 IU; giant breeds, 800 IU.

- **L-carnitine:** Dogs up to fourteen pounds, 250 milligrams daily; dogs up to eighty-four pounds, 500 milligrams; giant breeds, 750 milligrams.

- **Kelp:** Dogs up to fourteen pounds, 1/2 teaspoon per meal, mixed into food; dogs up to thirty-four pounds, 1 teaspoon; dogs up to eighty-four pounds, 1 1/2 teaspoons; giant breeds, 2 teaspoons.

Vitamin E, Selenium, and CoQ₁₀—Roger DeHaan, DVM

After graduating from veterinary school thirty years ago, I started practicing under an old veterinarian who had followed the work of Wilfrid Shute, M.D., the Canadian pioneer of vitamin E for heart conditions. We used the vitamin along with selenium, a mineral also important for the heart. The results were quite dramatic. A dog would come in with a weakened heart, an enlarged heart, or a murmur, and we would start them on the supplements. A month later, when we saw them again, they were new animals with more energy and clearly acting as if they were feeling better. I was never taught this in medical school, but I became a believer way back then and have been using this combination ever since for old animals and animals with weak hearts, cardiomyopathy, or any cardiac condition. More recently I added coQ$_{10}$, the vitamin that perks up the heart muscle.

I suggest the following program if you want to try a holistic approach for heart problems, perhaps when the condition is not advanced enough to necessitate drugs or when drugs are causing problems. You can also use this to support any conventional treatment. Along with a good diet, you should see solid improvement within a month.

DOSAGE
• **Vitamin E (preferably in the form of d-alpha tocopherol [natural vitamin E]):** Small and medium dogs, 100 IU daily; large dogs, 200 IU; giant breeds, 400 IU.

• **Selenium (preferably in the form of selenium methionate):** 100 to 400 micrograms daily, depending on size.

• **CoQ$_{10}$:** 1 milligram per pound of body weight. Cut back to half dose for maintenance when animal improves.

Antioxidants for the Heart—Wendell Belfield, DVM
If a dog's condition is not advanced, I recommend an antioxidant supplement I developed that helps strengthen the heart muscle and generate more vitality. The product is called Vital Tabs and is available from Orthomolecular Specialties (408-227-9334). The formula contains vitamins A and E, plus selenium. It can be used along with standard medication. Sometimes it will help eliminate the dry, hacking cough that accompanies the typical valvular insufficiency problems of older dogs. It may permit a reduction in medication. Follow dosage suggestions on the label.

MIXED AND MISCELLANEOUS APPROACHES
Hawthorn and CoQ$_{10}$—A. Greig Howie, DVM
I recommend adding beef or lamb heart to the food of animals with heart conditions. Studies have shown that proteins from a particular organ meat will actually be utilized by that organ.

The primary supplement in my heart program is hawthorn, an herb that comes from Europe. It is available in health food stores. Be sure to purchase a product that contains a standardized extract of the herb. Hawthorn is packed with potent compounds called vitexin, quercetin, and oligomeric procyanidins. These are phytochemicals—natural plant chemicals—that improve the flow of blood to the heart and extremities and also promote the pumping action of the heart muscle. Normally it takes different pharmaceutical drugs to dilate the coronary arteries and increase blood flow to the muscle. But hawthorn does it efficiently and safely, without building up and causing problems in the system. The heart is strengthened and the heartbeat is normalized if there is an irregular rhythm.

According to Michael Tierra, a prominent herbal expert and author of *Planetary Herbology* (Lotus Press, Santa Fe, 1988), hawthorn is "one of the most reliable herbs for heart problems." In Europe hawthorn is frequently recommended in general medical and cardiology practices to improve heart function. Scientific studies indicate that hawthorn is beneficial for congestive heart failure. In addition, studies on certain ingredients contained in hawthorn have shown that the compound also exerts a strong antioxidant action in the cardiovascular system.

I also use a good deal of coQ_{10}, particularly for dogs with cardiomyopathies. I don't stop any prescriptive medication; however, over a few months' time an animal may improve enough on the combination so that medication can be reduced and perhaps even discontinued. But always work with a veterinarian, and do not stop medication on your own. With heart diseases other than cardiomyopathy, you generally have more time to utilize natural approaches. In such cases medication keeps the animal alive long enough for the nutrition and natural remedies to help.

Dosage
- **Hawthorn:** Dogs up to forty pounds, one-quarter to one-half the human dose; larger dogs, up to a full dose, depending on size. Liquid tinctures may be easier to administer to small dogs and capsules to larger animals. Older dogs usually stay on it indefinitely. For an animal with heartworms or other heart-related problems, give as long as the problems exist.

- **CoQ$_{10}$:** Small dogs, 10 milligrams daily; larger dogs, up to 100 milligrams.

DOES YOUR DOG'S HEART PROBLEM START IN THE MOUTH?—JAN BELLOWS, DVM

If your animal's teeth are not cleaned properly, you may face the risk of not just gum disease, but heart disease as well. Animals with bad gums are more prone to heart problems.

Bacterial infections originating in the gums are known to spread into the body and attack the heart valves. The result is a condition known as "bacterial endo-carditis." It can be deadly. The disturbance to the tissue interferes with the proper function of the valves. Fluid may back up into the lungs and cause congestive heart failure.

Refer to the section on dental health for information on how to keep your pet's mouth healthy.

⚜ Heat Stroke and Hot Weather ⚜

Warning: Hot weather can cause heat stroke and even death if you don't use common sense. An animal going into heat stroke may collapse or appear very depressed. It may be panting frantically. The gums may be bright red. At any sign of heat stroke, use a fan to cool the air and wet the animal down with cool water.

Be sure your animals have access to shade (it's twenty degrees cooler than in direct sunlight) and plenty of water.

Long-haired dogs bred for colder climates, such as St. Bernards and Huskies, need regular brushing in hot weather to help thin out their undercoat of fur.

Feed Wet Food—Joseph Demers, DVM

Commercial dry pet food creates internal heat. The combination of hot weather and dry food can contribute to a heat overload. If you haven't done it before, hot weather is the time for sure to introduce more moisture into an animal's diet. That means green beans, spinach, broccoli, peas, and other green vegetables. Ideally, feed your animal a home-prepared diet.

Don't run or exercise your dog in blazing heat. Dogs don't sweat. It is easy for them develop a heat overload that can lead to heat stroke.

Feed Cooling Foods—Norman C. Ralston, DVM

The environment your animal lives in can exert a positive or negative health influence. We constantly put animals in situations for which they were not originally bred or acclimated. Asking them to perform in such an environment puts them in a terribly stressful situation.

An example is a St. Bernard, with a big, heavy coat, originally bred and suited for the Swiss Alps, who is brought to live in the Southwest. Then he is fed a high-protein diet. It's like putting a high-octane gasoline in a car not made for it and then racing the motor. The animal suffers terribly in hot climates. When it's hot, be sure to give your animals more cooling food such as tofu, fresh vegetables, and fruits.

But with Chihuahuas, dogs acclimated to the heat, you need to take another tack. I have actually seen a Chihuahua go into a coma after being left in an air-conditioned house. The breed doesn't tolerate cold very well. These dogs need more heat and concentrated food such as chicken and lean meat.

Animals Left in Cars—Pamela Wood-Krzeminski, DVM

I see a lot of heat stroke even during the Florida winters. The weather is sunny and pleasant, the temperature in the seventies. People will leave their animals in the car and close the windows, thinking there is no danger. Yet the majority of my heat stroke cases are in the winter, involving northerners who come to Florida for the season. The weather may not be sizzling, but don't think it's not hot in the car.

Don't leave any animal in a car unless someone is sitting in it and you leave on the air conditioner or the windows are wide open. Even with the air conditioner running, it may not be entirely safe. As an example, one March a client came to the clinic to see me and left his two dogs alone in the car with the air conditioner running. He was in the clinic for twenty minutes. Shortly after he left the car, the engine stopped. When he returned to the car, he encountered an emergency situation. The younger dog was alert, but you could see it was experiencing heat stroke. The older dog was much more critical, and we came close to losing him. We had to do intravenous fluids, enemas, and alcohol baths. Happily we got them both around, but it was a good example about not leaving animals alone in a car.

The Alcohol Cooler—Alfred Plechner, DVM

If the temperature is over 90 degrees and the animal is showing signs of being bothered by the heat, such as panting or drinking excessively, apply some rubbing alcohol to the pads of the feet. This will help bring down the temperature.

⅏ Hip Dysplasia ⅏

See also Arthritis

The word "dysplasia" means improper growth. In dogs, dysplasia refers to the abnormal formation of the hip complex, a pivotal structure that include muscles, tendons, ligaments, cartilage, and the joint capsule that holds together the ball of the thigh bone and the socket of the hip. The problem originates in puppyhood, when the skeleton grows more rapidly than the supporting soft tissue. This results in unstable hip joints. The ball and socket are not held together normally.

One minute a dog can be a picture of health, jumping, running, and chasing a ball under a full head of steam. With one vigorous leap on unstable joints, the ball of the thigh bone can be wrenched out of the hip socket, and you now have a dysplastic dog.

The condition usually affects both hips and ranges from very mild, with no apparent symptoms, to severe, painful, and crippling. Signs of hip dysplasia include hind leg lameness, a wobbly or swaying gait, difficulty upon rising (particularly in the morning), and reluctance to walk up stairs or to run or jump as normal.

As dogs age, abnormal movements within the dysplastic joints cause cartilage erosion and degenerative arthritis.

Although most common among bigger dogs, hip dysplasia may strike an animal of any size. In the past, many veterinary researchers contended that the primary reason for hip dysplasia was genetic, and therefore it was important to evaluate the hips of prospective breeding animals to determine the potential for problems in offspring. But recent evidence has indicated the condition is more complex and that major nutritional factors are involved.

A variety of surgical options exists for dysplastic dogs, including total hip replacement. Holistic veterinarians utilize methods such as acupuncture, chiropractic, massage, homeopathy, and nutrition to help relieve affected dogs (refer to the section on arthritis). They also emphasize nutritional strategies to help prevent the condition.

NUTRITIONAL SUPPLEMENTS

Vitamin C for Prevention—Wendell Belfield, DVM

I consider hip dysplasia to be a biochemical condition easily prevented with good nutrition, and particularly with supplementation of vitamin C. In 1976 I first reported in a medical journal how I used a nutritional supplement to prevent hip dysplasia in eight litters of German Shepherd puppies born to parents with dysplastic hips. In these cases, the bitches were maintained on the supplement through pregnancy and the pups fed the supplement until adulthood.

The formula I developed many years ago and still use with great success is called Mega-C Plus and contains, as the name implies, large amounts of vitamin C, plus other essential nutrients. The form of vitamin C used in the formula is nonacidic sodium ascorbate. The product is available through Orthomolecular Specialties (408-227-9334).

The supplement has worked for hundreds of clients over the years, including many breeders. For twenty-five years people with German Shepherds, Golden Retrievers, Rottweilers, Great Danes, and other large-breed animals have been telling me they no longer have hip problems and that their litters are strong.

The supplement, in powder form, is given to the bitch during pregnancy. For the pups you use a liquid version of the product—

called Mega-C Drops—starting within a few hours of birth and continuing until weaning. After weaning, the pups can be switched to the crystals.

Why is vitamin C so important and so effective? It is well-known that most animals produce their own vitamin C in the liver (notable exceptions are humans and guinea pigs, who must obtain vitamin C in their diets). However, dogs—and cats as well—are not particularly good producers. They benefit greatly from supplementation. Adequate vitamin C is required for the development of strong collagen, the main structural protein in tendons, bone, cartilage, muscle, and connective tissue. Think of collagen as the cement that binds the body together. Vitamin C performs a critical biochemical role by transforming iron in the body into a form that permits the production of collagen. Without enough vitamin C, iron would inhibit the process.

Stress depletes vitamin C. Puppies are under constant stress: environmental, when young animals are placed in new surroundings; emotional, when separated from mother and litter mates; toxicological, when subjected to vaccines and dewormers; physical, when teething and undergoing dewclaw removal and tail docking. Large-breed dogs, in particular, have an additional load of stress due to their rapidly growing bodies.

By supplementing these animals during pregnancy, and throughout puppyhood, we are able to dramatically fortify their nutritional input and build the strong connective tissue necessary for good hip joints and supportive ligament tissue to sustain their big bodies. This has been my consistent experience for years.

The genetic theory has never been conclusively proven as the sole cause of canine hip dysplasia. In recent years many scientific papers have demonstrated the role of vitamin C in collagen synthesis. Until this issue is resolved, I continue to recommend a very simple solution that prevents crippling arthritis and suffering, avoids drug therapies with side effects, and offers an alternative to expensive surgical procedures.

Dosage
- For pregnant large-breed bitches, use enough Mega-C Plus crystals mixed into moist food to provide 3,000 milligrams of

vitamin C. See label for the amount per teaspoon. For pups, use Mega-C Drops. For the first five days, give 66 milligrams of the mixture by mouth with a dropper. From five to ten days, give 100 milligrams. From then until weaning, give 132 milligrams daily. After weaning, give Mega-C Plus in food, gradually increasing amount. For animals up to twenty pounds, give 750 to 1,500 milligrams; larger breeds, increase slowly to bowel tolerance level. Note that excess doses may cause diarrhea. If the initial dose triggers soft stool, withhold the vitamins for two to three days or until stools become firm, and then begin at a lower level. Each animal is individual, and some may require more time to adjust to these levels of vitamin C. If the stool remains firm, increase the vitamin C level 750 milligrams every third day, until the stool begins to soften and loses its cylindrical shape. When this occurs, reduce the level by 750 milligrams and the stool should return to its previous firm shape. This is known as the "individual bowel tolerance level" for the particular animal. Always proceed slowly to reach the individual tolerance level—which is the optimum level—for your particular animal. Maximum dosage of vitamin C should not exceed 10,000 milligrams daily.

80 Percent Preventable—Roger DeHaan, DVM

I find hip dysplasia showing up much earlier than before. These problems used to appear at 1 1/2, 2, or 3 years or older. I now have animals at 6 months having trouble walking up steps from dysplasia, weak ligaments, and bone structure that isn't holding them up anymore. I attribute 80 percent of this to malnutrition and the rest to inbreeding. Practically speaking, it means too much high-protein and low-quality puppy food. I consider hip dysplasia 80 percent nutritional and therefore 80 percent preventable. The greatest success you can have against this problem is to put the parents on a good diet. Then you seldom have problems with the progeny.

If a puppy comes in at about eight weeks, I always check the hips. Even though nothing unusual may be found through X-rays, an examination can determine if there is any laxity in the joints and the beginnings of problems. I manipulate the legs in and out, and if there is any pain and if the animal is a larger-breed dog, I interpret this as a strong indicator of dysplasia and arthritis ahead. I then suggest the following preventive program.

- Feed less protein.

- Give Mega-C Plus, a nutritional supplement high in vitamin C developed by veterinarian Wendell Belfield (see previous Belfield comments).

- Try also Missing Link, made by Designing Health (800-774-7387), a whole-food nutritional supplement with many important nutrients and enzymes.

When I reexamine animals a month or two later, the pain is usually gone. If the owners continue the program on a long-term basis, especially for the puppy's growth phase, they can greatly reduce the chance of hip problems.

Relief for Pain—Thomas Van Cise, DVM

Often, the hip dysplasia I see involves animals who have had the condition for months or even years. The situation has gotten to the point where the owner sees an animal limping badly or in obvious pain. Perhaps the dog has bitten somebody who got too close to its rear end. Until these things happen, owners frequently don't bother seeing a veterinarian for an evaluation. Even though they know their animal has hip dysplasia, people believe there is little that can be done outside of an expensive hip replacement.

I can't create a new hip, but I can substantially help the functionality of the joint—getting up, walking around, and reducing pain. My approach involves acupuncture and Dismutase, a powerful antioxidant supplement made by Bio Vet International (800-788-1084). In most cases the animal improves significantly (see Van Cise's entry under arthritis). Treatment involves one to fifteen sessions of acupuncture (one session a week), depending on the severity of the condition. For dogs with hip dysplasia I recommend seeing a veterinarian skilled in acupuncture. If acupuncture isn't feasible, Dismutase by itself is very helpful. It also benefits muscles and tendons, thus giving additional support to the affected joint.

DOSAGE
- Small to medium dogs, 6 tablets; larger dogs, 8 tablets. The supplement must be given regularly and is best taken on an empty stomach.

⚜ Incontinence ⚜

Urinary incontinence means an animal loses the ability to hold urine normally in its bladder. It pees involuntarily, perhaps where it sleeps, or when lying down and awake, or when excited. There are many possible causes, including spaying, bladder infections, bladder stones, behavioral responses to stress and excitement, the use of steroid medication, or diseases such as diabetes, kidney failure, or urinary tract cancer that result in an increased amount of urine or a heightened urge to urinate. If your dog has a persistent problem, see a veterinarian.

There is often a spay connection to incontinence. "Many female dogs are spayed too young, resulting in underdeveloped muscles and supporting tissue that control the bladder," says Lynne Friday, DVM. "In these cases, the muscles and excretory openings from the bladder may not mature sufficiently for a lifetime of control."

The muscles are matured by ovarian hormones, she points out. They become stronger if the female is allowed to have its first season or at least one week of it before being spayed. Bones also develop more fully in response to estrogen and results in fewer joint problems later on, particularly for large breeds that are more prone to get them, she adds.

"You rarely have incontinent neutered males," says Friday. "The reason is that they have a longer urethra with more control than the female. But I prefer waiting to neuter the male until after the animal starts lifting his leg to urinate, indicating the presence of testosterone, which helps mature muscles and bones."

HOMEOPATHIC MEDICINES
(See chapter 10 for general dosage guidelines.)

Causticum—Charles Loops, DVM

About half of the older animals I treat with incontinence respond to the homeopathic remedy Causticum. If it works, you will see immediate alleviation. If it doesn't work, and you want to continue a homeopathic approach, you'll need to consult with a homeopathic veterinarian. Finding the right remedy for this condition, if Causticum doesn't help, can be difficult.

DOSAGE
- **Causticum 6 or 12C:** Give once daily for five days and then as needed.

NUTRITIONAL SUPPLEMENTS

Acidify the Urine with Methionine—Nancy Scanlan, DVM

Acidifying your dog's urine can often improve, and sometimes eliminate, incontinence. Many animals with this problem have alkaline urine. One simple way to acidify the urine is to add supplemental methionine, an amino acid, to the diet. You can purchase methionine in a health food store. For mild cases, this method alone may solve the problem. For severe incontinence, it may help, but you will probably have to consult with a veterinarian. Methionine is a safe and simple approach that I recommend before trying other things.

First check the urine, using a simple litmus paper test. Litmus paper strips determine the acidity or alkalinity of a substance. They are coated with an organic dye that changes color in the presence of acid and alkaline substances. You can purchase litmus paper through science, laboratory, or chemical supply stores, or ask your local pharmacist. Simply place a strip in a spot where the dog has just urinated. Observe the color change. Pink represents acid. Blue is alkaline. Lavender is in between. Your goal with the methionine is to make the urine *slightly* on the acidic side; thus you are aiming for a litmus color reaction between lavender and pink. Keep in mind that urine turns more alkaline with time, so test the urine as soon as possible. If you have any doubts, bring the animal or a sample of the urine to your veterinarian for more precise testing.

A note of caution: Don't do this procedure if your dog has oxalate stones. Oxalate stones are present in strongly acidic urine. You would not want to make the urine more acidic if such a condition exists.

DOSAGE
- Give methionine twice daily. Smaller dogs, 100 milligrams each time; larger dogs, 200 milligrams. Crunch tablet and add to food, or give directly. Check urine level again in a few days. If the level is not yet acidic, give same amount of methionine three times a day. If you give too much methionine, an animal will throw up, but for most cases this is a very safe range.

⚜ Infectious Illnesses ⚜
(Colds, Viruses, Bacterial Infections)

Stress, poor diet, and environmental toxins are major factors that undermine a dog's resistance to bacterial and viral infections. Genetics, of course, plays a big role. Some dogs are hardier than others. Some, as we have seen in chapter 2, have weaker immune systems because of the way they are bred.

Holistic veterinarians emphasize good nutrition above all, with additional support from a supplement program, as the primary means of keeping animals healthy and resistant to the many germs that come their way. Supplement recommendations vary among practitioners but typically include a quality pet multi-vitamin/mineral formula with extra vitamins C and E, and other anti-oxidants.

Treatments for infections are highly variable. Some holistic veterinarians emphasize vitamins, others emphasize herbs, and still others tailor an individualized program around homeopathic remedies. Conventional treatments for infections often include antibiotics. Antibiotics can cause vomiting and stomach and intestinal disorders in animals, the result of the destruction of beneficial bacteria normally present in the gut.

To prevent this, give your animal yogurt, which contains the beneficial bacteria acidophilus, or a good probiotic supplement available at health food stores. Do this after any course of antibiotics. (see comments on antibiotics and probiotics in section on digestive disorders).

FLOWER ESSENCES
(See chapter 11 for general information on essences.)

Essences for Kennel Stress—Paul McCutcheon, DVM
Being boarded in a kennel is an extremely stressful experience for animals. The stress and anxiety involved may lower the resistance of the animal so that it becomes more susceptible to viruses and other infectious microorganisms that abound in kennels. Help your dog by fortifying it emotionally with Bach flower remedies. The two that work very well together are Rescue Remedy and Walnut, both available in health food stores.

DOSAGE
• Take a 1-ounce bottle with an eyedropper lid and fill with spring or filtered water. Add 5 drops of Rescue Remedy and 3 of Walnut. Give animal a half dropperful of the mixture several times, beginning the day before it is to be boarded. Instruct the kennel staff to administer a similar dosage during the boarding period. Continue for a day or two after your return, depending on the stress level of the animal.

HERBS

Echinacea to Boost Immunity—Mark Haverkos, DVM
Echinacea is a major healing tool in my program to boost and normalize the immune system. It is excellent for humans and for animals. I use it for any chronic infections, such as ear and respiratory conditions, sores that won't heal well, autoimmune illnesses or deranged immunity, and allergic skin problems, and for animals who have been on long-term steroids, antibiotics, or any medications that deplete or suppress the immune system. I recommend a liquid tincture form of echinacea, prepared by Winter Sun Trading Co. (520-774-2884).

DOSAGE
- Give one to three times a day. Small dogs, 1 to 5 drops of the tincture diluted in a teaspoon of water; medium dogs, 10 to 15 drops in a tablespoon of water; large dogs, 30 to 40 drops in 2 tablespoons. Use for two weeks, then stop for two weeks. If the case is severe, use for three weeks, then discontinue for one week, and repeat as necessary. You can use this approach long term as long as you stop the echinacea at intervals. Reports in the herbal literature indicate that continual use may overly stimulate and exhaust the immune system. If the dog won't take the echinacea directly in the mouth because of the taste, than put the diluted remedy in a small bowl, add a little water, and dribble in some honey for a slightly sweet taste.

OSHA ROOT FOR VIRAL CONDITIONS AND GENERAL DEBILITATION
Osha root, known by Native Americans as "bear root," is one of the most powerful herbs on the planet. According to Michael Moore, director of the Southwest School of Botanical Medicine in Albuquerque, osha is one of the only botanicals that is truly virucidal—that is, it kills viruses. The name of the herb derives from a Native American tradition in which it was noted that bears were seen to dig up the root and eat it when not feeling well. Osha root is a blood purifier, immune stimulant, and expectorant (for coughs). It is strong but safe. Osha root, in the same liquid tincture form that I use, can be purchased from Winter Sun Trading Co. (520-774-2884).

I recommend this remedy for any viral-related condition or for chronic debilitation, where an animal's health status worsens no matter what you do for it. I use it in cases where an animal has been to half a dozen veterinarians, is taking four or five drugs, and is not improving. Most of the time the vital force in these animals is blocked. Even if the animals remain on their prescriptions, you will notice an increase in vitality with osha. It can be used along with standard medication.

DOSAGE
- Give once a day. Small dogs, 1 to 5 drops diluted in 1 teaspoon of water; medium dogs, 10 to 15 drops in 1 tablespoon of water; large dogs, 20 to 30 drops in 2 tablespoons. If the dog

won't take the remedy, add it to some water and honey in a small bowl, as described previously under "Echinacea to Boost Immunity." Can be used indefinitely. Try reducing dosage or discontinue when animal improves.

PLEURISY ROOT FOR KENNEL COUGH OR BRONCHITIS

Pleurisy root is an expectorant herb for chronic respiratory conditions such as kennel cough or bronchitis, where the dog is coughing for weeks. Again, I recommend a liquid tincture form made by Winter Sun Trading Co. (520-774-2884).

Expect a temporary increase in coughing as a result of the expectorant breaking up the congestion. Unlike familiar cough medicines, expectorants do not suppress the cough. They work with the body to stimulate the cough and eliminate the contaminants or germs in the mucous lining. It is the body's natural response to cough up— and out—the disturbing foreign matter. Suppressing the cough counteracts the body's own natural detoxification process.

For a less severe condition, without fever and where the animal is somewhat off its food, you can use pleurisy root by itself with great effect. Improvement usually comes within three days to three weeks. If an animal is under conventional treatment with antibiotics, pleurisy root will support the therapy by helping to clear out the debris.

DOSAGE

- Give 1 to 3 times a day. Small dogs, 1 to 5 drops of the tincture diluted in a teaspoon of water; medium dogs, 10 to 15 drops in a tablespoon of water; large dogs, 30 to 40 drops in 2 tablespoons. Use additional water, along with honey, as previously described, for a slightly sweet taste that dogs will accept.

Head Off Viruses with Chinese Herbs—Jody Kincaid, DVM

Gan Mao Ling, a combination of Chinese herbs, works well to abort full-blown viral infections. You can purchase this product, made for humans but safe for animals, at health food stores, Chinese pharmacies, or herbal emporiums. It is available in tablet or capsule form. If your dog develops fever, starts coughing, goes off its food, or otherwise displays signs of becoming sick, the formulation is effective in stopping the illness. This is a human product. Use it for at least a week, or as long as needed. If your animal's symptoms worsen, see a veterinarian.

Dosage
- Adjust dosage according to the size of the animal in relation to humans.

HOMEOPATHIC MEDICINES
(See chapter 10 for general dosage guidelines.)

Homeopathy for Puppy Colds—Joseph Demers, DVM

FIRST STAGE

If a dog starts to sneeze, with a runny clear discharge from the eyes, that is the first stage of a cold. I recommend the remedy Aconitum napellus. Another good indicator for Aconitum is if the dog is somewhat fearful or jumpy.

SECOND STAGE

Arsenicum album, another homeopathic remedy, is appropriate against more frequent sneezing, coughing, and an increased but still thin discharge. These signs indicate the infection is still of a mild nature but is somewhat stronger. This may now be the second or third day of a cold. The dog may be rubbing its nose or eyes as if there is a burning sensation or discomfort. It would not be very thirsty and perhaps feel somewhat cold. When you pick up the dog, the ears and the belly may be hot, but the paws and the rest of the body feels cold. This is what we would call a "chilly fever."

For puppies with acute head colds and high fevers, who have thick discharges and are very weak, with perhaps shaking legs, the homeopathic remedy Gelsemium works very well.

If the condition does not improve, a different homeopathic remedy is needed. Ideally, consult with a homeopathic veterinarian.

Dosage
- Use remedies in pellet form. Crush the pellets in a folded piece of paper or mix it in 1 ounce of distilled water; and give the dog half an eyedropperful in the mouth.

- **Aconitum napellus:** Give 2 or 3 pellets of 6C potency, six or seven times a day (every two hours) for two to three days. This usually stops the cold. If not, try a 30C potency two to three times daily.

- **Arsenicum album:** Give 2 or 3 pellets of 6C potency, six or seven times for two to three days. If no decrease in symptoms by the third day, use a 30C potency three times daily for three days.

- **Gelsemium:** Give 2 or 3 pellets of 6C potency, five times daily until the symptoms are better. Use a 30C potency, two or three times a day if no improvement after twenty-four to forty-eight hours.

Homeopathy Vs. Puppy Parvo—Charles Loops, DVM

Homeopathic remedies can often turn around puppies suffering from parvo, a viral condition that causes gastrointestinal symptoms, despondence, and frequently blood in the stool. I recommend homeopathics as an adjunct to standard administration of fluids. It is always best to try one remedy at a time.

DOSAGE
- **Arsenicum album:** Give 30C potency twice a day if the animal is vomiting and has diarrhea.

- **Phosphorus:** Give 30C potency twice a day if there is also blood in the stool.

- **China:** Give 30C potency twice a day if animal has collapsed and is weak to the point where it can't raise its head.

MIXED AND MISCELLANEOUS APPROACHES

For Susceptible Animals—Donna Starita Mehan, DVM

For animals prone to chronic infections, I use a combination of several nutritional supplements and herbs that can abort or significantly shorten the duration of infectious episodes. The combination consists of a good multi-vitamin/mineral formula for pets, colloidal silver, Spectra Probiotic, and EHB. Spectra is a multistrain beneficial bacteria product that replenishes the good bacteria that the body needs. EHB is a supplement containing echinacea, goldenseal, and barberry, important herbal immune boosters. Spectra and EHB are made by NF Formulas (800-547-4891).

DOSAGE

- **Multi-vitamin/mineral formula:** Follow label instructions.

- **Colloidal silver:** 2 to 10 drops twice daily. Use product with 500 parts per million of silver.

- **Spectra:** Small dogs, 1/4 capsule daily; larger dogs, up to 1 capsule, depending on size of animal.

- **EHB:** 1/4 to 1 capsule twice daily, depending on size.

➤ Kidney and Urinary Tract Conditions ➤

Nature never designed canine kidneys to cope with the flood of impurities that come their way during the lifetime of a modern dog. Years of eating poor-quality food and exposure to numerous toxic chemicals eventually damage these critical organs that remove wastes from the blood. Kidney disease affects a large number of dogs, many of them older. Usually the disease involves chronic inflammation and scar tissue formation, with a progressive loss of the kidneys' critical filtering capacity. If the kidneys do not effectively eliminate wastes, internal poisoning (uremia) develops, a buildup of toxicity that can be fatal.

Signs of diminished kidney function include the following:

- Excessive thirst
- Weight loss and wasting
- Poor appetite
- Vomiting
- Poor coats, scratching, loss of hair, heavy shedding
- Smell of urine on the skin and in the mouth

Annual checkups, with bloodwork, can detect a kidney problem even before symptoms appear. Outward signs may not become apparent until the disease is well advanced.

Veterinarians usually recommend fluid therapy to correct dehydration and flush the body of wastes, thus reducing the risk of internal poisoning: Treatment generally includes medication to reduce inflammation and pain, and increase appetite, as well as a prescription diet low in protein. The kidneys remove the waste products left after the body breaks down protein, so a diet lower in protein eases the burden on weakened organs.

Diet and Natural Remedies—Robert Goldstein, VMD
Holistic therapies can help a good deal. Specific natural remedies and proper nutrients nourish the kidneys and strengthen the entire body's efficiency.

I prefer a home-cooked kidney diet to the prescription diets, which often contain by-products and wastes from the human food industry. I feel these commercial diets tax the kidneys. The diet I developed may be served alone or mixed with any natural, low-protein food. It meets all the needs of a kidney patient.

Ingredients:
2 egg yolks (organic, if possible)
1 cup brown rice or millet
3 cups filtered or distilled water
1/2 cup boneless, skinless chicken, cubed (preferably hormone and antibiotic free)
2 tablespoons minced parsley
2 tablespoons grated asparagus
1 tablespoon sesame oil (unrefined)
Multi-vitamin/mineral (Daily Health Nuggets, from Earth Animal at 800-711-2292, or Maximum Protection Formula, from Dr. Goodpet at 800-222-9932)

Directions: Cook rice or millet well with 2 1/2 cups of water for about 45 minutes. With remaining water, cook chicken slightly for 5 minutes. Add finely chopped raw vegetables, eggs, and oil to cooked grain. The parsley and asparagus act as gentle diuretics, helping the kidneys flush out impurities. If the eggs are organic, add them raw. If not organic, soft boil them first. Add supplement to cooled mixture (crush tablet if tablet form is used). If your animal has a poor appetite, flavor the mixture with raw, organic liver or organic fat-free yogurt (1 1/2 tablespoons). Use as a whole meal or topping over a base of a natural senior-type food. Reduce the amount of commercial food by the amount of "topper" recipe added. As a meal, feed up to 1/2 cup to small dogs, 1 cup to medium-size dogs, 2 cups to large dogs, and 2 1/2 to 3 1/2 cups to giant breeds.

I also recommend a number of nutritional and natural remedies, which can extend and improve the day-to-day quality of your animal's life. When trying this program, watch your animal's appetite closely. That's a good way to tell if wastes are increasing in the blood. If the appetite weakens, even slightly, see your veterinarian at once.

To create an individually tailored nutritional and remedy program for patients with kidney failure and other life-threatening conditions, I use a special test I developed years ago. The test is called the Bio-Nutritional Analysis and is available to veterinarians at 800-670-0830 (for more details see chapter 16).

PRODUCTS AND DOSAGE

- **Renatrate,** an extract of kidney tissue, made by Progressive Laboratories (800-527-9512). Tablets are given twice daily. Small dogs, 1/2 tablet each time; medium dogs, 1 tablet; large dogs, 1 1/2 tablets; giant breeds, 2 tablets.

- **Renal Drops,** a combination homeopathic liquid remedy to help rebuild kidneys, made by Professional Health Products (800-929-4133); ask your veterinarian to order it for you. Give twice daily apart from food. Small dogs, 3 to 5 drops each time; medium dogs, 7 drops; large dogs, 10 drops; giant breeds, 12 drops.

- **Solidago, Inflammation, and Exhaustion,** three homeopathic remedies in tablet form made by BHI Laboratories (800-621-7644) and available through health food stores or pharmacies. Dissolve 6 tablets of each remedy in a 2-ounce glass eyedropper bottle filled with distilled water. Shake well. Give three times daily apart from food. Small dogs, 1/3 dropperful each time; medium dogs, 1/2 dropperful; large dogs, 3/4 dropperful; giant dogs, 1 dropperful. Store in refrigerator after mixing.

Methionine for Bladder Infections—Nancy Scanlan, DVM

Dogs with chronic bladder infections are typically treated with repeated antibiotics. I have found an effective alternative for my patients—a combination of the amino acid methionine and cranberry extract, both available in health food stores. The combination usually clears up the infection so that antibiotics are no longer needed. Often infections don't return. If they do, they are less frequent and severe.

Methionine helps by making the urine acidic, but you want the urine to be only *slightly* acidic. Check the acid-alkaline level with litmus paper strips (see Scanlan's entry under incontinent dogs).

DOSAGE
- **Methionine:** Give twice daily. Small and medium dogs, 100 milligrams each time; larger dogs, 200 milligrams. If the urine isn't acidic on two doses of methionine, increase to three times.

- **Cranberry extract:** Give three times daily. Small dogs, 100 milligrams each time; medium dogs, 200 milligrams; large dogs, 300 milligrams; giant breeds, 400 milligrams.

⚜ Liver Disease ⚜

The liver is the largest gland in the body and one of the most important organs. It carries out essential chemical processing, including the handling of nutrients from digestion and the elimination of toxic substances. When its complex mechanisms go wrong, the body can suffer in many ways.

First and foremost, you need a diagnosis to determine the exact nature of the problem. Liver disease frequently affects older dogs; however, signs of a liver ailment can be confused with, or associated with, many other medical problems. Common signs include vomiting, tiring easily, decreased appetite, irritability, jaundice, and swollen abdomen. Regular checkups, including bloodwork, can help spot liver trouble at an early date. If you see the signs, be sure to see a veterinarian right away.

HERBS

Milk Thistle Protects the Liver—A. Greig Howie, DVM

For any liver condition—such as hepatitis, chronic liver disease, or inflammation of the bile ducts—I recommend the herb milk thistle, available in health food stores. This herb has amazing healing effects and can actually regenerate the liver.

You can add milk thistle to any treatment program, and it may very well be the only thing that will help. I don't know of any drug we veterinarians have that will regenerate the liver, but milk thistle will definitely do it. You will see big improvement with this herb. Your veterinarian will gauge improvement by doing standard liver enzyme tests, and I am sure that he or she will be surprised, as I was in the beginning, at how well this herb improves the status of the liver. This is a very organ-specific herb. Once the enzyme level normalizes you can stop the herb.

Studies have validated milk thistle's protective effect against poison. It works protectively and also repairs the liver from exposure to poisons. If the animal is on any medication that puts a particular burden on the liver, use milk thistle daily. Heartworm medication, for instance, is hard on the liver. I start animals on milk thistle prior to the medication for added protection against the chemicals that kill the heartworms. Some of the cancer drugs are toxic to the liver, and again, milk thistle offers protection.

If an animal has a damaged liver or a history of liver problems, I suggest giving milk thistle daily for a week each month.

DOSAGE
- One-quarter to one-half the human dose for a forty-pound dog. Start at the lower dose to avoid any possible stomach upset, and work up to higher level. Start with a lower or higher dose depending on animal's size.

Ayurvedic Herbs for the Liver—Tejinder Sodhi, DVM

I have had excellent results with an Ayurvedic herbal combination called Livit-2, prepared by Ayush Herbs (800-925-1371). The product is available in liquid form for small dogs and in tablet form for larger animals. The formula contains multiple herbs, among them kutli (*Picrorhiza kurroa*), which has been shown by research to detoxify the liver, eliminate excess or impure bile, and purify the blood; and amla (*Emblica officinalis*), which helps rejuvenate the immune system and increase the red blood cell count. Amla is the richest source of vitamin C among all fruits and also contains phytochemicals recognized for antioxidant properties and immune enhancement.

I recommend this formula when blood tests reveal elevated liver enzymes, a sign of trouble in the liver that could indicate such problems as acute hepatitis, congestion, or a buildup of toxicity from medication. Livit-2 protects, nourishes, and detoxifies the liver. I believe it is more effective than milk thistle alone. Within two to three weeks animals usually feel better, although it will often take longer for tests to show a normalization of the liver enzymes. Blood tests done a month after starting on the product usually show a decrease toward normalization of the enzyme levels. After another two months there is typically a dramatic drop.

This product is very protective against the toxicity of drugs when animals undergo chemotherapy. We see improved appetite, more energy, less vomiting, and in general fewer problems related to the medication. Livit-2 supports any therapy and medication by fortifying and protecting the liver.

DOSAGE
- Small dogs, give 10 drops of Livit-2 liquid twice daily per ten pounds of body weight; dogs up to thirty pounds, 1 tablet twice daily; dogs up to sixty pounds, 1 tablet three times daily; larger dogs, 2 tablets twice daily. Use formula for at least three months or until liver enzymes normalize, or long-term while animal is taking strong medication such as phenobarbital for epilepsy or chemotherapeutic drugs.

MIXED AND MISCELLANEOUS APPROACHES

Glutamine and Milk Thistle—Ron Carsten, DVM
I have found that a majority of liver problems are closely linked to a digestive tract that is not functioning as well as it should. To help here, I recommend the amino acid glutamine, a primary energy

source for intestinal cells, along with milk thistle, an excellent herbal agent for the liver that acts both protectively and restoratively.

This simple two-part supplement program can substantially enhance any treatment your veterinarian has prescribed. Animals often start to look and eat better, be more energetic, and become more interactive with their environment and members of the household.

You may also want to add a good probiotic supplement to aid the digestive process. Probiotics contain billions of beneficial bacteria that play important roles in the digestive process. They are often destroyed by antibiotic treatment (see comments on probiotics in section on digestive disorders).

DOSAGE
- **Milk thistle:** 250 to 500 milligrams twice a day for dogs, depending on size and severity of the condition.

- **Glutamine:** 500 milligrams twice a day for all animals.

Homeopathic and Chinese Remedies—Roger DeHaan, DVM

Several natural remedies can powerfully enhance the healing process and treatment program for liver failure. Conventional medicine doesn't have very good answers for this condition, and I have found that many veterinarians are open to this supportive approach. Keep in mind that most cases are chronic in nature and do take months to heal.

The products in this program can be purchased through Holistic Veterinary Services (218-846-9112). The first remedy is Theratox, a homeopathic combination to detoxify the liver, made by HoBon. Sick livers are always loaded with toxins. Cleansing is an essential first step to restoration of liver health.

The second remedy is Liv-C, a Chinese herbal combination (known as Tiao-he) from Nature's Sunshine. This formulation builds up the liver on a nutritional level. The two major ingredients are bupleurum root and peony root.

The third part of the program is Liver Liquescence, a homeopathic combination remedy made by Professional Health Products, intended for building up the liver on an "energy" level.

The length of time to use these remedies will vary. I recommend having your animal's liver function tested at two weeks and then again after a month, or at your veterinarian's suggestion. You can taper off the remedies as the liver becomes healthier.

You might also try raw beets, which help detoxify the liver. Just grate up a small piece of beet and add to food. Feed 1 teaspoon daily for a sixty-pound dog.

DOSAGE

- **Theratox:** 10 to 15 drops daily, depending on severity of condition. Gently pull away the animal's lips and apply drops to the mucous membranes inside. In a crisis, give the drops hourly for four hours and then three to four times a day until symptoms are relieved.

- **Liv-C:** Give daily with meals for one to three months. Dogs up to fifteen pounds, 1 capsule; dogs up to forty pounds, 1 capsule twice; dogs up to eighty pounds, 2 capsules twice; giant breeds, 2 to 3 capsules twice daily.

- **Liver Liquescence:** Give twice daily, before meals. Smaller dogs, 1/4 teaspoon each time; larger dogs, 1/2 teaspoon.

⋙ Motion Sickness ⋘

To eliminate the anxiety and motion sickness associated with transporting animals, the popular flower essence Rescue Remedy and/or homeopathic medicines are often recommended.

As a general rule, don't feed animals before traveling. They may throw up during the trip. If you are going on an extended car ride, feed only at night when you arrive at your destination. You can offer water on stops.

Calm with Rescue Remedy—Pamela Wood-Krzeminski, DVM

I've had good success with Rescue Remedy, a liquid product available in health food stores. You can give it directly in the mouth, add to the drinking water, or put a couple of drops on the dog's ears and rub gently into the skin.

DOSAGE
- Give before departure and use as often as needed—every half hour or couple of hours to keep animal calm.

Homeopathics for a Smooth Ride—Roger DeHaan, DVM

I like CalmStress, a homeopathic liquid formula from Dr. Goodpet (800-222-9932) that works quite well for motion sickness and stress. I often mix CalmStress and Rescue Remedy, the flower essence. The combination appears to be even more effective than either one individually.

DOSAGE
- Use either product singly and follow label instructions. Or, to combine the two, add 6 drops of Rescue Remedy to a bottle of CalmStress. Shake well. Whether combined or separately, start remedy a day or two before departure on an extended automobile or air journey. Add to animal's drinking water as well as giving directly in the mouth several times a day. Give remedy two hours before, one hour before, and just prior to getting into the car. One reason for starting ahead of time is that many animals become anxious when they sense an upcoming trip. Some animals pick up readily on a "traveling vibe." During an extended ride in the automobile, adding the remedy to drinking water is helpful, as is giving it orally every two to four hours.

◣ Neuromuscular Collapse or Paralysis ◢

Electromagnetic Poisoning?—Donna Starita Mehan, DVM

I am seeing a disturbing number of dogs, involving all breeds, but particularly large animals, who have developed a strange and sudden form of neuromuscular collapse. An otherwise healthy animal suddenly develops neurological symptoms such as on-and-off tremors, general weakness, hindquarter paralysis, or the tendency to collapse, or acts as if it is punch-drunk or poisoned. It may wobble back and forth or perhaps be unable to put one foot in front of the other.

Owners are stunned. A dog may go outside to urinate and then doesn't come back. The owner looks in the yard and sees the dog crawling back as if paralyzed. I have seen many dogs with sudden onset paralysis that could be traced to a disc misalignment, meningitis, or trauma. But now I see a problem apparently generated on the electromagnetic level of the body, at a more subtle level.

I believe this may be related to changes in the ozone layer and magnetic field of the planet and the fact that our nervous systems are being blitzed with pathological radiation from overhead power lines, microwaves, car phones, and X-rays.

I have found that vitamin B_{12} helps to stabilize the nervous system and prevent a "toxic electric reaction" in the body. I usually give an affected animal a series of three injections of 500 to 1,000 micrograms of B_{12}, depending on the size of the dog. I give the shots every other week. B_{12} orally doesn't always work as consistently. The vitamin makes a tremendous difference in the vitality and the bioelectrical integrity of these animals. In many instances it has the impact of a miracle cure. If these kinds of symptoms suddenly occur, consult your veterinarian. Consider the B_{12} shots as a primary treatment.

I also recommend the use of a ceramic catalyst bead that can be attached to an animal's collar. The bead acts as a buffer or absorption point for electromagnetic pollution. Such beads are available through Cascadia Creations (425-788-2315).

⩗ Obesity ⩔

Obesity is common among adult dogs and increases the risk of medical problems. One survey found more than 20 percent of animals were too heavy.

"There is no question that a lean dog is healthier and lives longer," says Edmund Dorosz, DVM. "The primary reason for this widespread problem is too many calories and not enough activity."

Of course, genetic makeup also exerts a large role. Some pets are simply going to lose and maintain their weight better than others, and laid-back animals may gain more readily than supercharged dogs. Disorders of the adrenal and thyroid glands, as well as over-medication with steroids, may be associated with weight gain.

Obesity in animals, just as in people, "is a frightening disease, because, in addition to causing serious discomfort and body dysfunction, it exacerbates and contributes to other diseases," says Susan Wynn, DVM, of Marietta, Georgia. Obesity-related problems include the following:

- Difficulty breathing.
- Higher danger for animals with heart or lung disease.
- Extra discomfort for arthritic dogs.
- A causal factor for liver disease, hypertension, constipation, heat intolerance, and increased risk under anesthesia.
- Abnormal life expectancy.
- In general, weaker immunity and greater susceptibility to tumors.

Obesity is a serious medical and nutritional problem. See your veterinarian, who can help you develop an appropriately individual program to improve the quality of your pet's life.

HOW TO TELL IF YOUR DOG IS TOO HEAVY

- Stand above your dog. Look down and see if the dog has a "waist"—that is, a visible indentation behind the ribs. You want to see an "hourglass figure," with the rib cage wider than the abdomen. The stomach should be tucked up, not loose and flabby.
- Gently place the palms of both hands against the animal's ribs. You want to be able to feel the ribs. If you can't feel the ribs, your dog is probably too heavy.
- Many obese animals have fatty pouches in the groin area.

FOOD AND SPECIAL DIETS

Three Recipes for Heavyweights—Edmund Dorosz, DVM

If your dog has no medical problem, such as congestive heart failure, hypothyroidism, or diabetes, which may be the cause of the excess weight, there are a few effective measures you can follow to promote loss of fat while conserving lean muscle tissue. First, be sure to provide a diet supplying high-quality protein and fat (see chapter

7). Always feed the best quality, which contains maximum nutrition. This way animals get quality without needing quantity. They eat less.

Feed less—up to 30 percent less—and more often. Small, more frequent portions often can be very effective.

A periodic fast helps lose weight.

Don't feed table scraps high in fat.

Don't give snacks between meals. Give love and attention instead.

Increase exercise and play to avoid boredom. Exercise burns calories.

The following recipes are excellent for weight loss:

Low-Fat, High-Fiber Diet

This recipe provides balanced proteins, vitamins, and minerals. It is low in calories and high in fiber to give a feeling of fullness.

Ingredients:
4 ounces lean ground beef
1/2 cup dry cottage cheese
2 cups cooked carrots
2 cups green beans
1 teaspoon bone meal
1/2 teaspoon garlic powder

Directions: Cook beef. Drain fat. Mix with other ingredients. Sprinkle with garlic. Feeds a thirty-to-forty-pound dog for one day.

Beef Tongue

This is a tasty low-calorie, high-fiber reducing diet.

Ingredients:
1 pound diced beef tongue
2 sliced carrots
2 celery stalks, with leaves chopped
1 cup low-sodium tomato juice
1 cup water
1 teaspoon bone meal
2 teaspoons cornstarch
3 teaspoons chopped parsley

Directions: Mix first six ingredients in a blender. Simmer for 1 hour. Mix cornstarch with 2 tablespoons of water and add slowly to

tongue mixture. Stir and cook until thickened. Add parsley. Cool.
Feeds a thirty-to-forty-pound dog for two days.

MEAT LOAF
Ingredients:
1 1/2 pounds lean ground beef
1 beaten egg
3/4 cup water
1 cup rolled oats
1 tablespoon brewer's yeast
1 teaspoon bone meal
1 teaspoon kelp
1/2 teaspoon garlic powder
1/2 cup grated cheddar cheese

Directions: Put all ingredients except cheese into large bowl.
Mix well. Place into a loaf pan 9 x 5 x 3 inches (23 x 12 x 7 cen-
timeters). Bake uncovered at 350 degrees F (180 degrees C) for 1
hour. Spread cheese over meat and return to oven to melt. Cool.
Serves thirty-to-forty-pound dog for four days.

Three More "Losers"—Paul McCutcheon, DVM
These three reducing diets have been used successfully by my clients
for years. Each yields a daily ration for a twenty-five-pound dog.

Diet #1 Ingredients:
1/2 cup lean meat, cooked
1/4 cup dry-curd cottage cheese
1 cup cooked oatmeal
1/2 cup grated or chopped vegetables
1/2 cup bran

Directions: Mix ingredients together and serve slightly warm.
Add daily supplements. Yield: 2 3/4 cups.

Diet #2 Ingredients:
1/4 pound ground round or other lean beef
1/2 cup cottage cheese (uncreamed)
2 cups drained canned carrots
2 cups drained canned green beans

Directions: Cook beef in skillet, stirring until lightly browned. Pour off fat and cool. Add remaining ingredients and mix well. Keep covered in refrigerator. When feeding, add daily supplements.

Diet #3 Ingredients:
1 cup low-fat cottage cheese
1 cup cooked brown rice
1 slice whole-grain or whole-wheat bread
1 cup frozen corn (thawed) or 1 jar corn (baby food)
1 cup frozen peas (thawed) or 1 jar peas (baby food)
1 hard-boiled egg
1/2 to 1 teaspoon garlic powder (not garlic salt)

Directions: Mix ingredients together. To this mixture, add the following:

First week: 1/4 pound leanest ground beef, browned, with the water and fat removed.

Second week: 1/4 pound white-meat chicken.

Third week: 1/4 pound white-meat turkey.

Store mixture in a tightly sealed container in refrigerator. Heat slightly before serving. Add supplements when serving.

The Green Bean Diet—Mark Haverkos, DVM
A simple weight-loss strategy for dogs has worked quite well for my overweight patients. Just add canned green beans to the regular food. A medium-size dog takes a half can a day, a large dog a whole can. Whatever the amount of green beans you feed, reduce the volume of the regular ration by the same amount.

I learned about green beans eight years ago from a client. I had mentioned to her that I was seeing a lot of fat dogs.

"Feed 'em green beans," she said.

I laughed when she said it. But she was serious and said it really worked. The next time I saw an overweight dog I told the owner about the green beans. He said he would try it. Two months later he brought the animal back and I was amazed to see a slim dog.

Since then I've put hundreds of overweight dogs on the green bean diet, and well over half of them lose weight. It takes about two to six weeks before you start to notice a change. Many of these heavy dogs really need to lose pounds because of bad hips. This simple approach has helped many animals unable to lose weight on restricted diets.

I don't know why it works, but it works. Most animals have no problem eating the beans. Some, in fact, like the taste so much that they wait for the can of beans to come out. Cooked, frozen beans don't seem to be as effective.

After seeing their dogs slim down, people are curious and want to know if the beans will do the same for them. I don't know the answer. Most people won't stick to a green bean diet long enough to find out.

The One-Day Fast—Nancy Scanlan, DVM

In the wild, dogs naturally fast about one out of seven or ten days. If you find your dog doing that on its own, that's quite okay. Many people worry when their dog stops eating for a day. They may change the diet or put gravy on the food to entice the dog. No need for it. You might want to consider fasting your dog for a day every week or ten days as a simple way of addressing an obesity problem. It is in tune with the animal's own nature.

If an animal doesn't eat for more than twenty-four hours, that's the time to become concerned. See a veterinarian. By no eating, I mean *no food*, not just a decrease. Dogs will decrease the amount of food they eat when the weather is too hot.

MIXED AND MISCELLANEOUS APPROACHES

The Second Dog Solution—Michele Yasson, DVM

Contemporary pets often lead solitary and sedentary lives cooped up in small apartments with owners away working much of the day. For many such animals, weight gain is a natural result of this unnatural existence. For those fat dogs stuck inside, try the second dog solution—get them a playmate. Dogs are pack animals, and there usually isn't a problem.

A second animal will stimulate activity and movement and is often curative for obesity. This approach works as well for animals who are depressed and don't eat well. A little competition at the dinner plate stimulates interest in food.

A variation on this theme is day care for pets. If you have a friend with a dog and both animals are alone during the day, arrange to have the animals spend time together during the work week. I have many New York City clients who do this. They find other people in their buildings, or nearby, with single animals. They arrange day care "matches" that bring play partners together, thus providing for some calorie-burning social opportunities for the animals.

The Spay and Neuter Connection—Roger DeHaan, DVM

If you have an animal fixed, be sure to allow it to rest and recover properly after the operation. Don't fix an animal immediately after you obtain it from the shelter. Let it first become adjusted to its new surroundings. Don't have it vaccinated at the same time. You want to separate and stretch out such stressful events. Too much stress can overwhelm the immune and endocrine (hormonal) systems, and you may wind up with a sick and/or fat animal. Weight gain is often related to a hormonal imbalance, particularly the pituitary, thyroid, and adrenal glands.

Cut back on food if necessary, and be sure your animal gets exercise! Animals love order and purpose in their lives. Purpose is especially important to working breeds, and if you park them in an apartment all day, their purpose goes to pot. They need daily exercise. Twice a day for ten or fifteen minutes at a time is better than twice a week for an hour. Throw sticks. Stroll with them around the corner. But do it regularly. Consistency is important for their weight, their psychological well-being, and their overall physical health. It's great for bonding and healing.

I have found it particularly useful to supplement animals with kelp before and after fixing. Kelp contains iodine and other important minerals that give nutritional support to the thyroid gland. When the thyroid becomes overly stressed, metabolism suffers and weight gain is a frequent result.

DOSAGE
- 1 teaspoon of kelp powder per fifty pounds of body weight. Start a week before fixing. Continue for a month or two afterward. Kelp can also be given long-term five days out of a week.

⇘ Old Age ⇙

Age-related changes are inevitable, but a lifetime of good nutrition, exercise, and proper veterinary and home care can make the difference between your dog living an average life span or a maximum one. The antiaging suggestions offered here by veterinarians can help boost the health and energy of an older pet.

NUTRITIONAL SUPPLEMENTS

Antiaging Magic of Chlorella—Clarence Hardin, DVM

In more than forty years of veterinary practice, I have never come across any natural or synthetic agent with the systemic-enhancing potential of chlorella, a human nutritional supplement available in health food stores. Chlorella is a single-celled, freshwater algae that packs a storehouse of vitamins, minerals, amino acids, and a high level of chlorophyll, one of nature's most effective cleansers and detoxifiers. In addition, it contains a unique ingredient called "chlorella growth factor," rich in nucleic acids. The quantity of nucleic acid in the body decreases with age, a decline associated with the aging process and weakened immunity.

Chlorella offers great benefits for aging dogs. When added regularly to the diet, it markedly slows down the aging process, maintains a youthful energy level longer, helps to normalize an animal's blood picture, improves liver and kidney function, and offers significant detoxifying effects. Some of my clients have taken chlorella after seeing the improvement in their animals, and they have told me they feel more energized with it. Research on chlorella indicates that it improves the hemoglobin count, meaning improved ability of the blood to deliver oxygen throughout the system, and boosts immune cell activity.

Dogs fed chlorella just don't seem to age like other animals. One typical case several years ago involved an aging dog with a heart murmur and an early cataract. Today the dog still plays actively with the household cat and hasn't slowed down. He still has the heart murmur, but there are no signs of heart-related coughing and short-ness of breath, and the cataract has remained stable.

I recommend chlorella as a long-term antiaging, health-boosting agent and as an accompaniment to any treatment program for cancer, colitis, and liver or kidney disease. It will also benefit skin conditions, speed up healing of wounds (when taken either internally or used locally as a poultice), and help clear up smelly skin infections very quickly. Chlorella is available in powder or tablet form.

Numerous studies with chlorella show it is safe at very high levels. I normally recommend 1 gram a day for smaller dogs. I once prescribed 6 grams of chlorella for a fifteen-year-old Yorkshire Terrier who was passing blood from the bladder and bowel. Another veterinarian had said the dog only had a short time to live. The owner was considering euthanasia. He decided, however, to get a second opinion and made an appointment with me. I suggested chlorella. We started the dog on the supplement. The owner called a short time afterward to say the bleeding had stopped. A few weeks later the overall condition and energy level showed improvement. It appeared that we bought the animal some extra time with improved quality of life.

Dosage
- For general use, give small dogs 1 gram of powder daily, mixed into food; larger dogs, up to 3 grams. As a nutritional support for dogs under treatment, the amount can be doubled and in many cases given up to five times the regular dose.

Vitamin E—Wendell O. Belfield, DVM
More than half a century ago the late Canadian physician Wilfrid Shute, M.D., a pioneer of vitamin E therapy and an ardent dog breeder, found that supplementation with vitamin E could revitalize older animals. Shute was at one time president of the Doberman Pinscher Club of America and used doses of 300 to 400 IU daily to create an optimum physiology and vitality among his dogs.

Vitamin E has worked reliably for me over the years to help energize aging animals. Studies have shown that older animals need more of this important antioxidant vitamin in order to slow down the oxidative damage of tissue associated with aging. Additional animal research has shown that vitamin E improves circulation, the immune system, endurance, stamina, skin problems, and libido.

DOSAGE
- Small dogs, 100 international units (IU); medium and large dogs, 200 IU; giant breeds, 400 IU.

Whole-Food Supplements—Roger DeHaan, DVM

I recommend two whole-food pet supplements that work very well to reenergize older animals and build up their health. Either one is excellent. If an animal doesn't like the taste of one, try the other.

1. Missing Link, from Designing Health Inc. (800-774-7387). It contains enzymes, fatty acids, fiber, beneficial bacteria, vitamins, trace minerals, and health-boosting compounds from plants. Follow label instructions.

2. Vita-Dreams Daily Greens, from Halo (800-426-4256). It contains vitamins, minerals, amino acids, chlorophyll, barley and alfalfa juice, bee pollen, bee propolis, and royal jelly. Follow label instructions.

MIXED AND MISCELLANEOUS APPROACHES

Herbal/Flower Essence Pick-Me-Up—Shannon Hines, DVM

Senior Support for Dogs has helped many of my geriatric animals. This liquid combination of herbs and flower essences is made by Tasha's Herbs (800-315-0142) and promotes health, appetite, and energy. Hawthorn, nettles, oatflowers, chamomile, dandelion root and leaf, kelp, and garlic are components of the formula.

DOSAGE
- Follow label instructions.

Exercise More, Feed Less—Alfred Plechner, DVM

Give them more exercise and fewer calories and supplement with digestive enzymes.

FOOD AND SPECIAL DIETS

Lower Protein, Supplement the Diet—Carvel Tiekert, DVM

Lower the amount of protein in the diet. Be sure the protein you do feed is high quality. I often supplement older animals with a good multi-vitamin/mineral, because as they get older they do not absorb the nutrients from their food as they did when younger, and their needs for nutrients may be higher.

Vegetable Power—Norman C. Ralston, DVM

It is very helpful if you can get them to start eating fresh vegetables. Fresh vegetables clean up the gut and act like a broom, sweeping out toxins. Don't overcook the vegetables. Just steam or lightly cook them.

⚜ Parasites ⚜

GIARDIA

Herbs for Relief—Tejinder Sodhi, DVM

Giardia is a common protozoan parasite that reproduces in the intestines of animals and causes diarrhea. Infections are typically picked up from feces, exposure to infected animals, or contaminated water. Giardia is usually treated with Flagyl (metronidazole), an antiparasitic drug that unfortunately has many side effects. Among other things, it affects balance and the ability to walk.

I have successfully used a combination of two herbal formulas. One is called AP Mag, made by Ayush Herbs (800-925-1371), and includes bael fruit, bitter melon, China berries, berberis, and basil leaf. The other formula is DGL Plus, from Pure Encapsulations (800-753-2277), with licorice root and unripe plantain. Start with DGL Plus and AP Mag. Use DGL Plus for about two to three weeks to firm up the stool and calm the intestine. AP Mag is used for two to three months or as long as it takes to resolve the condition. If an animal goes through cycles of improvement and relapse,

I then strengthen the program with another Ayush product called Neem Plus, an Ayurvedic formula containing neem and several potent antiparasitic herbs.

This herbal program can be discontinued once repeated testing of the feces is negative for parasites and there is a complete resolution of symptoms.

DOSAGE

- **DGL Plus:** Dogs up to thirty pounds, 1 capsule twice daily; dogs up to sixty pounds, 2 capsules twice daily; larger dogs, 2 capsules three times daily.

- **AP Mag:** Dogs up to thirty pounds, 1 capsule twice daily; dogs up to sixty pounds, 1 capsule three times; larger dogs, 2 capsules twice a day.

- **Neem Plus:** Dogs up to thirty pounds, 1 tablet twice daily; dogs up to sixty pounds, 1 tablet three times daily; larger dogs, 2 tablets twice a day. For smaller animals, the product is also available in liquid form from Ayush.

WORMS

About Worming Treatment and Medication

If you suspect your animal has worms, or you live in an area with a known worm problem, it is best to work closely with your veterinarian to develop a prevention, diagnosis, or treatment strategy. Ideally, have your dog examined twice annually for worms. Internal parasites can wreak much havoc in the intestinal tract and elsewhere in the body.

Many holistic practitioners recommend the new chemical dewormers used today by veterinarians to quickly rid an animal of an infestation. They are regarded as generally effective and less toxic than the older generation of products. Use the best of both worlds, the holistic vets say, a combination of the new dewormers along with natural approaches. "Worms tend to be hard to treat naturally," explains Michele Yasson, DVM. "We work with conventional medications to clear out the problem first and then focus on building up the health of the animal with natural means."

In the treatment of hookworm, for instance, "a good strong chemical dewormer can knock down the infection, and then a program of natural remedies can be initiated to rapidly restore the blood and vitality of the puppy," says Joseph Demers, DVM. "In my experience this dual approach works best."

Any heavy parasite infestation, adds Karen Bentley, DVM, "probably requires a chemical deworming agent first, which can then be followed with a natural remedy, such as an herbal product, for prevention."

Be wary of store-bought chemical dewormers, veterinarians advise. It is best to check with your veterinarian before using one. "They are generally old products and may contain very potent chemicals, including toluene, an organophosphate," warns Pamela Wood-Krzeminski, DVM. "I have seen dogs die of liver failure on this. Other dewormers may be purgatives that get rid of the worms but cause cramps for twelve hours. They work but are too harsh."

Hookworms

These bloodsucking parasites cause ulcerations in the digestive tract. In puppies, where the problem is most common, a severe infestation can lead to anemia and death. Animals become infected from maternal milk that contains worms, through eating hookworm eggs, or through penetration of the skin.

Dewormer Plus Natural Remedies—Joseph Demers, DVM

Mature animals are usually immune to hookworms but may be affected if they are exposed to kennels, crowded environments, dog shows, or other stressful situations. If hookworms are detected through a stool test, the veterinarian can prescribe the appropriate dewormer medication. Some holistic-minded pet owners may balk at the suggestion of using a chemical dewormer; however, it works very well to quickly eliminate a worm overload. You need use it only for a day or two. After the treatment, you can start rebuilding the animal's health with a comprehensive supplement program. Most of the products I recommend are available in health food stores or pet stores.

PRODUCTS AND DOSAGE

- **Pet digestive enzymes.** They aid the digestive system. Follow label instructions. Give for two to three months.

- **Probiotic supplement.** This restores beneficial microorganisms that have been destroyed in the gut by the dewormer. For instructions on use, see comments on probiotics in section on digestive disorders. Give for two weeks.

- **Hematinic.** This is a blood-building nutritional supplement with B-complex vitamins and iron. Follow label instructions. Use for one month.

- **Tang kuei,** a Chinese herbal blood-building preparation that helps to boost the immune system and recovery of your animal. You can purchase this product in a Chinese pharmacy or grocery. Tang kuei comes in liquid form in a single-dose vial, similar to how ginseng is often packaged. Give 1/4 to 1/2 vial twice daily for ten days to puppies.

Wormwood vs. Hookworm—Karen Bentley, DVM

Wormwood Combination, developed by herbalist Hanna Kroeger, is beneficial for mild cases of hookworm. This parasite should always be treated chemically first. The Kroeger herbal combo can then be used for two weeks to help prevent reinfestation (see details under Bentley's entry for roundworms).

ROUNDWORMS

Ninety-five percent of dogs are born with roundworms or become infected shortly after birth, according to studies. The parasites are passed through both the placenta and the milk. Regardless of the cleanliness in the household or breeding facility, the parasite skillfully transfers itself from one generation to the next. Textbooks say the most common roundworm sign is a skinny dog with bloated belly.

In Colorado's Rocky Mountains, Ron Carsten, DVM, treats more roundworm cases than any other parasites. "I tend to see this problem associated with heavy dogs having trouble keeping their weight in a normal range," he says. "They seem to be bloated all over, not just the stomach. But bloat could be an indication of other conditions, such as a heart or adrenal problem. So it is important to get a veterinarian's opinion whenever you notice a change in the animal's usual state of health or habits."

Untreated roundworms can lead to inflammation of the gut, digestive disorders, and the absorption of toxins into the body. They can be lethal to puppies. If enough of them pass into the body from the digestive tract, they can also cause serious damage to the liver and lungs.

Chemical Dewormer Plus Enzymes—Ron Carsten, DVM

I have had excellent results with Zymex II, made by Standard Process (800-848-5061; sold through veterinarians). This supplement, containing digestive enzymes, literally consumes parasites present in the upper intestinal tract. It can be given by itself, but it takes about six weeks to work and is much more expensive than many of the new safe and effective chemical dewormers. I typically use a chemical dewormer to get rid of the worms quickly and then recommend Zymex II preventively once a week. This approach works well as a general strategy, particularly if you live in an area with a roundworm problem or if your animal is constantly exposed to roundworms (from contaminated soil in kennels, for instance) and runs the risk of reinfection.

Unfortunately, stool examinations for roundworms do not have a good record for accuracy. Such tests are only 50 percent reliable for adult dogs and 20 percent for puppies. And unlike other worms, with roundworms you won't see the typical warning signs such as worms in the stool or animals scooting around on their rear ends.

DOSAGE
- **Zymex II.** Small dogs, 1 capsule daily; medium dogs, 2 capsules; larger dogs, 3 capsules. Give on a empty stomach.

Wormwood vs. Roundworms—Karen Bentley, DVM

Hanna Kroeger, the world-famous herbalist, developed herbal wormers that work very well. For roundworms, I recommend her Wormwood Combination, containing black walnut leaves, wormwood, quassia, cloves, and male fern. The product is available through Hanna's Herb Shop in Boulder, Colorado, at 800-206-6722. This combination can be used alone for two weeks at a time twice yearly, or even four times a year if necessary, for animals that are constantly reinfecting themselves.

DOSAGE
* Small dogs, 1/4 capsule; medium dogs, 1/2 capsule; larger dogs, 1 capsule. Give daily for two weeks twice (spring and fall) or more a year. Open capsule and mix in food.

SCREW WORMS (MAGGOTS)

Clear Skin Wounds with Charcoal   Roger DeHaan, DVM

Maggots that develop at the site of an injury or wound can burrow into the skin, devour flesh, and create infections. You can effectively get rid of them by using wood ash or charcoal. First clean out the wound with a Q-tip soaked with hydrogen peroxide. Then apply the charcoal or ash. Do this twice a day. The charcoal or ash is very alkaline and will kill the maggots.

TAPEWORMS

Dogs typically develop tapeworms by swallowing fleas during grooming that have in turn eaten tapeworm eggs. You may notice ricelike particles in the stool or sticking to the anal hair of your dog. Those may be tapeworm segments. Tapeworms are large parasites that live in the gut. They often migrate to the anus, which leads to irritating itching. Often an infected dog will drag its rear end on the ground because of the itching. In large numbers, tapeworms can cause weight loss, diarrhea, and debility.

Granatum (Homeopathic)—Charles Loops, DVM

The homeopathic remedy Granatum works effectively to rid animals who have occasional tapeworm problems. I find it works as well as Dronsit or Cestex, the standard chemical products.

DOSAGE
* **Granatum 6X or 12X,** four times a day for five days. It may be difficult to give that many doses a day, but in my experience it requires that much. In some cases you may have to repeat the process the following week. If an animal has a continual tape-

worm problem, it will require an individualized homeopathic program beyond Granatum.

Homeopathic Combination—Stan Gorlitsky, DVM

For more than ten years I have use a homeopathic mother tincture combination of Gnaphalium and Filix mas that is highly effective in ridding animals of chronic tapeworm problems. The remedy, called Tape Away, is available through my clinic at 803-881-9915. It has no side effects. Generally I recommend first using one of the standard tapeworm medications to clean out the animal and then following with the remedy on a regular basis for prevention. However, the remedy can be effective without the medication. Worms are usually eliminated within a week.

DOSAGE
- If used in connection with a conventional dewormer, give a few drops for two or three days twice a month after having completed treatment with the medication. If used by itself, give a few drops twice daily for a week to ten days on a monthly basis.

Antitapeworm Recipe—Carolyn Blakey, DVM

A client who operates a kennel of Great Danes uses the following recipe to rid her animals of tapeworms. After a couple of days the dogs pass tapeworms.

Ingredients:
2 cups canned pumpkin
1/2 cup wheat germ
1/4 cup blackstrap molasses

Directions: Mix together and then mix well into food. Give once a day for two days. Small dogs, 1 to 2 tablespoons; large dogs, such as a Great Dane, 3/4 cup.

Prevent Tapeworm with Herbs—Karen Bentley, DVM

To help prevent tapeworms, I recommend Hanna Kroeger's Rascal herbal worming formula, available at 800-206-6722. It contains pumpkin seed, garlic, crampbark, capsicum, and thyme. The formula can be effectively used alone for animals who are prone to reinfections, including dogs with chronic flea problems. In such cases, the product can be given preventively on a daily basis for two weeks twice or even four times a year.

DOSAGE
- Small dogs, 1/4 capsule; medium dogs, 1/2 capsule; larger dogs, 1 capsule. Give daily for two weeks twice a year (spring and fall) or more, if necessary. Open capsule and mix in food.

⚶ Pregnancy, Nursing, and Beyond ⚶

If ever there was a time to improve the nutrition of an animal, this is it. Holistic veterinarians encourage clients to provide the best possible diet to pregnant and lactating females and to supplement the diet with at least a high-quality multi-vitamin/mineral formula for pets. See the diet chapters in part 1 for guidelines on improving quality of food. Pregnancy and lactation cause severe biochemical stress. The bitch is providing for anywhere from two to a dozen pups. She must herself be nutritionally fit if she is to pass on the necessary nutrients to her progeny.

FLOWER ESSENCES
(See chapter 11 for general guidelines on flower essences.)

Rescue Remedy for Weak Puppies—A. Greig Howie, DVM
Rescue Remedy, the popular flower essence, can help reinforce weak puppies and enable them to overcome stress, shock, and trauma.

Dosage: Dilute it according to the directions and then give a couple of drops. You can give it as often as every few minutes, if needed, until animal perks up.

HERBS

Raspberry Leaves for Easier Birthing—Lynne Friday, DVM
Red raspberry leaf tea helps accelerate and ease the birthing process. I recommend it for any pregnant animal. It is available in health food stores.

Start giving it a month before breeding and throughout the pregnancy, and to help clean out the insides, for several weeks afterward. This simple step consistently helps animals. I once recommended this to the owner of a Miniature Schnauzer who had to deliver the first time by C-section. The second time around, on red raspberry tea, she just popped out the litter.

DOSAGE
- Put 3 raspberry leaf teabags in 1 quart of boiling water. Let steep until the color resembles maple syrup. Cover well and store in the refrigerator. Dole out the quart during one week. Pour onto the animal's food.

Chamomile Eases Teething—Jan Bellows, DVM
For the discomfort of teething, chamomile works very well to decrease swelling and soothe the disturbed gum tissue. A sign of discomfort is an animal pawing at its mouth.

Boil a teabag. Then put the bag in the refrigerator and apply it cold to the gums. Do this two or three times a day for a few moments at a time until the teeth come in.

HOMEOPATHIC MEDICINES

To Strengthen Whelping—A. Greig Howie, DVM
For females whose contractions need to be strengthened or who tend to become exhausted during whelping, the homeopathic remedies Caulophyllum and Cimicifuga racemosa can be quite effective. They have worked very well for a number of my breeder clients over the years.

DOSAGE
- **Caulophyllum 30C:** 3 drops in the mouth once a week during the last month of pregnancy to help strengthen the uterus.

- **Cimicifuga racemosa 30C:** A few drops at the time of whelping, where the cervix is not dilating.

TO RELIEVE MASTITIS
The homeopathic remedy Phytolacca, in my experience, alleviates about 75 percent of cases. The condition is characterized by redness

and swelling, usually of one particular gland. The bitch will not want any of the little ones to nurse from that gland. You can also apply hot packs to the area to help resolve the problem. If the animal goes off food or develops a fever, be sure to see a veterinarian at once.

DOSAGE
- **Phytolacca 30C:** A few drops three times a day until the condition improves.

FOOD AND SPECIAL DIETS

Avoid Puppy Defects with Diet—Norman C. Ralston, DVM

There is no substitute for anything less than the best possible nutrition. Because we feed our animals so much nutrient-poor food, I continually see young animals who are "incompletely developed." The female young will have a juvenile vagina and not come in heat perhaps until 2 or 2 1/2 years of age, and perhaps not come in heat at all. I see males with one testicle or testicles that do not descend from the body. The testicles are totally retained inside the body.

To me, these are not signs of a genetic problem, as some people like to say. Rather, they represent poor nutritional status during pregnancy. It's a matter of prenatal nutrition. And it is also a matter of prevention.

Once I treated a Doberman female who produced a litter of seven puppies, five of whom were males. All of them had either one or both testicles retained. I took this dog under my care and put her on a good diet. I bred her every time she came in heat, including to the same male with whom she produced the "incomplete puppies." There was never a problem again. You must supply the good nutrition.

INTRODUCING SOLID FOOD TO THE PUPS
A good way to introduce solid food is to take a small amount of raw ground beef, about the size of a pea, and then dip it into an egg yolk, previously separated from the white matter. The yolk and beef bit is then placed in the mouth of each puppy. This seems to stimulate the average puppy's appetite for solid food.

For Chihuahua puppies, use ground chicken meat. For St.

Bernards, use a larger portion of ground beef and possibly add a little cottage cheese before dipping the meat into the egg yolk.

Golden Retriever pups often seem to have a periodic lameness in
their legs. That is an indication they are not getting enough calcium.
You can correct this by adding some seaweed, available in health
food stores, to their diets. Aduki beans, lentils, chickpeas, and leafy
greens are other good sources of calcium that can be used regularly.

MIXED AND MISCELLANEOUS APPROACHES

Massage Away Back Pain—Nancy Scanlan, DVM
Pregnant dogs, just as pregnant humans, often experience low back
pain. A gentle back massage helps provide relief (see chapter 14).

⚜ Prostate ⚜

Older male dogs, just as their human counterparts, may develop
enlarged prostate glands. Signs to watch for include straining to urinate and defecate and producing very small, pencil-like stools. The
animal may also urinate more frequently and dribble afterward.

Homeopathic Remedies—Charles Loops, DVM
The homeopathic remedy Pulsatilla is indicated if the animal is
clingy and wants to be in your company. If the animal is more
aggressive, restless, or irritable and seeks cool places, then use the
remedy Iodium. You should see relief of symptoms within a few
days. The remedies can be used by themselves or along with any
regular medication.

DOSAGE
- **Pulsatilla 30C or Iodium 30C:** Once or twice a day for five
days.

Saw Palmetto—Joseph Demers, DVM
I recommend saw palmetto, the same herbal preparation used by
men. It can be used long-term preventively or as a therapeutic aid to

any treatment. I have had good results with combinations of saw palmetto, acupuncture, and homeopathy. For additional relief, I suggest a "male glandular" product from the health food store that contains prostate and testicular tissue.

DOSAGE
• Small dogs, one-quarter the human dosage; larger dogs, full human dosage.

☙ Skin Disorders and Allergies ❧

See also Fleas, Ticks, and Insect Pests; Food Allergies

The sight of an animal constantly scratching or chewing on its skin drives pet owners to distraction…and to veterinary clinics en masse for help. Skin disorders are the number one problem that veterinarians treat.

Causes are varied, including flea-bite sensitivities, food or airborne allergies, reactions to vaccinations, and chemicals in the environment and diet. Finding an effective treatment is often quite challenging. Typical conventional treatments involve steroids, antibiotics, antihistamines, and even tranquilizers. While these drugs usually provide temporary relief, prolonged use can create other serious problems such as adrenal, liver, and kidney disease.

Holistic veterinarians often say that the sole use of drugs for symptoms of chronic skin problems merely drives the disease deeper into the body. "Hot spots" often develop as a result of the body trying to rid itself of toxins or of inner heat generated by poor-quality dry food being constantly fed to an animal. Drug treatments may help for a while, but months later animals are frequently back at the veterinarian with a new symptom, this time perhaps involving the kidneys or wherever there is a genetic weakness. Such new symptoms may appear to be unrelated, but in reality they are part of an unaddressed continuum of the same disease process still raging inside the animal.

Properly used steroids can relieve inflammation and control itching, but they are often misused and overdosed. Problems occur when animals are put on arbitrary levels that are beyond what they need.

The skin is the body's largest organ of detoxification, and a rash or irritation is also a common way the body tries to eliminate a toxin. "When the condition is treated with drugs, the activity of the immune system is suppressed, and the toxin is prevented from leaving the body," says Robert Goldstein, VMD. "Sometimes giving drugs is appropriate, but reliance on drugs alone over the long term is asking for a chronic, never-ending skin condition as well as other health problems."

WHY SKIN ALLERGIES?

Medical dictionaries define an allergy as "a hypersensitive state acquired through exposure to a particular allergen." An allergen is any substance that can cause an immediate or delayed reaction. Such substances include pollen, dust, mold, food, chemicals, or an insect bite, such as a flea bite.

Humans sniffle, sneeze, cough, and wheeze when their bodies have been "insulted" by an allergen. Dogs most frequently itch and scratch. The difference has to do with mast cells, specialized cells in the body that respond to allergens by production of a chemical called histamine. It is the release of histamine that triggers symptoms by causing small blood vessels to leak and ooze fluid, resulting in a swelling of tissue. In humans, the mast cells are highly concentrated in the area of the eyes, nose, and windpipe. That's why people with hay fever experience nasal congestion, a result of leaky vessels and swelling in the nose. In animals, the cells are concentrated on the sides of the face, paws, armpit, and groin. "A common saying is that if your pet is a face rubber, foot licker, and armpit scratcher, then he's probably allergic to something," says Ernest K. Smith, DVM, secretary of the Academy of Veterinary Allergy and Clinical Immunology, as quoted in a 1994 article in the *Orange County (California) Register.*

Many sensitive people are intolerant to multiple substances. This can cause unique combinations of physical, mental, emotional, and behavioral symptoms. The same is true for animals. Skin is affected most frequently, but intestinal disorders, behavioral disturbances, seizures, and other problems also occur, both with or without a concurrent skin problem. New allergies can arise any time an animal is exposed to any substance for a period of time. Some allergic reactions appear after exposure to a single allergen. Others appear only after exposure to multiple substances. It depends on an animal's individual resistance.

A GROWING PROBLEM IN YOUNGER ANIMALS

In 1986 Los Angeles veterinarian Alfred Plechner, DVM, and I collaborated on a book about pet allergies (*Pet Allergies: Remedies for an Epidemic*). It was Plechner's opinion, based on years of clinical experience, that an unrecognized allergy epidemic was ruining the health of millions of pets. The situation hasn't changed, he says, and, if anything, it has only gotten worse.

Plechner continually sees dogs with inferior or damaged immunity, who are seriously affected by environmental input. "The problem is larger than anybody realizes," he says. "Perhaps one out of two animals brought into veterinary hospitals may be suffering from some degree of allergic malady, a hypersensitive state that can cause death and not just everyday scratching problems. Allergies are so common that pet owners probably face the problem sometime or another during the life of their animals."

Adds Joseph Demers, DVM: "I now see many more allergies than before, the result, I believe, of a confused or out-of-balance immune system underreacting or overreacting, or otherwise just not doing its normal job. Years ago I used to see this in animals two or more years of age, and now I see allergies in animals as young as six months of age. Dogs under a year of age are coming in with severe skin allergies."

The main reasons for this situation, according to the experts, are the following:

- **Flawed food.** Commercial pet foods are loaded with highly processed, inferior-quality ingredients, and chemicals that may contribute to overall ill health or trigger allergic sensitivities.

- **Cosmetic breeding.** Increasing numbers of dogs have genetic weaknesses due to selective breeding practices and puppy mills, where animals are bred for a certain look and no longer for hardiness and function. Many hunting dogs, for instance, have lost their nose to hunt as a result of this practice. Selective breeding creates fashionable features valued by fanciers and judges. This translates into prestige and maximum sales prices for breeders, whose standards are then duplicated in assembly-line fashion by puppy mills. The result is animals who often have endocrine and immune system imbalances and other serious defects. These animals enter life less able to cope and begin to have problems early on. Biological flaws are passed on to purebred offspring and to mixed-breed descendants as well.

- **Overvaccinating.** The current use of powerful and multiple vaccines creates a massive insult to the immune system, leading to general dysfunction and allergies.

- **Proliferation of chemicals.** This is an age of unprecedented proliferation of chemicals and pollutants that many experts say is weakening our immune systems and undermining health. Doris Rapp, M.D., an expert on environmental medicine, says that "if this had happened over hundreds of years, perhaps we could have adapted. Unless our nutrition is good we can't hope to detoxify these things. But our nutrition has deteriorated over the last half century as well. The food is processed, pesticided, and poor in nutrients. What we drink is full of chemicals. The result is that our bodies have become toxic dump sites." The same situation applies to our companion animals. Dogs, with their noses close to the ground and carpets, are intimately exposed to a multitude of toxins: lawn and garden chemicals, rat poison, pesticides, cleaning and disinfectant chemicals, lead in paint and water, building and decorating chemicals, and the fumes outgassing from synthetic carpets. The food they eat is full of chemical additives.

WHY DOES AN ANIMAL DEVELOP SYMPTOMS AT A CERTAIN TIME?

Problems can develop at any time in an animal's life. Imagine your body, or your animal's body, as a barrel that can hold a specific amount of stress and toxins. Each barrel has a different capacity—or threshold—depending on individual genetic strengths or weaknesses. Lifestyle, diet, environmental factors, and chemical exposures are common elements in our lives that cause the barrel to overflow or not. When the barrel overflows, symptoms appear.

If, for instance, you are exposed to a small amount of dust and mold, your barrel—if it is normal—should have the capacity to hold it. But if on another occasion you are exposed to too much of any one or more pollutants, your barrel may overflow. You develop symptoms. Another person in the same circumstances may develop symptoms earlier or later, depending on the size of his or her barrel. If there is much stress in your life at one particular point, or if the weather is very hot, or you are constantly exposed to a certain chemical, your barrel may fill up and overflow faster.

For animals, the combination of poor food, vaccinations, and the advent of flea season offers an obvious seasonal explanation for the barrel spilling over. For many animals, the barrel may always be close to overflowing because of genetic weakness. In such cases, it doesn't take much for symptoms to appear. A genetically weak animal on a poor diet and exposed to stress and multiple chemicals is a prime candidate for allergies and illnesses early on.

HOW TO TELL IF YOUR DOG IS ALLERGIC

The following symptoms are typical signs, but not necessarily the only ones, indicating an allergic problem:

- Persistent biting, licking, or scratching of skin.
- Inflamed skin, lumps, bumps, or sores that recur.
- Inflamed ears with repeated infections.

GENERAL TIPS TO CONTROL SKIN DISORDERS
AND ALLERGIES

There are often no simple answers to allergies. But the following tips will help:

- Feed a better diet. Supplement the diet with vitamins and minerals. This should boost resistance so that fewer drugs may be needed for control. With luck, you may even be able to eliminate medication altogether. Whatever the level of your animal's resistance, you have the power to improve it and lessen the potential or intensity of skin allergies.

- Switch to higher-quality and lower-quantity protein foods. Better-quality protein has fewer potential allergenic offenders. Changing to a more natural or wholesome diet may reduce allergic reactions (see section on food allergies).

- "Usually there is a combination of things relating to allergic conditions, such as pollen, food, and fleas," says A. Greig Howie, DVM. "If you can eliminate just one of the things, then you may be able to bring the allergy back down below the problem threshold."

- Vaccines are increasingly associated with chronic disorders (see chapter 15), and animals with recurring skin problems may be reacting to past vaccinations.

- Animals are exposed to many toxic chemicals that may cause reactions. If possible, use natural, nontoxic products.

- Keep down dust levels inside the house. Consider filtration systems.

- Frequent shampooing can provide temporary relief by getting offending "stuff" off the haircoat. If a shampoo is going to help, it should give relief for twelve to forty-eight hours. If not, try another shampoo.

- If you have an allergic animal, consider switching from plastic to ceramic feeding bowls. "I have seen cases where plastic bowls have caused local allergic reactions around the face," says Carvel Tiekert, DVM. "Red bowls seem to evoke more reaction than other colors, but we don't know why."

Chinese Herbs for Itchy Skin—Stan Gorlitsky, DVM

For any kind of itching skin problem, I developed a Chinese herbal combination called Skineze, available through Good Communications at 800-968-1738. The product contains angelica root, the fruit of the burdock plant, calamus gum, Chinese foxglove root, and licorice root. It comes as a chewable tablet with liver flavoring and whey added to make it palatable. The tablets can be crumbled and mixed into food or given intact. Skineze can be used in conjunction with any medication prescribed by a veterinarian.

The formula has a powerful effect. More than two thousand animals have used the product to date, and I estimate that it has significantly helped up to 75 percent of them. It reduces itching that may be due to pollen and food allergies and flea or other insect bites. It does not cure the cause of the itching, but it usually provides relief and comfort.

Many dogs experience relief within four to twenty-four hours, but some have taken up to a month, particularly in cases involving major "hot spots." In about 12 percent of cases, the formula has had no effect. In a handful of animals, there were minor gastrointestinal side effects that cleared up when the formula was stopped or given in smaller amounts.

Because the product contains whey (for sweetness), don't give it to an animal allergic to dairy. More scratching may result. For such cases, we have the same product available in capsule form without any flavoring. The taste is bitter, but sensitive animals usually respond well.

DOSAGE
• Follow label instructions.

Topical Relief with Ayurvedic Gel—Jody Kincaid, DVM

For dealing on the outside with a wide variety of skin problems, including minor injuries, infections, eczema, and "hot spots," I have been impressed by Phytogel, an Ayurvedic herbal gel from India that significantly enhances healing. The product is available from Ayuvet (888-881-8767). A small amount goes a long way. It has a pleasant cedar smell that comes from the Himalayan cedarwood oil used in the formulation. Research has shown that cedarwood has antibacterial and antifungal activity. The product also contains neem seed oil, a phytochemical known for its antibacterial and healing properties.

Phytogel has a first-class disinfectant and soothing action and reduces itching and irritation. It works as well as any cortisone cream I have used. One of its features is that once you put it on, it will usually stay on. Most dogs will not lick it off as they will the average skin cream.

DOSAGE
• Follow label instructions.

Ayurvedic Relief from the Inside—Tejinder Sodhi, DVM

To help skin problems from the inside out, I recommend an Ayurvedic herbal combination called Neem Plus, available from Ayush Herbs (800-925-1371). The product comes in liquid form for small dogs and in tablets for larger animals. It features neem, a well-known Indian herb with a long healing tradition for skin conditions. Research has demonstrated neem's antifungal, antibacterial, and antiviral properties. The product also contains amla, bahera, and haritaki, the three fruit components of triphala, the traditional Indian herbal preparation used as an intestinal cleanser. Triphala adds effectiveness to the formula because many skin conditions are related to intestinal disorders.

Neem Plus is also helpful in cases of yeast infections that many animals develop as an aftermath of antibiotic treatments. There is a typical strong sour smell. You may see a black exudate from the ears. I see this problem often in Golden Retrievers, Cockers, and Beagles.

DOSAGE
• Small dogs, 10 drops per ten pounds of body weight twice daily; dogs up to thirty pounds, 1 tablet twice daily; dogs up to sixty pounds, 1 tablet three times daily; larger dogs, 2 tablets twice daily.

Free Backyard Relief!—Mark Haverkos, DVM

Plantain, the broad-leaf weed that grows in most people's backyards, is a great topical healer. If you aren't sure what plantain looks, ask someone who knows about herbs or refer to a book. Plantain reduces redness, inflammation, and itching. It's a great natural healer, and it's free! Take a leaf, chop it up, and mash it into a paste. Apply the paste to the affected area. You will usually see quick relief for rashes, lesions, pimples, and raw areas of skin.

HOMEOPATHIC MEDICINES
(See chapter 10 for general dosage guidelines.)

Cooling "Hot Spots" with Arnica—Thomas Van Cise, DVM

"Hot spots," also known as "wet eczema," refers to the all-too-common condition of open sores that are constantly being bitten, scratched, or chewed by animals. Arnica is a good homeopathic remedy to defuse the intensity of itching. The remedy seems to "put out the fire" in the skin.

DOSAGE
- **Arnica 30C:** Give twice daily for two or three days. Observe the results. Don't repeat the remedy as long as you see signs of improvement. If the problem persists, give again for two to three days. Follow this approach as long as you have the problem.

SULFUR FOR SMELLY OR SWEATY SKIN

If you are dealing with a chronic seborrhealike odor that is not the usual dog or cat smell, use the homeopathic remedy Sulfur.

DOSAGE
- **Sulfur 30C:** Give once a day for two or three days.

NUTRITIONAL SUPPLEMENTS

B Complex Plus Amino Acids—Nino Aloro, DVM

I recommend a combination of B-complex vitamins and a multiple amino acid formula to improve the health of the skin and support any medical treatment. The B-complex product I use is called

Lipocaps, made by Vetus Animal Health and distributed by Burns Veterinary Supply (800-922-8767). The amino multi is Amino Plex, from Tyson Neutraceuticals (800-318-9766).

These supplements can be used long-term if necessary. Some clients have used them for years and told me that skin problems return whenever they run out of the supplements.

DOSAGE
- **Lipocaps:** 1 capsule for each twenty pounds of body weight.

- **Amino Plex:** Smaller dogs, 1 tablet daily; larger dogs, 2.

Vitamin C, Antioxidants—Wendell Belfield, DVM

I have developed a simple protocol in my practice, and animals typically show great improvement with it. The total elimination of steroids and other medications is often possible. But it is not a quick fix. The body requires approximately six weeks to adjust to the biochemical changes brought about by this program.

First, feed the best possible diet to your animal. The dry foods I recommend to my clients are made by Natura Pet Products (800-532-7261). For wet food, I suggest Nature's Recipe, available at most pet and food stores.

Add Mega-C Plus, an effective supplement with vitamin C and extra vitamins and minerals. Supplemental C acts as an antihistamine and also strengthens the immune system. The product is available from Orthomolecular Specialties (408-227-9334).

I also recommend Vital Tabs, an antioxidant combination of vitamins E, A, and selenium, also available through Orthomolecular Specialties. This formula protects against stress and oxidative damage and helps raise the efficiency of key thyroid and adrenal hormones to boost resistance.

Give both supplements with food.

DOSAGE
- **Mega-C Plus:** Small dogs, start with 750 milligrams of the powder daily; medium dogs, 1,500 milligrams; large dogs, 3,000 milligrams. Every third day, increase dosage by 1/8 teaspoon for small dogs and 1/4 teaspoon for medium and large dogs. Monitor the stool. When it loses its firmness and cylin-

drical form, decrease amount by one increment level and remain at this daily dosage. This is the bowel tolerance level—the optimum level for your particular animal. At this level the stool should maintain a firm, cylindrical form. Tolerance varies from animal to animal. Once the animal is asymptomatic, return to the starting level as a routine maintenance dose.

- **Vital Tabs:** Small dogs, 800 international units (IU) of vitamin E, 10,000 IU of vitamin A, 20 micrograms of selenium; medium dogs, 1,600 IU of E, 20,000 IU of A, and 40 micrograms of selenium; large dogs, 2,400 IU of E, 30,000 IU of A, 60 micrograms of selenium. When animal is asymptomatic, continue maintenance supplementation as follows: small dogs, 100 IU of E, 1,250 IU of A, and 2.5 micrograms of selenium. Maintain larger animals at one-fourth of the therapeutic dose.

- **Note:** Animals who have immune weakness or imbalances will often regress under stress conditions. In such a case, you need to return immediately to the starting treatment protocol.

Vitamin C, Pantothenic Acid, Fatty Acids—Carvel Tiekert, DVM

Vitamin C, pantothenic acid (a B-complex vitamin), and fatty acids represent a simple, inexpensive, and helpful approach. C and pantothenic acid can have a significant effect. They are important immune boosters with the potential to increase resistance to allergens. Allergic response is basically the result of a dysfunctional immune system. Vitamin C and pantothenic acid alone generate good results fairly quickly in about 30 percent of cases. If you don't see improvement in a week, this approach is not going to have any major benefits. If response is good, reduce the dose and frequency to the lowest effective level. Vitamin C can be given in any form, although I like nonacidic sodium or calcium ascorbate in the powder form.

Omega-3 fatty acids are well documented in veterinary research literature to help against skin-related allergies by promoting the production of natural anti-inflammatory substances in the body. I use Opticoat II, made by Natural Animal Nutrition (800-548-2899), as my fatty acid supplement. It contains flaxseed oil, marine lipids, and vitamin E and will control allergic dermatitis in 10 percent of cases. About half of the time, this product allows me to cut back on other therapies.

DOSAGE

- **Vitamin C:** Give in divided doses with food. Small dogs, up to 500 milligrams daily; medium dogs, up to 1,000 milligrams; large dogs, up to 1,500 milligrams; giant breeds, up to 2,000 milligrams.

- **Pantothenic acid:** Give with food two to three times daily. Small dogs, 100 to 200 milligrams each time; medium dogs, 200 to 300 milligrams; large dogs, 300 to 400 milligrams; giant breeds, 500 milligrams.

- **Opticoat II:** Follow label instructions.

Enzymes Plus Trace Minerals—Alfred Plechner, DVM

In combating skin problems, a plant-based digestive enzyme supplement for pets is very beneficial. Add it directly into the food. The enzymes improve nutritional absorption. Older or sickly animals are very often deficient in digestive enzymes. Supplementation benefits the entire system, including the skin.

I also recommend a good nutritional supplement with trace minerals because the soil we grow our food in is often deficient in minerals. Minerals are the building materials of strong bones, tissue, teeth, nails, and hair coat. Along with the major minerals, such as calcium, magnesium, potassium, and zinc, there are dozens of other lesser-known elements—needed in tiny, trace amounts—that are important for health. Mineral deficiencies are involved in many common disorders. I reached this conclusion through the simple step of supplementing the diets of animals with natural products containing seventy or so different minerals. Supplementation with minerals is highly beneficial. Within a six-month period I usually see the following results:

- Improvement in general health.
- Darker, thicker hair coat with increased luster.
- Reduced scratching.
- Reduced flakiness.

- Better maintenance of body weight with reduced caloric intake.
- In geriatric dogs, increased activity and improved condition of hair coat.
- Animals plagued by fleas appear to be less attractive to insects. You can see that effect usually within a few weeks.

Many of my clients supplement enzymes and trace minerals for both healing and general prevention. I recommend a palatable product called Power for Life, made by Terra Oceana (805-563-2634), which contains an effective array of enzymes, nutrients, and trace minerals. When dealing with a skin problem, use the enzymes and minerals therapeutically for seven days straight and check for progress. If you don't see improvement by that time, continue the supplements but switch your animal to a simple diet such as cottage cheese and potatoes. If you start seeing improvement, then start adding back individual foods, a single food a week at a time (see Plechner's add-back plan in the food allergies section). If that approach doesn't work, you probably need to look at imbalances in the animal's hormonal system (see chapter 16).

Over the years dry, itchy, scaly skin has often been treated with fatty acid supplements. Fatty acids can indeed help the quality of the skin and hair coat if there is a deficiency, which is, in fact, fairly common. However, food allergies, deficiencies in digestive enzymes, and imbalances in hormones can also often create this same unhealthy skin condition. And if there is an enzyme deficiency or imbalance, the fatty acids may not become absorbed and reach the skin. Instead they bind with minerals and fat-soluble vitamins and go out with the stool.

DOSAGE
- **Power for Life:** Follow label instructions.

Fish Oils—Stan Gorlitsky, DVM

If an animal has dry skin with obvious signs of flaky dandruff, I recommend fish oil capsules. You can purchase them in most grocery, drug, or health food stores.

DOSAGE
- 1 to 4 capsules daily, depending on size of dog. Prick capsules and squeeze contents onto food or give to animal directly.

MIXED AND MISCELLANEOUS APPROACHES

Oxygen for Hot Spots—Thomas Van Cise, DVM

A stabilized oxygen spray product called Earth Bounty Oxy Mist from Matrix Health Products (800-736-5609) works very well for hot spots. This is a human product available in health food stores. You can spray it on the most purulent drippy sores, the kind where the animal doesn't want you to touch it.

Relief is rapid. Animals often will stop licking or chewing the sore by the end of the first day. Within two to four days you will see substantial healing under way.

For long-haired animals, first trim the long hairs hanging down into the sore. There is no need to do this with short-haired animals.

I previously used calendula topical sprays for this problem and found that they worked better than most commercial veterinary sprays (such as cortisone). But the oxygen spray provides even more rapid and effective relief.

DOSAGE
- Spray sores three times daily.

Healing Oil for Hot Spots—Stan Gorlitsky, DVM

For raw or hot spots, or wounds of any kind, I suggest Healing Oil, a formula I developed with the homeopathic remedies Urtica urens, Symphytum, Calendula, Hypericum, and Arnica in a base of extra-virgin olive oil, plus lavender, chamomile, and geranium oils. The product is available through Good Communications at 800-968-1738. The oil is applied directly to the affected area of the skin. It helps to clean the wound and speed the healing process. I also use it for "dirty" ears and minor ear conditions.

DOSAGE
- Follow label instructions.

Healing from Outside and Inside—Robert Goldstein, VMD

For skin flare-ups and hot spots, I have had good success with a double-barreled inside-outside approach.

OUTSIDE

* First, to soothe skin irritations and help stop the scratching and lick cycle, apply a wet, warm black teabag on the affected spot. This acts in place of a cortisone cream. The tannic acids in the teabag ooze onto the skin and have a soothing, itch-relieving effect. Hold the bag to the skin for four or five minutes. Do this twice daily for three days. It is very effective.

* Following the teabag treatments, apply aloe vera gel, either fresh from an opened leaf or from a purchased gel. Aloe speeds the healing process.

INSIDE

Any of the following products can help break the scratch cycle from the inside by strengthening your animal's immune system and increasing the ability to eliminate toxins. Choose one or a combination of these recommendations. When the animal stops scratching, and sore spots on the skin begin to heal and dry over, this is an indication that the itching is gone. At this point, the remedies can usually be reduced or discontinued.

* **Vitamin B$_6$,** a natural antihistamine.

* **Scratch Free,** made by Dr. Goodpet (800-222-9932); or **Skin and Seborrhea,** by Homeopet (800-423-2256). These liquid combination homeopathic remedies work quickly, particularly on acute irritations that cause animals to be very uncomfortable and irritable.

* **Rhus tox,** a homeopathic remedy, for extremely irritated, red, and itchy skin.

* **Kai Yeung,** a Chinese herb, for clearing up chronic dermatitis marked by continuous irritation and either dry, flaking skin or skin clogged with a greasy material (seborrhea). The herb is available through Asia Herbs (415-989-9268).

* For general health and to give the skin extra nourishment, I suggest the regular use of a good multiple vitamin, mineral,

and fatty acid supplement. My own formula, Daily Health Nuggets, is available through Earth Animal (800-711-2292).

DOSAGE

- **Vitamin B$_6$:** Small and medium dogs, 25 milligrams twice daily with food; larger dogs, 50 milligrams twice daily. Give for seven to ten days and then reduce dosage or eliminate as condition improves.

- **Scratch Free** or **Skin and Seborrhea:** Give 3 times daily for three to four days. Small dogs, 7 drops; medium dogs, 10 drops; larger dogs, 12 drops. When incessant scratching has subsided and animal is calmer, give same number of drops twice a day for seven to ten more days. Then discontinue. Follow this procedure for any future flare-ups.

- **Rhus tox 6X:** Small and medium dogs, 1 pellet; larger dogs, 2 to 3 pellets. Give twice daily or as often as every two to three hours until you see improved appearance and less itching, usually by the end of the first day. Continue for one week.

- **Kai Yeung:** Small and medium dogs, 1 caplet; larger dogs, 2 caplets. Give daily for three to four weeks or until symptoms abate. Reduce the dosage by half for the following month. Then discontinue.

- **Daily Health Nuggets:** Follow label instructions.

Herbs and Essences Plus Supplement—Shannon Hines, DVM

For animals with dry, scaly, and itchy skin and poor hair coat, I recommend two helpful products. They can be used by themselves or, as I prefer, in combination. One is Skin & Hair for Dogs, a liquid blend of herbs and flower essences made by Tasha's Herbs (800-315-0142). This formula helps to remove toxins and stimulate a healthy exterior. It contains burdock root, red clover, nettles, yellow dock, and red raspberry leaf.

The other product is Missing Link, made by Designing Health (800-774-7387), a whole-food nutritional supplement supplying important nutrients and enzymes for better skin and digestion.

DOSAGE
- Follow label instructions.

Make Your Own Healing Shampoo—Roger DeHaan, DVM

For a great antiseptic shampoo—that both kills fleas and soothes irritated skin—try this simple approach:

Add 10 drops of tea tree oil and 1 tablespoon of aloe vera into an 8-ounce bottle of your regular pet shampoo. Then, separately, add 1 tablespoon of apple cider vinegar to 1 pint of water.

Shampoo the animal as normal and let the shampoo stand for six to ten minutes. Rinse off well.

Then rinse again with the apple cider spiked water. The purpose of this is to restore the natural pH of the skin. Dogs and cats have a slightly acidic skin. Most shampoos are somewhat alkaline. This difference many times leaves animals with irritated and itchy skin after shampooing. Rinsing with an apple cider vinegar solution after a shampoo often eliminates the problem.

FOOD AND SPECIAL DIETS
(See section on food allergies.)

The Healthy Skin Diet—A. Greig Howie, DVM

For many years I have recommended a home-prepared meal that helps nourish and heal problem skin. Be sure that your animal is not sensitive to any of the contents. After a month on this diet, there is usually great improvement.

Ingredients:
3 cups brown rice
2 cups barley
2 cups carrots
2 cups beets
1 cup beet tops
1 cup spinach
2 cups chicken livers or giblets
3 cloves garlic
1/2 teaspoon sage
8 to 12 cups water

Directions: Combine ingredients in a large pot. Bring to a boil. Simmer for 1 1/4 hours. Keep pot covered; stir every 15 minutes, and add water if needed. Using this diet, feed the quantity of food that was previously being fed.

Switch to Puppy Diets?—Wendell O. Belfield, DVM

An interesting case involved two dogs living in the same household. One of the animals was a puppy eating puppy kibble. The young dog had no scratching problem. The other animal was an older dog, eating regular kibble and scratching continually. The owner told me that one day he ran out of the adult kibble and began feeding the puppy food to both dogs. Soon thereafter the older dog stopped scratching.

Coincidence? Maybe not.

After hearing similar stories several other times, I suggested to some dog owners that they put their older scratching animals on a puppy chow and see if that works. Often, just changing to the puppy diet alone has worked, even though I like to add a good nutritional supplement program. Puppy diets have more fat than the adult diet, and the addition of more fat in the system may be what is making the difference.

⚊ Stress ⚊

See also Behavioral Problems

You may not think of it, but stress could be causing your animal's health problem.

"Stress is too often the unrecognized problem behind the problem," says Toronto veterinarian Paul McCutcheon, DVM. "It can play a tremendous role in nearly every condition that a veterinarian treats."

Stress is a nonspecific reaction of the body to demands put on it. Reactions to demands are widely varied, from emotional disturbances to wear and tear of the system that contributes to illness. For humans, stress could come in the form of not having enough money to pay the mortgage, difficulties on the job, or marital discord.

For an animal, stress can be brought on by boredom, an owner who doesn't provide enough attention, variety, or exercise, interpersonal relationships with members of the family or other animals in the household, and unpleasant environmental conditions. All of these factors start to add up and can undermine the immune system. As the burden of stress grows, the immune system becomes overworked, and the potential for problems increases. Chronic stress also impacts the adrenal glands, the body's stress organs. In time the adrenals may become exhausted, which lessens the animal's ability to deal with any new or continuing stress. Weakened adrenals also erode immune function.

Anything from skin problems to behavioral disorders can result from this simplified scenario. Unless you act to lessen the stress in the animal's life, a sick animal may not respond well to treatment, says McCutcheon.

Donna Starita Mehan, DVM, suggests evaluating the level of stress in your animal in the same manner that you would for people. She offers the following points:

- Is your animal relaxed or tense in its environment?
- Is your animal content or happy or constantly concerned or fearful that something is going to happen? Defensive, angry, or jealous?
- Is your animal suspicious of other animals and people or interacting with others well?
- Does your animal smile? Animals do smile.

"These are important considerations in assessing your animal's level of contentment—or lack of it," she says. "Remember that your level of physical health is dictated by your level of stress. If you have an animal who is easygoing, well balanced, interactive, and playful, that animal is going to be less prone to chronic illness. The mind/body connection applies to animals just as it applies to us."

McCutcheon, who routinely educates his clients about stress, tells pet owners to put themselves in their animal's place and consider possible sources of stress.

"Examine the animal's lifestyle, and relationship with you, other people, or other animals in the household," he says. "Is there discord in your house? Stress in the household may very well be transmitted to the animals who live there. Is there a new addition or major change in the household that is affecting the pet? Are you spending more time away from home? If you take the time to look beneath the surface of symptoms, you will often find the real reason for the animal's stress. Then you can try to modify the situation in some way."

COMMON SIGNS OF STRESSED DOGS

- Lick granuloma, the constant gnawing on feet and legs.
- Pica, eating of nonfood objects.
- Diarrhea or vomiting.
- Skin problems.
- Behavioral problems.

What to Do About Stressed Pets—Paul McCutcheon, DVM

Here are some practical considerations for lowering the stress level in your animal's life:

- Feed a good diet, with as high-quality ingredients and as few chemical additives as possible. Poor-quality food can stress an animal's body.

- Consider the physical environment that you offer a pet. Is it reasonable for the animal? If you are about to choose an animal, try to match the surroundings to the animal. A Jack Russell terrier, for instance, is a high-energy animal and needs more room to frolic than would be available in a small apartment. On the other hand, a large, complacent dog might do well in an apartment.

- Animals need an outlet for their energy. They need to be exercised regularly or stimulated with toys and activity.

- Avoid unnecessary medication. Drugs cover up symptoms and do not address root problems.

- In my practice I use homeopathic or Bach flower remedies to help stressed or anxious animals. The appropriate remedy depends on each individual situation. Many combination homeopathic and flower essence remedies are available in the marketplace; try these on your own first. If they do not work, see an animal behaviorist or holistic veterinarian. And remember this important point: You may be able to calm down a stressed animal with a natural remedy, but you really want to locate and correct, if possible, the source of stress.

• When considering any healing program for your animal, do not overlook the possibility that stress may be contributing to the condition; therefore you may need to deal with the stress to have a successful outcome.

• Reduce puppy stress. Try to match an animal's temperament to the lifestyle and environment you have in mind for it. Choose your animal well. Once you choose, try to reduce the stress level. This is an extremely stressful time for an animal. There are many drastic changes, beginning with separation from mother and litter, but also a rapid growth cycle. Consult with an obedience trainer or behaviorist for help training and integrating the animal into its new surroundings. Poor training results in added stress for the animal—and you. Added stress increases the risk of illness and makes for an unhappy animal. If your animal will be alone much of the time, you need to train it that way. Look ahead.

St. John's Wort and Other Aids—Donna Starita Mehan, DVM

In severely stressed animals, I am having excellent results with St. John's wort, the same herbal that has become very popular for people as a natural treatment for depression. For me it is the number one antianxiety, adrenal-supportive remedy. We see changes in a couple of days. It can be a lifesaver for animals by naturally reducing anxiety without causing drowsiness or suppression of mental activity. Persistent anxiety can lead to depression through adrenal and physical burnout.

The adrenal glands are intimately related to the nervous system. They are packed with nerve endings. If the adrenals become exhausted, the central nervous system will suffer. To protect the nervous system, I frequently use phenylalanine, an amino acid with a calming effect. This substance is regarded as a natural antidepressant and mood elevator. Phenylalanine contributes to a series of biochemical transformations that exert a strong and positive effect on mood and behavior, favoring a state of relaxation and increased mental activity.

Vitamins B_{12} and folic acid, two members of the B-complex vitamin family, are important nutrients for the normal functioning of the nervous system. I recommend these vitamins as well to help stressed animals.

St. John's wort and phenylalanine can be purchased at the health food store. For B_{12} and folic acid, I use a combination called B_{12} Folic, made by Pure Encapsulations (800-753-CAPS; sold through health professionals). If you are not able to obtain this particular formula, look for B_{12} and folic acid supplements at a health food store, and use the dosage suggestion that follows.

DOSAGE
- **St. John's wort:** Smaller dogs, 100 milligrams twice a day; larger dogs, 200 to 400 milligrams twice or three times daily, depending on size.

- **Phenylalanine:** Give twice a day. Smaller dogs, 100 milligrams; larger dogs, 500 milligrams.

- **B_{12} Folic:** Each capsule contains 800 micrograms of both nutrients. Small dogs, give 200 micrograms daily of each factor—1/4 capsule; larger dogs, up to 1 full capsule.

⚜ Surgery ⚜

Many holistic veterinarians recommend Arnica, a popular homeopathic remedy well-known for its ability to speed recovery from trauma, bruising, and surgery. Refer to chapter 10 on general guidelines for administering homeopathic medicines.

"There is much less scarring, stiffness, and soreness with Arnica," says Thomas Van Cise, DVM. "Many pet owners say their animals are back acting normally very soon. Even for serious surgery, Arnica speeds healing and helps animals rapidly get back up to full steam."

It is not necessary to give Arnica before surgery. Giving it before, as some people do, may create a need for somewhat more anesthesia.

"Give Arnica as soon as possible after surgery," says Van Cise. "I always stick a couple of Arnica 30C pellets right under the tongue of the anesthetized animal when surgery is completed."

Holistic veterinarians also frequently recommend variations of vitamin C and E and other nutrients to promote healing nutritionally.

BEFORE SURGERY

Milk Thistle for the Liver—Pamela Wood-Krzeminski, DVM

I routinely do a presurgical blood screening. If there is a mild elevation of liver enzymes, I recommend milk thistle on a daily basis for three or four weeks. Milk thistle is a magnificent herb for protecting and purifying the liver. A mild elevation of enzymes indicates some irritation or sluggishness in the liver. I prefer to have the liver operating maximally before it has to deal with the chemical onslaught of an anesthetic drug. I find that this short course of milk thistle noticeably improves the enzyme levels in more than half the cases. I use a milk thistle extract made by Twin Labs, available in health food stores.

DOSAGE
- Small dogs, 1 capsule; medium dogs, 2; large dogs, 3 or 4; giant breeds, human dosage on the label. Empty the contents of the capsule in the animal's food or drinking water.

Multivitamins—Wendell O. Belfield, DVM

Animals should be routinely maintained on a good multivitamin/mineral supplement. If your animal is facing surgery in the immediate future and is not receiving a daily supplement, start supplementing well in advance of the procedure. This type of nutritional fortification enhances recovery and healing.

Rescue Remedy for Anxiety—Paul McCutcheon, DVM

To help relieve an animal's anxieties and fears, use the popular flower essence Rescue Remedy before surgery. It can be given several times during the day of the anticipated surgery. The animal will appear calmer and less anxious as an effect of the remedy. See chapter 11 on flower essences.

AFTER SURGERY

Arnica—Michele Yasson, DVM

I have seen some remarkable recoveries from surgery simply by using this great homeopathic remedy. Sutures sometimes can come out in half the normal time.

DOSAGE
- **Arnica 30C:** For minor procedures, such as dental treatment with one extraction, give twice a day following surgery for two days. After major surgeries, give three times daily for four days, or longer if needed.

Make Your Own Arnica Formula—Paul McCutcheon, DVM

To encourage healing and relief from pain, try this homeopathic combination:

Drop 10 pellets each of Arnica 6X, Hypericum 6X, and Staphysagria 6X in 1 ounce of spring or filtered water. Give a half dropperful several times a day for several days, starting right after surgery.

Arnica is a well-known homeopathic remedy for bruising. Hypericum is beneficial for nerves, incisions, and pain. Staphysagria works on the level of deeper pain.

Arnica Plus Hypericum Plus Vitamin C—Charles Loops, DVM

The combination of the homeopathic remedies Arnica and Hypericum, along with vitamin C, has worked well to speed recovery of my patients. Hypericum is effective against pain.

DOSAGE
- **Arnica 30C** and **Hypericum 30C:** Alternate remedies hourly or every two hours the day after surgery. Decrease dosage over the next several days.

- **Vitamin C:** Give twice daily a few times before surgery and throughout the healing period afterward. Smaller dogs, 500 milligrams each time; larger dogs, 1,000 milligrams.

B Complex Plus Vitamin C Plus Amino Acids—Nino Aloro, DVM

A simple supplement program of B-complex vitamins, vitamin C, and amino acids helps speed healing and recovery. The B-complex product I use is Lipocaps, made by Vetus Animal Health and distributed by Burns Veterinary Supply (800-922-8767). Use any vitamin C product. The amino multi I recommend is Amino Plex, formulated by Tyson Neutraceuticals (800-318-9766).

If your animal isn't taking supplements regularly, start this program a week or at least several days before surgery, and maintain for a month afterward. Inform your veterinarian. These supplements do not interfere with the medical procedure or any medication.

DOSAGE

- **Lipocaps:** 1 capsule for each twenty pounds of body weight.

- **Vitamin C:** Smaller dogs, start at 250 milligrams; larger dogs, start at 1,000 milligrams. Increase slowly to where you notice the stool has become soft, and then reduce slightly. Ideally, divide the dose and give twice a day with food.

- **Amino Plex:** Smaller dogs, 1 tablet daily; larger dogs, 2.

Speed Healing with Vitamins C and E—Nancy Scanlan, DVM

The simple addition to vitamins C and E to a dog's food after surgery is always helpful.

DOSAGE

- **Vitamin C:** Give twice daily. Small dogs, 125 milligrams each time; medium dogs, 250 milligrams; large dogs, 500 milligrams; giant breeds, 1,000 milligrams.

- **Vitamin E:** Small dogs, 50 international units (IU) once a day; medium dogs, 100 IU; large dogs, 200 IU; giant breeds, 400 IU.

Topical Relief: Vitamin E and Magnets—Roger DeHaan, DVM

Prick a vitamin E capsule and apply the oil to the site of an incision. It will help speed the healing process at the site. If the animal licks the vitamin, no problem.

Magnets can accelerate healing. Use "flexi-pad," North Pole negative polarity or circular north-south magnets, but never a straight South Pole magnet. Apply the magnet to the surgery point for a minimum of twenty minutes at a time twice a day. If the animal is bandaged, you can slip it under the bandage. This will help against pain and inflammation and dramatically cut down healing time, often in half. I obtain my magnets from Mid-America Marketing in Eaton, Ohio (800-922-1744).

⚜ Toxicity and Drug Side Effects ⚜

(For acute cases of poisoning, see a veterinarian immediately. Refer to section on first aid. For problems related to antibiotic use, see "Diarrhea and Vomiting" in section on digestive disorders.)

As horrible as it sounds, many of us are toxic waste dumps, our inner machinery clogged with environmental chemicals, pharmaceutical drugs, and contaminants from the environment. Unfortunately, most people are unaware that accumulated toxicity in the body is a common underlying cause for many conditions and symptoms of fatigue, pain, and general unwellness. Unless we rid the body of these poisons, they continue to build up and erode health and vitality. Marshall Mandell, M.D., an expert in environmental medicine, puts it this way: "Everything that we eat, drink, or inhale is now polluted with chemical agents that are foreign to our bodily chemistry, and we are suffering the consequences of possessing a body that is incapable of handling the by-products of our own amazing chemical technology."

The same holds true for our companion animals.

"I see this in my practice all the time," says Mark Haverkos, DVM. "The sick animals I see are very toxic, a result of the toxic food and medicine they take and the less than pure air and water."

Holistic veterinarians consider the problem of toxicity in their treatment strategies. Here are some suggestions they offer for measures you can take on your own to reduce the toxic level in your animals.

Nux Vomica (Homeopathic)—Mark Haverkos, DVM

Increasingly I have to detoxify animals as a first step in the healing process. A big tip for keeping animals healthy or when starting them on the road to recovery is to do a periodic detoxification. That's a great place to start any kind of an alternative program. All you need is a bottle of the homeopathic remedy Nux vomica, available at any health food store.

In more than half the cases I see, a round of Nux vomica lessens the severity of the symptoms, whatever they are. Animals have more energy, interest in their surroundings, and just plain more wellness when they are cleaned out. Nux is good for most cases except when an animal is very weak or near death.

Unless an animal has been totally organic, never been vaccinated, fed only clean food since early in life, and provided a lot of fresh air and exercise, I almost automatically reach for the Nux vomica whenever the animal comes in the door.

DOSAGE
- **Nux vomica (6C to 30C potencies):** Once a day until you start to see changes and then stop the remedy.

Herb and Flower Combo Detoxifier—Shannon Hines, DVM

For a general detoxification of the system, I use Detoxifier for Dogs, a liquid formula combining herbs and flower essences made by Tasha's Herbs (800-315-0142). It helps clear up animals who have been on long-term medication or who are exposed to constant low-grade toxicity in the environment, such as lawn chemicals. The formula includes cornsilk, burdock root, Siberian ginseng, licorice root, milk thistle seed, yellow dock, and dandelion root.

DOSAGE
- Follow label instructions.

BETTER NUTRITION EQUALS FEWER SIDE EFFECTS— ROGER DEHAAN, DVM

All pharmaceutical drugs are toxic to the body. All create side effects, major or minor. Some animals do fine on prescription drugs. Others do not. Over the years I have learned that animals with good nutritional status have a better ability to handle drug toxicity. If they are poorly nourished, they generally have a poorer ability to detoxify drugs. Good nutrition is vital, whether your animal is on drugs or on herbs. The more malnourished they are, the more likely the chance of reactions.

Milk Thistle Detox—Pamela Wood-Krzeminski, DVM

The herb milk thistle (*Silymarin*) is a magnificent protector and detoxifier of the liver. It is used to treat acute liver toxicity in people. I recommend the Twin Labs silymarin extract, available in health food stores, for these kinds of situations:

- Any animal who has been on medication.
- Any animal who is being maintained on long-term medication.
- Any animal who has undergone surgical or dental procedures involving the use of anesthesia.

I consider milk thistle a *must* for any epileptic animal maintained on anticonvulsive drugs. The animal should stay on the milk thistle for as long as it is on the drug. There is no known contraindication or interference with medications.

I recall the case of a Greyhound diagnosed with epilepsy who was taking four different kinds of medication—phenobarbital, potassium bromide, Prednisone, and an immune-suppressant drug called Imuran. As a result, the dog had become a dull, bloated, drugged creature who stayed in the corner. True, he had fewer seizures, but he still had them nevertheless.

The dog's owner came to see me because the animal had basically gone from one problem to a new drug-induced set of problems. I suggested weekly acupuncture treatments at the start, along with daily milk thistle. Within three months the dog was off Prednisone and the immune-suppressant medication. A year later the dog had dropped twenty pounds and his active personality had returned. He is now being maintained on 50 percent of his previous anticonvulsant prescriptions, along with the milk thistle. Here is a good example of the marriage between "conventional" and alternative medicine. Often you need to use the best of both.

Milk thistle specifically helps heal liver cells damaged from medication or anesthesia. In the case of short-term medication, milk thistle may not be necessary, but it can't hurt.

DOSAGE
- Small dogs, 1 capsule daily; medium dogs, 2; large dogs, 3 or 4; giant breeds, follow the suggestions for human dosage on the label. You can empty the contents of the capsule in drinking water or the animal's regular food.

⚜ Vomiting ⚜

See Digestive Disorders

⚜ Yeast Infections ⚜

See also Digestive Disorders, Ear Problems, and Skin Disorders and Allergies

Yeast infections are rampant conditions that stem from an imbalance of the bacteria population of the intestines. They often manifest as:

- itchy skin.
- itchy toes and a reddish black discoloration between the toes that smells of smelly gym socks.
- a similar-colored vaginitis in young dogs and a constant licking of the area.
- digestive disorders.
- chronic itchy ears, particularly if there is a reddish black discharge.

"Be careful with the ears," cautions Donna Starita Mehan, DVM. "Some cases may involve ear mites. Ear mites show up as a clumpy, grayish black granular discharge. Sometimes you can see the tiny white mites crawling around in this debris. By comparison, a yeast infection will smell yeasty and have a greasy, reddish black color to it."

Adds Karen Bentley, DVM: "Many ear problems are yeast based. If there is a chronic combination of ear and skin problems, suspect a yeast infection. Most of the time, the animal has had a history of antibiotics."

Holistic veterinarians frequently treat yeast infections that have developed after antibiotics or vaccinations and a resultant depression of the immune system.

"Conventional veterinary treatments can often be a cause of yeast infections," Mehan points out. "If you bring in an animal for treatment with itchy skin or a bowel upset, a veterinarian will often prescribe an antibiotic. This will further upset the digestive tract, and then you have new problems—a double whammy. In my practice, yeast infections are more often involved in digestive disorders than any other cause, including parasites."

Probiotics and Vinegar vs. Yeast—Donna Starita Mehan, DVM

A major weapon against yeast infections is a probiotic supplement containing billions of beneficial bacteria, such as acidophilus, that can restore proper bacterial balance in the intestines. I also suggest adding and mixing in a small amount of nonpasteurized apple cider vinegar to the animal's food or water. Yeast do not grow well in an acid environment.

There are a large number of other products designed to help balance the bowels in a healthy manner. See your holistic veterinarian for guidance, as you need to match the products to the specific requirements of the patient. It's also important to eliminate foods from the diet, such as wheat, sugar, and yeast, which tend to encourage the growth of yeast in the body.

DOSAGE

- **Probiotic:** If you use a human product, calculate an animal's dose according to its size.

- **Apple cider vinegar:** 1/4 to 1/2 teaspoon two times daily.

Grapefruit Seed Extract Plus Enzymes—Karen Bentley, DVM

I have had good results using a combination of grapefruit seed extract along with Canine Digestive Enzymes from Dr. Goodpet (800-222-9932). Improvements are usually seen within two to three months. Both supplements should be taken long-term, for at least six months to a year, if the problem is long-standing. Be sure the animal is eating a high-quality diet and taking a good multi-vitamin/mineral supplement.

DOSAGE

- **Grapefruit seed extract:** one 100-milligram capsule three times a day for any size. Mix into food.

- **Canine Digestive Enzymes:** Follow the label instructions.

APPENDIXES

APPENDIX A

LIST OF CONTRIBUTING VETERINARIANS

This book is based on the expertise generously provided by the veterinarians listed below. Behind each of their names you will see the initials DVM or VMD, abbreviations meaning doctor of veterinary medicine. Listed beside the veterinarian's name are his or her special interests. Many of the veterinarians offer general medical services, such as surgery, in addition to a variety of alternative specialties. Some also offer telephone consultation.

- Nino Aloro, DVM, Aloro Pet Clinic, 2212 Laskin Rd., Virginia Beach, VA 23454. Phone: 757-340-5040. Herbs and nutrition.

- Wendell O. Belfield, DVM, Bel-Mar Veterinary Hospital, 3091 Monterey Rd., San Jose, CA 95111. Phone: 408-227-9944. Orthomolecular medicine, nutrition. Web site: www.belfield.com.

- Jan Bellows, DVM, All Pets Dental Clinic, 9111 Taft St., Pembroke Pines, FL 33024 Phone: 954-432-1111. Dental and general veterinary medicine. Web site: www.dentalvet.com.

- Karen Bentley, DVM, 1 Simcoe St., Guelph, Ontario, Canada N1E 3B7. Phone: 519-821-8859. Homeopathy, nutrition, herbal medicine, magnetic therapy.

- Carolyn S. Blakey, DVM, Westside Animal Clinic, 1831 West Main St., Richmond, IN 47374. Phone: 765-966-0015. Acupuncture, nutrition, homeopathy, herbs, flower remedies.

- Ron Carsten, DVM, Birch Tree Animal Hospital, 1602 Grand Ave., Glenwood Springs, CO 81601. Phone: 970-945-0125. Acupuncture, chiropractic, homeopathy, nutrition.

- Christina Chambreau, DVM, 908 Cold Bottom Rd., Sparks, MD 21152. Phone: 410-771-4968. Homeopathy.

- Roger DeHaan, DVM, 33667 Peace River Ranch Rd., Frazee, MN 56544-8818. Phone: 218-846-9112. Acupuncture, chiropractic, nutrition, homeopathy, herbs, magnetic therapy. Web site: www.aholisticvet.com.

- Joseph Demers, DVM, Holistic Animal Clinic, 496 North Harbor City Blvd., Melbourne, FL 32935. Phone: 407-752-0140. Acupuncture, homeopathy, herbs, Chinese medicine.

- Edmund R. Dorosz, DVM, P.O. Box 2094, Fort MacLeod, Alberta, Canada T0L 0Z0. Phone: 403-553-4140. Nutrition. Web site: www.ourpets.com.

- Lynne M. Friday, DVM, Lexington Veterinary Clinic, 5346 Main St., Lexington, MI 48450. Phone: 810-359-8828. Acupuncture, chiropractic, applied kinesiology, flower essences, homeopathy, herbs, nutrition.

- Maria Glinski, DVM, Silver Spring Animal Wellness Center, 1405 W. Silver Spring Dr., Glendale, WI 53209. Phone: 414-228-7655. Acupuncture, Chinese herbs, homeopathy, nutrition.

- Robert Goldstein, VMD, Northern Skies Veterinary Center, Westport, CT 06880. Phone: 203-222-0260. Nutrition.

- Stan Gorlitsky, DVM, Shem Creek Animal Hospital, 461 Coleman Blvd., Mt. Pleasant, SC 29464. Phone: 843-881-9915. Acupuncture, homeopathy, nutrition, herbs.

- Clarence E. Hardin, DVM, California Mobile Veterinary Service, 1921 Park Ave., Hemet, CA 92544. Phone: 909-658-6075. General veterinary medicine.

- Mark Haverkos, DVM, Village Veterinary Clinic, P.O. Box 119, 22163 Main St., Oldenburg, IN 47036. Phone: 812-934-2410. Acupuncture, chiropractic, nutrition, herbs, homeopathy.

- Shannon Hines, DVM, Orchard Animal Clinic, 3305 S. Orchard Dr., Bountiful, UT 84010. Phone: 801-296-1230. Nutrition, homeopathy, chiropractic.

- Jean Hofve, DVM, P.O. Box 22302, Sacramento, CA 95822. Currently involved in animal advocacy work. Not in active practice. Nutrition, flower remedies, homeopathy. Web site: www.spiritessence.com.

- A. Greig Howie, DVM, Dover Animal Clinic, 1151 S. Governors Ave., Dover, DE 19901. Phone: 302-674-1515. Acupuncture, nutrition, Chinese herbs, homeopathy.

- Jody Kincaid, DVM, Anthony Animal Clinic, 901 E. Franklin, Anthony, TX 79821. Phone: 915-886-4558. Acupuncture, herbs, nutrition.

- Charles Loops, DVM, 38 Waddell Hollow Rd., Pittsboro, NC 27312. Phone: 919-542-0442. Homeopathy.

- Paul McCutcheon, DVM, East York Animal Clinic, 805 O'Connor Dr., Toronto, Ontario, Canada M4B 2S7. Phone: 416-757-3569. Bach flower essences, nutrition, homeopathy.

- Donna Starita Mehan, DVM, A Country Way Veterinary Care, 27728 S.E. Haley Rd., Boring, OR 97009. Phone: 503-663-7277. Herbs, nutrition, chiropractic, electroacupuncture, homeopathy, magnetic therapy, flower essences.

- Alfred J. Plechner, DVM, California Animal Hospital, 1736 S. Sepulveda, Los Angeles, CA 90025. Phone: 310-473-0960. Nutrition, endocrine-immune dysfunction.

- William Pollak, DVM, Fairfield Animal Hospital, 1115 E. Madison Ave., Fairfield, IA 52556. Phone: 515-472-6983. Nutrition, herbs, homeopathy, Ayurveda. Web site: www.healthyvet.com.

- Pedro Luis Rivera, DVM, Healing Oasis Veterinary Hospital, 2555 Wisconsin St., Sturtevant, WI 53177. Phone: 414-886-1100. Nutrition, herbs, homeopathy, flower essences.

- Nancy Scanlan, DVM, Sherman Oaks Veterinary Group, 13642 Moorpark St., Sherman Oaks, CA 91423. Phone: 818-784-9977. Acupuncture, flower essences, Chinese herbs, nutrition, homeopathy, chiropractic. Web site: www.hibridge.com.

- Allen Schoen, DVM, Veterinary Institute for Therapeutic Alternatives, 15 Sunset Terrace, Sherman, CT 06784. Phone: 203-354-2287. Acupuncture, chiropractic, herbs, Chinese medicine, nutrition.

- Tejinder Sodhi, DVM Animal Wellness Center, 2115 112th N.E. #100, Bellevue, WA 98208, and 6501 196th St., Lynnwood, WA 98036. Phone: 425-455-8900. Ayurveda, homeopathy, nutrition.

- Carvel Tiekert, DVM, Animal Clinic of Harford County, 2214 Old Emmorton Rd., Bel Air, MD 21015. Phone: 410-569-7777. Acupuncture, chiropractic, nutrition, homeopathy, applied kinesiology.

- Thomas E. Van Cise, DVM, All Animals Exotic or Small Hospital, 1560 Hamner Ave., Norco, CA 91760. Phone: 909-737-1242. Acupuncture, chiropractic, homeopathy, herbs.

- Pamela Wood-Krzeminski, DVM, VCA Boca Del Mar Animal Hospital, 7076 Bera Casa Way, Boca Raton, FL 33433. Phone: 561-395-4668. Nutrition, acupuncture, herbs, flower essences.

- Susan G. Wynn, DVM, Greater Atlanta Veterinary Medical Group, 1080 North Cobb Pkwy., Marietta, GA 30062. Phone: 770-424-6303. Acupuncture, herbs, homeopathy, nutrition. Web site: www.altvetmed.com.

- Michele Yasson, DVM, Holistic Veterinary Services, 1101 Route 32, Rosendale, NY 12472. Phone: 914-658-3923. Homeopathy, acupuncture, herbs, nutrition.

APPENDIX B

RESOURCES

Veterinary Organizations

- American Holistic Veterinary Medical Association, 2214 Old Emmorton Rd., Bel Air, MD 21015. Phone: 410-569-0795. Fax: 410-569-2346. E-mail: AHVMA@compuserve.com.

  This flagship organization publishes the *Quarterly Journal of the American Holistic Veterinary Medical Association*, available for $65 per year. Contact the association for the name and number of holistic veterinarians in your area.

- The Academy for Veterinary Homeopathy, 1283 Lincoln St., Eugene, OR 97401. Phone: 541-342-7665. The AVH provides training in classical homeopathy for veterinarians, leading to certification. For the names of veterinarians who practice homeopathy, refer to the Internet Web site http://www.acadvethom.org or call 305-652-1590. The list is maintained by Miami veterinarian Larry Bernstein, VMD.

- International Veterinary Acupuncture Society, P.O. Box 1478, Longmont, CO 80502. Phone: 303-449-7936.

- American Veterinary Chiropractic Association, 623 Main St., Hillsdale, IL 61257. Phone: 309-658-2920. Fax: 309-658-2622.

Internet Web Sites of Interest

- Alternative Veterinary Medicine on the Internet: www.altvetmed.com. This supreme Internet Web site is the labor of love of Jan Bergeron, DVM, and Susan Wynn, DVM. It features a state-by-state directory of holistic veterinarians that enables you to quickly look up the nearest practitioner to you. You will also find excellent articles here on important pet health issues and conditions written by Wynn. Other features: alternative medicine resources, books and book suppliers, periodicals, and a list of premium natural pet foods.

• Critter Chatter: www.nwga.com/members/crchat. This excellent Web site is a full plate of information on puppy mills, shelters, rescues, pet food, diseases, people's experiences with veterinary drugs, veterinary commentaries, and even a chat room for kids to talk about pets.

Newsletters

• Bob and Susan Goldstein's *Love of Animals*. This jam-packed monthly gem of information is written by a pioneer holistic veterinarian and his wife, an expert on animal nutrition and behavior. Contains reader-friendly commentary on latest developments in veterinary medicine, regular ratings, analyses and recommendations on food, creative recipes, and a cornucopia of nutritional and natural care product tips. Published by Earth Animal LLC, 372 Danbury Rd., P.O. Box 809, Wilton, CT 06897-0809. Phone: 800-211-6365. Subscriptions: $69 per year.

Special Services

• The endocrine-immune imbalance blood test. National Veterinary Diagnostic Services, 23361 El Toro Rd., Suite 218, Lake Forest, CA 92630-6929. Phone: 949-859-3648.

• Bio-Nutritional Analysis. Robert Goldstein, VMD, Bioanalytics, Inc., Westport, CT 06880. Phone: 800-670-0830.

• Seminars on Holistic Health and Homeopathy for Animals, Christina Chambreau, DVM, 908 Cold Bottom Rd., Sparks, MD 21152. E-mail: cbctina@aol.com.

• Top Dog Instructor and Training Camps, Wendy and Jack Volhard, 30 Besaw Rd., Phoenix, NY 13135. E-mail: topdog@aiusa.com. Web site:www.volhard.com.

• Natural Breeders Association, Marina Zacharias, P.O. Box 1436, Jacksonville, OR 97530. Phone: 541-899-2080. This organization publishes newsletters and directories for breeders and animal aficionados "who care and pride themselves in the health of their animals...special people who have chosen to learn and incorporate natural health care methods for their animals."

Manufacturers, Distributors, and Stores

Some companies listed below sell products only through health professionals, in which case you will have to ask your veterinarian or a licensed practitioner to make the purchase for you. Some manufacturers and distributors can help you locate individual stores in your area that carry the products you want.

Animal Nutrition, Inc.
(Pat McKay)
Food, supplements, books
396 W. Washington Blvd.
Pasadena, CA 91103
626-296-1120
800-975-7555 (orders only)
Web site: home1.gte.net/patmckay

Animals' Apawthecary
Herbs
P.O. Box 212
Conner, MT 59827
406-821-4090

Ayush Herbs, Inc.
Ayurvedic herbals
2115 112th Ave. N.E.
Bellevue, WA 98004
800-925-1371

Azmira Holistic Animal Care
Nutritional supplements,
neutraceuticals, pet food
2100 N. Wilmot Rd. #109
Tucson, AZ 85712
800-497-5665
Web site: www.azmira.com

BHI Homeopathics
11600 Cochiti S.E.
Albuquerque, NM 87123
800-621-7644

Bio Vet International
Dismutase
5152 Bolsa Ave. #101
Huntington Beach, CA 92649
800-788-1084

Coastside Bio Resources
Sea cucumber supplements
P.O. Box 151
Stonington, ME 04681
800-732-8072

Designing Health, Inc.
Nutritional supplements
28310 Ave. Crocker Unit G
Valencia, CA 91355
800-774-7387

Dr. Doolittle
A Health Food Store for Pets
572 Dundas St.
London, Ontario, Canada N6B
1W8
519-642-1130
1-888-CHEESIE
Web site: www.drdoo.com

Dr. Goodpet
Homeopathic remedies for
animals, nutritional supplements,
digestive enzymes, shampoo, stain
control garments
P.O. Box 4547
Inglewood, CA 90309
800-222-9932
Web site: www.goodpet.com

DVM Pharmaceuticals, Inc.
4400 Biscayne Blvd.
Miami, FL 33157
305-575-6200

Earth Animal
Retail store and distributor natural
pet health care products
606 Post Rd. East
Westport, CT 06880
800-711-2292

Emerson Ecologics
Nutritional supplements
18 Lomar Park
Pepperell, MA 01463
800-654-4432

Flower Essence Society
Flower essences
P.O. Box 459
Nevada City, CA 95959
800-736-9222
Web site: www.flowersociety.org

Flower Essence Therapy for
Animals
Flower essences
P.O. Box 9046
Denver, CO 80209-6046
Web site: www.spiritessence.com

Gaia Herbs, Inc.
12 Lancaster Country Rd.
Harvard, MA 01451
800-831-7780

Good Communications, Inc.
Nutritional supplements
P.O. Box 10069
Austin, TX 78766
800-968-1738

Green Foods Corporation
Barley Dog and Barley Cat
320 N. Graves Ave.
Oxnard, CA 93030
800-222-3374

Green Hope Farms
Flower essences for people and
animals
P.O. Box 125
Meriden, NH 03770
603-469-3662

Halo, Purely for Pets
Nutritional supplements, herbal
dips, herbal eye wash
3438 East Lake Rd. #14
Palm Harbor, FL 34685
800-426-4256

Hanna Kroeger Herbs
Hanna's Herb Shop
5684 Valmont
Boulder, CO 80301
800-206-6722

Health Concerns
Chinese herbal formulas
8001 Capwell Dr.
Oakland, CA 94621
800-233-9355

Holistic Pet Center
A health food store for pets
15599 S.E. 82nd Dr.
Clackamas, OR 97015
800-788-PETS
Web site:
www.holisticpetcenter.com

HomeoPet
Homeopathic remedies for animals
P.O. Box 147
Westhampton Beach, NY 11978
800-434-0449

Jo-Mar Labs
Nutritional supplements
251 "B" E. Hacienda
Campbell, CA 95008
800-538-4545

Morrill's New Directions
Natural pet health care products
P.O. Box 30
Orient, ME 04471
800-368-5057
Web site: www.morrills.com

Mt. Capra Cheese
Capra Mineral Whey
279 S.W. 9th St.
Chehalis, WA 98532
800-574-1961

Natural Animal Nutrition (NAN)
Nutritional supplements,
shampoos, pet food
2109 "A" Columbia Park Dr.
Edgewood, MD 21040
800-548-2899

Natural Pet Care Company
Retail store, mail order, food,
supplements, and remedies
8050 Lake City Way
Seattle WA 98115
800-962-8266

Natur Vet
Nutritional/neutraceutical
supplements
27461-B Diaz Rd.
Temecula, CA 92590
888-628-8783

New Action Products
Nutritional supplements
145 Ontario St.
Buffalo, NY 14207
716-873-3738

Newton Labs
Homeopathic remedies
2360 Rockaway Ind. Blvd.
Conyers, GA 30012
800-448-7256

NF Formulas
Nutritional supplements
805 S.E. Sherman
Portland, OR 97214
800-547-4891

Noah's Ark
Nutritional supplements
6166 Taylor Rd. #105
Naples, FL 34109
800-926-5100

Nutramax Laboratories
Neutraceutical products
5024 Campbell Blvd.
Baltimore, MD 21230
800-925-5187
Web site: www.nutramaxlabs.com

Orthomolecular Specialties
Nutritional supplements
3091 Monterey Rd.
San Jose, CA 95111-3204
408-227-9334

Pacific BioLogic
Chinese herbal formulas
P.O. Box 520
Clayton, CA 94517
800-869-8783

Perfect Health Diet (PHD)
Pet food
65 Court St.
White Plains, NY 10602
1-800-PHD-1502

Pet's Friend
Nutritional supplements, digestive
enzymes
5871 N. University Dr., Suite 720
Tamarac, FL 33321
954-720-0794
800-868-1009 (orders only)

PetSage
Natural pet health care products
and books
4313 Wheeler Ave.
Alexandria, VA 22304
1-800-PET-HLTH
Web site: www.petsage.com

Pets, Naturally
Retail store for holistic pet
products
13459 Ventura Blvd.
Sherman Oaks, CA 91423
1-818-784-1233

Professional Health Products
Manufactures/distributes
homeopathics, herbals, glandulars,
and supplements through
health professionals
211 Overlook Dr.
Sewickley, PA 15143
800-929-4133

Progressive Laboratories
1701 W. Walnut Hills Lane
Irving, TX 75038
800-527-9512

Prozyme Products, Ltd.
Digestive enzymes
6600 N. Lincoln Ave.
Lincolnwood, IL 60645
800-522-5537

Pure Encapsulations
Nutritional supplements
490 Boston Post Rd.
Sudbury, MA 01776
800-753-CAPS

Quantum Herbal Products
Flea and tick repellents
20 Dewitt Dr.
Saugerties, NY 12477
800-348-0398

Seroyal International, Inc.
Nutritional supplements
44 E. Beaver Creek Rd. #17
Richmond Hill, Ontario, Canada
L4B 1G8
800-263-5861

Seven Forests Chinese Herbs
Available through I.T.M.
2017 S.E. Hawthorne
Portland, OR 97214
800-544-7504

Sojourner Farms
Pet food and nutritional
supplements
11355 Excelsior Blvd.
Hopkins, MN 55343
800-TO-SOJOS
Web site: www.sojos.com

Solid Gold Health Products for
Pets
Pet food and nutritional
supplements
1483 N. Cuyamaca
El Cajon, CA 92020
1-800-DOG-HUND
Web site: http://www.solid-gold-
inc.com

St. Jon's—VRX Pharmaceuticals
St. Jon's sold over-the-counter;
VRX through veterinarians
Dental chews, natural toothpastes,
dentifrices, toothbrushes
1656 W. 240th St.
Harbor City, CA 90710
310-326-2720

Standard Process
Nutritional supplements sold
through health professionals
1200 W. Royal Lee Dr.
Palmyra, WI 53156
800-848-5061

Tasha's Herbs
Herbs for dogs and cats
P.O. Box 9888
Jackson, WY 83002
800-315-0142

Terra Oceana
Nutritional supplements
1187 Coast Village Rd. #485
Santa Barbara, CA 93108
805-563-2634

Tyson Neutraceuticals
Amino acids and nutritional
formulations
12832 Chadron Ave.
Hawthorne, CA 90250
800-318-9766

VetriScience Labs
Nutritional supplements sold
through veterinarians
20 New England Dr.
Essex Junction, VT 05453
800-882-9993

Whiskers Holistic Pet Products
Retail store and distributor of food
and natural health care products
235 E. 9th St.
New York, NY 10003
212-979-2532
800-WHISKERS (orders only)
Web site: choicemall.com/whiskers

Winter Sun Trading Co.
Western wild-crafted and organic
herbs and herbal books
107 N. San Francisco St., Suite 1
Flagstaff, AZ 86001
520-774-2884
Web site: www.wintersun.com

Wow-Bow Distributors
Natural pet health care products
13B Lucon Dr.
Deer Park, NY 11729
1-800-326-0230

APPENDIX C

RECOMMENDED READING

- *Complementary and Alternative Veterinary Medicine: Principles and Practice*, edited by Allen M. Schoen, DVM, and Susan G. Wynn, DVM (Mosby, 1998). This 820-page whopper is the first real textbook to cover in depth a wide variety of holistic approaches in veterinary medicine. Chapters are written by veterinarians and other experts. You'll find detailed information on nutrition, supplements, Chinese medicine, acupuncture, chiropractic, massage therapy, bioenergetic medicine, magnetic therapy, botanical medicine including Chinese, Ayurvedic and Western herbs, homeopathy, aromatherapy, flower remedy therapy, and strategies for integrating holistic methods into conventional practices. Although the book is intended more for professional consumption, the "serious" layperson will find it a treasure of information. One of many books available through the American Holistic Veterinary Medical Association (410-569-0795).

- *How to Have a Healthier Dog*, by Wendell O. Belfield, DVM, and Martin Zucker, available through Orthomolecular Specialties, P.O. Box 32232, San Jose, CA 95152. Phone: 408-227-9334. This reprint of the original Doubleday nutritional classic showcases the many benefits of vitamin and mineral supplementation, and particularly of vitamin C, for dogs.

- *The Holistic Guide for a Healthy Dog*, by Wendy Volhard and Kerry Brown, DVM (Howell Book House). Written by Volhard, one of the most knowledgeable "dog people" in the world, in collaboration with a veterinarian. The book goes into great detail on dog food, nutrition, thyroid and adrenal gland function and laboratory tests and instructs you on how to use applied kinesiology on your animal. Volhard is famous for her seminars on behavior, training, and nutrition of the dog.

  What All Good Dogs Should Know, by husband Jack Volhard, is an excellent resource on training. Other Volhard publications and videos on training dogs can be obtained through Top Gun Training School, 30 Besaw Rd., Phoenix, NY 13135. Phone: 315-593-6115. Web site: http://jagunet.com.

- *Dr. Pitcairn's Complete Guide to Natural Health for Dogs and Cats*, by Richard H. Pitcairn, DVM, Ph.D., and Susan Hubble Pitcairn (Rodale Press), available in many book and health food stores. This is the gold standard book that even many veterinarians use for reference.

- *Pet Allergies: Remedies for an Epidemic*, by Alfred Plechner, DVM, and Martin Zucker (Very Healthy Enterprises, Inglewood, CA), available at 1-800-222-9932. This eye-opening book explains why dogs and cats get sick and die before their time and why there is a massive incidence of allergies among pets. It offers important solutions, such as the use of diet, digestive enzymes, trace minerals, and blood tests to determine endocrine-immune imbalances. The book was written in 1986, and according to Plechner, the epidemic has grown worse.

- *Food Pets Die For: Shocking Facts About Pet Food*, by Ann Martin (NewSage Press, 503-695-2211), P.O. Box 607, Troutdale, OR 97060. The title says it all.

- *What's Really in Pet Food*, a sixteen-page booklet prepared by the Animal Protection Institute, a nonprofit animal advocacy organization. The publication covers, in a quick read, many of the major problems with commercial pet foods. Full of good advice and caveats. Call the institute, located in Sacramento, at 916-731-5521.

- *Love, Miracles, and Animal Healing*, by Allen M. Schoen, DVM, and Pam Proctor (Simon & Schuster). This is a marvelously woven text full of tenderness, practicality, insights into the wondrous bond of companionship between animal and man, and finely crafted vignettes that make you want to read more and more. After you read this book you will be better equipped to know when a cherished pet is "ready to let go" and how you can deal with the situation.

- *Let's Cook for Our Dog*, by Edmund R. Dorosz, DVM. This book is an excellent primer on all you need to know about feeding your animals. Full of information, including how an animal's digestive tract works, how to tell if your animal is getting a good diet, and how to feed young, old, and overweight animals. Many recipes and solid, practical advice from a veterinarian written in a clear, easy-to-understand style. Available through Our Pets, P.O. Box 2094, Fort MacLeod, Alberta, Canada, T0L 0Z0. Web site: http://www.ourpets.com.

- *Reigning Cats and Dogs*, by Pat McKay (Oscar Publications, South Pasadena, CA). Animal nutrition expert McKay has long been a steadfast champion of raw food feeding and supplementation for pets. This book tells you how to feed with fresh, wholesome foods. Phone:

800-975-7555. Colorado veterinarian Ron Carsten gives a copy of the McKay book to all his clients for specific information on how to feed their animals. "Pat offers a wide variety of choices and ideas on how to prepare wholesome, health-giving meals for your pets," says Carsten. If you are interested in the issue of vaccinations, Pat has also put together a book entitled *Natural Immunity*, available at the same number. Web site: http://home1.gte.net/patmckay/index.html.

- *The Complete Herbal Handbook for the Dog and Cat*, by Juliette DeBairacli-Levy (Faber and Faber, London).

- *It's for the Animals Cook Book*, by Helen McKinnon A potpourri of good food recipes, basic holistic information, and directory of resources, available through It's for the Animals at 1-908-537-4144. Web site: http://members.aol.com/ifta2.

- *The Natural Remedy Book for Dogs and Cats*, by Diane Stein (Crossing Press, Freedom, CA, 1994).

- *Are You Poisoning Your Pets?* by Nina Anderson and Howard Peiper (Safe Goods, East Canaan, CT, 1995; phone: 860-824-5301). This is a useful guidebook on how *our* environmentally abusive lifestyles affect the health of pets…and what you can do about it.

- *Super Nutrition for Animals*, by Anderson, Peiper, and Alicia McWatters (Safe Goods, East Canaan, CT, 1996). Nutritional tips for dogs, cats, ferrets, horses, and birds, with many testimonials from animal owners.

- *Raising Healthy Pets: Insights of a Holistic Veterinarian*, by Norman Ralston, DVM (One Peaceful World Press, P.O. Box 10, Leland Rd., Becket, MA 01223; phone: 413-623-2322). At the time of his death in 1999, Dr. Ralston had practiced veterinary medicine for more than half a century. His book covers how macrobiotic principles can be applied to animal health care.

- *Natural Care of Pets*, by Roger DeHaan, DVM, a collection of nearly forty informative articles written by a longtime holistic veterinarian. Subject titles include "Understanding Nutrition," "What Is Acupuncture?" "Animal Chiropractic," "Herbal Medicine and Pet Health," "Skin Problems from a Holistic Viewpoint," "The Missing Ingredient—Food Enzymes," "Stress and Illness—Alleviating Stress," "Making Wise Diet Change Decisions," "Making the Medicine 'Go Down,'" "Puppy Sense—Your New Puppy," and "Home Remedies for Pets." To order this collection send a check or money order or $10.95 to Roger DeHaan, DVM, 33667 Peace River Ranch Rd., Frazee, MN 56544-8818. Phone: 218-846-9112

- *The Caring Pet Guardian's Guide to Complementary Therapies*, by Thomas Van Cise, DVM, is a fifty-four-page booklet prepared in a lively, concise, question-and-answer form by an experienced California veterinarian. The book covers frequently asked questions about some of the many alternative therapies performed by holistic practitioners, including acupuncture, acuscope therapy, aromatherapy, auricular medicine, color therapy, gold bead implantation, herbal and flower essence therapy, homeopathy, laser and magnetic therapy, Reiki and Tachyon energy. Available through Dr. Van Cise's clinic in Norco, California. Phone: 909-737-1242

- *The Natural Dog Book*, by Mary L. Brennan, DVM, with Norma Eckroate (Plume, 1994). A practical and wide-ranging review of canine health and problems from a holistic practitioner's experience.

Index

A.C.A. (nutritional supplement),
    98–99
acetaminophen poisoning, 156
acidophilus, 144–45, 188, 252
Aconite, 108
Aconitum napellus, 191–92
activated charcoal, 155–56
acupuncture, 60–63
    cancer, 119
    ear problems, 143
    heart problems, 173
    hip dysplasia, 184
adrenal gland disorders, 203
Advantage (antiflea medication), 159
aggression, 71
Agrimony (flower remedy), 106
Akitas, 44
alcohol cooler, 180
allergies
    ear problems, 141–42
    flea, 157
    skin, 20, 223–40
    from vaccinations, 74
    See also food allergies
aloe vera, 163, 237, 239
amino acids, 42, 231–32, 247
amla, 198, 230
animal fights, 154
Animal Protection Institute of
    America, 12
antibiotics
    adverse effects, 130
    for chronic bladder infections, 196
    for ear problems, 142

for infections, 187–88
for skin disorders, 223
yeast infections from, 230, 252
antibody tests, 76
antidepressants, 105
antihistamines, 223
anti-inflammatories, 90, 95, 102,
    116
antioxidants
    arthritis, 92
    cancer, 113–14, 117, 120
    heart problems, 176
    hip dysplasia, 184
    irritable bowel syndrome, 139
    skin disorders and allergies,
        232–33
anus, 21, 217
anxiety
    Arnica for, 154
    massage for, 72
    Rescue Remedy for, 246
    See also separation anxiety; stress
Apis, 162
Apis mellifica, 160
AP Mag (herbal remedy), 212–13
apple cider vinegar, 252
applesauce, for diarrhea, 133–34
Arnica
    arthritis pain and stiffness, 96, 97
    first aid, 154–55
    fractured teeth, 126
    "hot spots," 231, 236
    surgery, 244–45, 246
Arsenicum album, 191–92

arthritis, 62, 89–100
  back problems and, 101
  hip dysplasia, 7, 65, 180–85
ashwaganda, 90–91, 163
Aspen (flower remedy), 106
asthma, 100–101
autoimmune diseases, 8
autoimmune problems, from
     vaccinations, 74
Ayurvedic herbal remedies
  arthritis, 90–91
  giardia, 213
  irritable bowel syndrome,
     138–39
  liver disease, 197–98
  mange, 163
  skin problems, 229–30

Bach flower essences. *See* flower
     essence remedies
back problems, 101–3
  massage for pain of, 70, 222
bacterial infections. *See* infectious
     illnesses
bad breath, 104–5, 125
bahera, 230
barberry, 193
Barley Dog, 117
barley grass, 117
B-complex vitamins
  behavioral problems, 109
  cancer, 116
  neuromuscular collapse or
     paralysis, 202
  skin disorders and allergies,
     231–32, 233–34, 237, 238
  stress, 244
  surgery, 247
Beagle neck syndrome, 65–66

Beagles, 230
beets, raw, as liver detoxification,
     200
behavioral problems, 105–9
  chiropractic treatment for, 66
  flower essence remedies for,
     58–59
  massage for, 71
  See also stress
behavior, healthy diet and, 20
Benefin shark cartilage, 119–20
bentonite clay, 131, 132, 141
beta-carotene, 40
bile duct inflammation, 197
Biodent, 128
Bio-Nutritional Analysis, 83–84
birth defects, 13
birthing. *See* pregnancy and
     nursing
bladder infections, 196
bleeding, stopping, 154, 155
blindness, 7
boarding. *See* kennels
body temperature
  cooling measures, 178–80
  high fevers, 191–92
bones (food)
  as calcium source, 16
  for dental health, 127
  precautions, 40–41, 129
bones (of dog). *See* fractures;
     musculoskeletal problems
boswellia, 90–91, 96, 138–39
bowel problems
  constipation, 129
  diarrhea, 130–34, 212, 217
bowel tolerance
  vitamin C and, 89, 183
  See also stool

breast cancer, 112
breath. *See* bad breath
breeding problems, 226
brewer's yeast, 160
bronchitis, 190
bruising, 154
brushing of teeth, 124–25
Bryonia, 97–98
bupleurum, 149–50
burdock root, 238, 249

calcium, 44–45, 234
   malabsorption problems, 135
Calendula (homeopathic remedy),
   127–28, 155, 236
Calm Stress (homeopathic remedy),
   108, 201
cancer, 109–22
   chemical food additives and, 13
   spaying/neutering and, 112
cancer drugs. *See* chemotherapy
Capra Mineral Whey, 93
carbohydrates, dietary, 26, 37–38
cardiomyopathy. *See* heart problems
cars
   heat stroke potential, 179–80
   motion sickness, 200–201
cartilage-protective supplement, 96
cat's claw (uña de gato), 120
Caulophyllum, 220
Causticum, 186
cayenne pepper, 155
chamomile, 126, 211, 220
charcoal, 155–56, 217
chemical additives
   in commercial pet food, 10–13, 16,
      226
   food allergies from, 168
chemical dewormers, 213–14, 216

chemicals
   as skin disorder and allergy cause,
      226, 228
   See also toxicity and drug side
      effects
chemotherapy, 110
   Nux vomita for, 122
   toxicity protection, 197, 198
Chicory (flower remedy), 106
Chih-ko and Curcuma (herbal
      formula), 118–19
Chihuahuas, 179, 221
China (homeopathic remedy), 192
Chinese astragalus, 115
Chinese herbal remedies
   arthritis, 91
   cancer, 113–14
   diarrhea and vomiting, 133
   epilepsy, 149–50
   hookworm, 215
   infectious illnesses, 190–91
   liver disease, 199–200
   mammary gland tumors, 118–19
   skin problems, 229, 237–38
chiropractic, 64–68
chlorella, 104, 209–10
Chlorets, 104
Chlorowin, 104
chondroitin sulfate, 95–96
Chows, 170
Cimicifuga racemosa, 220
cloves, 126
Cocker ear, 146
Cocker Spaniels, 7, 145, 230
coenzyme Q10
   cancer, 113, 114, 116, 121
   eye problems, 152
   gum disease, 126–27
   heart problems, 173–78

colds. *See* infectious illnesses
Collies, 7
colloidal silver, 143, 163, 192–93
comfrey, 157
commercial dog food. *See* food, commercial
companions (second dog), 207–8
congestive heart failure, 203
constipation, 129
contusions, 154
convulsions. *See* epilepsy
cooling measures, 178–80
cornsilk, 249
cortisol level, measuring, 81–82
Cosequin, 98–99
cosmetic breeding, 226
cough, kennel, 190
cranberry extract, 196
Curing Pills (Chinese herbal remedy), 133
cuts, 155

Dachshunds, 101–2, 103
Dalmatians, 7
dandelion root and leaf, 211, 249
dandruff, 25, 235–36
day care, pet, 207–8
deafness, 7
degenerative joint disease. *See* arthritis
dehydration, 40
dental health, 122–28
  bad breath, 104–5, 125
  heart disease link, 178
dentrifrice, 127
dewormers, chemical, 213–14, 216
DGL Plus (herbal remedy), 212–13
diabetes, 203

diarrhea, 130–34, 212, 217
  dehydration, 40
  irritable bowel syndrome, 138
  as stress sign, 242
diet, 9, 10–41
  antiarthritis, 99–100
  antitapeworm recipe, 218
  bones, advantages of, 16, 127
  bones, precautions for, 40–41, 129
  cancer, 111, 112–13
  commercial brand recommendations, 22–23
  dental health, 123–24
  drug toxicity and, 250
  dry, adding moisture to, 25
  ear problems, 145
  fasting, 37, 131, 204, 207
  food allergies, 164–71
  foods to avoid, 19
  gas remedy, 137–38
  healing episodes, 39
  healthy, signs of, 20, 21
  hip dysplasia, 183–84
  homemade food, 17, 33–39
  hyperactivity, 108–9
  improvement measures, 15–21
  kidney and urinary tract conditions, 194–95
  natural commercial food, 17, 18, 23
  nutritional adequacy scale, 16–17
  obesity, 203–7
  old age, 212
  pregnancy and nursing, 221–22
  raw meat in, 16, 27–28, 30–32, 35, 37–38
  skin disorders and allergies, 228, 239–40

snacks, 40
stool-eating symptom, 140–41
stress and, 242
supplements. *See* nutritional
supplements; probiotic
supplements
table scraps, 29–30, 204
vegetarian, 39, 170–71
water's importance in, 40
yeast infection prevention, 252
See also food, commercial
digestive disorders, 129–41
bad breath from, 104–5
constipation, 129
diarrhea and vomiting, 63, 130–34,
212, 217
diet and, 20
enzyme deficiency, 134–37
gas, 137–38
irritable bowel syndrome, 138–40
stool eating, 140–41
See also food allergies
digestive enzymes, 42, 45
adding to diet, 25
arthritis, 97
back problems, 102–3
bad breath, 104
cancer, 116, 117
deficiency signs, 134–37
hookworm, 215
skin disorders and allergies,
234–35
stool eating, 140, 141
yeast infections, 253
disc disorders, 62, 101–2, 103
disc massage, 70–71
Dismutase, 92, 120
distemper, 75
dl-phenylalanine (DLPA), 95–96

Doberman Pinschers, 43, 136, 173,
210
drugs. *See* medications; toxicity and
drug side effects
Du Huo Jisheng Wan, 91
dyes, in commercial pet food, 12–13

ear problems, 141–47, 251–52
ears, diet appraisal and, 21
Earth Bounty Oxy–Max, 100–101,
146–47
echinacea, 162, 188–89, 192
eczema, wet. *See* "hot spots"
eggs, adding to diet, 25, 29, 31, 37
EHB (nutritional supplement),
192–93
electromagnetic poisoning, 201–2
enemas, 129
energy medicine, 57–58
English Bulldogs, 7
epilepsy, 63, 66, 147–51
essences, flower. *See* flower essence
remedies
essential fatty acids, 25, 27, 35, 42,
45; *See also* omega-3 fatty acids
Essiac tea, 116, 117, 121–22
estrogen measurement, 81, 82
ethoxyquin, 13
Euphrasia (eyebright), 152
exercise, 109, 179, 204, 208, 211,
242
eyebright (*Euphrasia*), 152
Eye-C, 153
eye problems, 7, 151–53
eyes, diet appraisal and, 21

fasting, 37, 131, 204, 207
fats
adding to diet, 38

fats (*cont.*)
  in commercial pet food, 14
  lowered in obesity diet, 204–5
fatty acid supplement, 25, 235; *See
    also* essential fatty acids; omega-
    3 fatty acids
fever, 191–92
first aid, 153–57
fish oils, 235–36
Five Flower Formula. *See* Rescue
    Remedy
Flagyl, 212
flaxseed oil, 25, 27, 45, 117
fleas, 157–61
  shampoo, 239
  skin disorders and allergies, 20,
    227, 228, 235
  tapeworm and, 217, 218
Flee Free (flower essence remedy),
    160
flower essence remedies, 56–59
  behavioral problems, 105–7, 108
  epilepsy, 148–49
  first aid, 153–54
  fleas, 160
  infectious illnesses, 188
  motion sickness, 200–201
  old age, 211
  pregnancy and nursing, 219
  skin disorders and allergies,
    238–39
  stress, 242–43
  toxicity and drug side effects, 249
folic acid, 244
food, commercial, 9, 10–14, 16–17
  allergies and, 14, 225
  brand recommendations, 23
  fresh food combined with, 17, 18,
    24–32

hazardous components of, 10, 11
  hot weather and, 178
food, homemade, 17, 33–39
food, natural, 17, 18, 23
food allergies, 164–71
  avoidance, 34
  bad breath and, 105
  behavioral problems and, 109
  from commercial pet food, 14,
    225
  ear problems and, 145
  irritable bowel syndrome and, 140
fractures
  bone, 157
  tooth, 126
Frontline (flea preparation), 159
fruits, in diet, 24, 30, 34

Gan Mao Ling, 190–91
garlic, 143, 158, 160, 211
gas, 137–38
Gelsemium, 191–92
genetics
  allergies and, 226, 227
  hormonal- (endocrine-) immune
    test for problems, 79–80
  purebreeds' problems, 7–8
German Shepherds, 7, 102, 136, 145,
    181
giant breeds, diet for, 23
giardia, 212–13
ginger snaps, 104, 138
gingivitis. *See* gum disease
glucosamine sulfate, 95–96
glutamine, 102–3, 153, 198–99
goat's whey, 93
Golden Retrievers, 7, 181, 222, 230
goldenseal, 192
Granatum, 217–18

grapefruit seed extract, 253
grapeseed extract, 115
Great Danes, 181
Great Pyrenees, 8
green bean weight-loss diet, 206–7
green-lipped mussels, 95–96
grieving dogs, 108
gum disease, 122–28
    heart disease potential, 178

hair coat, 20, 21, 228
halitosis. *See* bad breath
haritaki, 230
hawthorn, 173, 176–77, 211
healing crisis, 49, 53
healing episodes, 39
health decline, 7–9
heart problems, 7, 172–78, 203
heartworm medication, liver disease
    and, 197
heat stroke, 40, 178–80
hematinic, 215
hepatitis, 197
herbal remedies, 47–49
    arthritis, 90–91
    cancer, 115, 117–18, 121
    diarrhea and vomiting, 132
    ear problems, 143
    epilepsy, 149–50
    giardia, 212–13
    heart problems, 173, 176–77
    infectious illnesses, 188–91
    liver disease, 197–98
    old age, 211
    parasites, 212–13
    pregnancy and nursing, 219–20
    prostate, 222–23
    skin disorders and allergies,
        229–31, 237–39

stress, 243–44
tapeworm prevention, 218–19
toxicity and drug side effects,
    249–51
worms, 215–17
See also Ayurvedic herbal remedies,
    Chinese herbal remedies
hip dysplasia, 7, 65, 180–85
homemade food, 17, 33–39
homeopathic remedies, 50–55
    arthritis, 91–92, 96–99
    back problems, 101–2
    behavioral problems, 108
    cancer, 114–15
    dental health, 126, 127–28
    diarrhea, 131–32
    eye problems, 152
    first aid, 154–55
    flea and other insect bites, 160, 162
    gas, 137–38
    incontinence, 186
    infectious illnesses, 191–92
    liver disease, 199–200
    motion sickness, 201
    nosodes as vaccination alternative,
        78
    pregnancy and nursing, 220–21
    prostate, 222
    skin disorders and allergies, 231,
        236, 237
    stress, 242–43
    surgery, 244–45, 246
    tapeworms, 217–18
    tick-borne diseases, 161
    vaccinosis, 76–77
hookworms, 214–15
hormonal- (endocrine-) immune
    system
    common disorders, 80–81

hormonal- (endocrine-) immune
  system (*cont.*)
  genetic problems test, 79–80
  tests for genetic hormonal-
    (endocrine-) immune problems,
    79–83
hormonal replacement levels,
  81–83
"hot spots" (skin problems), 223,
  229, 231, 236
hot weather, 178–80
Huskies, 44, 178
hydrochloric acid deficiency, 140–41
hyperactivity, 20, 108–9
Hypericum, 236, 246
hypothyroidism, 203

Ignatia, 108
immune system, 63
  cancer and, 110, 111, 113
  disorders and problems, 8, 74, 117
  echinacea and, 162, 188–89, 192
inbreeding, 7–8
incontinence, 185–87
infectious illnesses, 187–93
inflammation, 231
insect bites, 157–64
"internal heat," 25
Iodium, 222
Irish Setters, 136
irritability, 20
irritable bowel syndrome, 138–40
itching, 229, 231, 237, 238

Jack Russell terriers, 242
joint misalignments, 64–68

Kai Yeung, 237–38
Kaopectate, 134

Keating, V. J., 35–36
kelp
  cancer, 117
  heart problems, 174–75
  mange, 164
  old age, 211
  stool eating, 141
  thyroid gland and, 208
kennel cough, 190
kennels, 188, 214
kidneys
  diet and, 14, 25
  ear problems and, 141
  urinary tract conditions, 193–96
kutli, 198

lactation. *See* pregnancy and nursing
lamb and rice diet, 164, 165–66,
  169–70
lameness, 62, 65, 180
L-carnitine, 173, 174–75
Ledum, 161–62
Lhasas, 103
licorice root, 249
light overexposure, epilepsy and,
  151
Liv-C, 199–200
liver
  bupleurum and, 149–50
  diet and, 14, 20, 25
  ear problems and, 141
  eye problems and, 152–53
  milk thistle benefits, 97, 153, 197,
    198–99, 245, 249, 250–51
liver, raw, in diet, 28–29
liver disease, 196–200
Liver Liquescence, 199–200
Livit-2, 197–98
Lyme disease, 161–62

maggots (screw worms), 217
magnesium, 234
magnets, 248
malabsorption, and digestive enzyme
deficiency, 135–37
Maltese, 124
mammary gland tumors, 118–19
manganese, 103
mange, 162–64
Martin, Ann, 10–11
massage techniques, 69–71, 222
mastitis relief, 220–21
Maximum Protection Formula, 27, 194
medications
avoidance of unnecessary, 242
for fleas, 159–60
for skin disorders, 223
for worms, 213–14
See also toxicity and drug side
effects
methionine, 186, 196
methylsulfonylmethane (MSM), 94
metronidazole, 138
milk thistle, 97, 153, 197, 198–99,
245, 249, 250–51
minerals. See nutritional supplements
misalignments, chiropractic for,
64–68
mites
as common misdiagnosis, 142–43
ear, 251–52
olive oil and yellow dock for,
145–46
skin appearance and, 20
morinda (noni), 113
motion sickness, 200–201
mullein, oil of, 143
multivitamins. See nutritional
supplements

muscles, 21
musculoskeletal problems, 62–63, 65
myelopathy, spinal, 101, 102–3

natural remedies, 87–89
adverse reactions to, 89
dosages, 88–89
how to administer, 87–88
See also flower essence remedies;
herbal remedies; homeopathic
remedies; specific remedies
neem and neem oil, 143, 163, 213,
230
nervousness, 20
nettles, 211, 238
neuromuscular collapse or paralysis,
63, 201–2
neutering. See spaying/neutering
Newfoundlands, 7
noni (morinda), 113
nose, 21
nosodes, 78
nursing. See pregnancy and nursing
nutrition. See diet; food; nutritional
supplements
nutritional supplements, 25, 27, 34,
36, 38, 42–46
arthritis, 92–96
asthma, 100–101
back problems, 102–3
bad breath, 104–5
cancer, 111, 113, 114–17
dental health, 128
ear problems, 143–45
epilepsy, 150
eye problems, 152
hip dysplasia, 181–85
incontinence, 186–87
infectious illnesses, 192

old age, 209–12
pregnancy and lactation, 219
pre-surgery, 245
skin disorders and allergies,
    231–36
stool eating, 141
See also specific vitamins
Nux vomica
    chemotherapy, 122
    digestive disorders, 132–33
    toxicity and drug side effects, 249

oatflowers, 211
obesity, 202–8
oil of mullein, 143
older dogs, 209–12
    acupuncture for, 62
    arthritis, 90, 97
    chiropractic for, 65
    digestive enzyme supplements,
        134, 137, 234
    nutritional supplements, 45
    prostate, 222–23
    prostate cancer, 112
    puppy diets for, 240
    stool eating, 140–41
olive oil, 27, 30, 145–46, 236
omega-3 fatty acids, 25, 35, 113–14,
    115, 233–34
osha root, 189–90
osteoarthritis. *See* arthritis
oxygen
    for asthma, 100–101
    for chronic ear infections, 146–47
    for hot spots, 236

pain relief
    acupuncture as, 62
    back problems, 22, 70

cancer, 115
first-aid measures, 153–55
hip dysplasia, 184–85
post-surgery, 246–47, 248
teething, 126
tooth, 126
pantothenic acid, 233–34
paralysis, neuromuscular, 63, 201–2
parasites, 212–19
parvo, 75, 192
pau d'arco, 117–18, 121
paws, 21
Pearl Drops, 127
pectin, 133
peppermint oil, 104–5
Pepto-Bismol, 133
periodontal disease. *See* gum disease
pet food. *See* food, commercial
phenobarbital, 150
phenylalanine, 243–44
phosphorus, 192
phytochemicals, 47, 177
Phytolacca, 220–21
pica, 137
plantain, 157, 231
plaque, dental, 122, 123–24, 125, 127
pleurisy root, 190
poisoning, 155–57, 201–2
Poodles, 103
potassium, 234
potentization, 53
Power for Life (product), 235
Power Mushrooms, 113–14
pregnancy and nursing, 219–22
    dietary requirements, 38
    vitamin C as hip dysplasia
        preventive, 181–82
    water needs, 40
    See also puppies

probiotic supplements
  arthritis, 97
  back problems, 102–3
  diarrhea, 130–32, 188
  hookworm, 215
  infectious illnesses, 188, 192
  yeast infections, 252
Program (antiflea medication),
  159–60
prostate, 222–23
prostate cancer, 112
protein
  adding to diet, 26, 34, 36, 37, 39
  for heart problems, 176
  in puppy food, 23
  reducing in diet, 19, 97, 109, 183,
    184, 212, 228
  in vegetarian diets, 39
Pulsatilla, 222
puncture wounds, 161, 162
puppies
  colds and high fevers, 191–92
  defects avoidance, 221–22
  diet, 38, 221–22, 240
  homeopathic remedies, 191–92
  introducing solid food to, 221–22
  parvo, 192
  prenatal and postnatal care,
    219–22
  stress in, 182, 243
  teething relief, 126
  weak, 219
purebreeds, genetic problems of, 7–8
pyometra, 112

qi, 61

radiation, 110
raspberry leaves, 219–20, 238

raw meat. *See* diet, raw meat in
Red Chestnut (flower remedy),
  106–7
red clover, 121, 238
Regeneration (Chinese herbal
  remedy), 114
rescued dogs, flower essence
  remedies for, 107
Rescue Remedy (flower remedy), 56
  behavioral problems, 106, 108
  epilepsy, 148–49
  first aid, 153–54
  kennel stress, 188
  motion sickness, 200–201
  pre-surgery, 246
  for weak puppies, 219
Rhus tox, 91–92, 97–98, 160,
  237–38
rice. *See* lamb and rice diet
ringworm, 20
Rocky Mountain spotted fever,
  161
Rottweilers, 181
roundworms, 215–17
rubbing alcohol, to reduce body
  temperature, 180
Ruta, 91–92, 96, 97

sad dogs, 107
St. Bernards, 178, 179, 222
St. John's wort, 243–44
saw palmetto, 222–23
scratching. *See* skin disorders and
  allergies
screw worms (maggots), 217
Sea Jerky, 92–93
Sea Meal, 117, 164
seizures. *See* epilepsy
selenium, 175–76

separation anxiety, 105–7
shampoo, 228
  recipe, 239
shark cartilage, 119–20
Shar-peis, 170, 173
Shih Tzus, 103
shock, Arnica for, 154
Siberian ginseng, 249
skin
  healthy diet signs, 20, 21
  raw, 155
  wounds, 217
skin disorders and allergies, 223–40
  causes, 225–27
  control tips, 228–29
  food and special diets, 239–40
  herbal remedies, 229–31, 237–38
  homeopathic remedies, 231–32
  nutritional supplements, 232–36,
    237–38
  as stress sign, 242
  topical remedies, 236–37
  See also fleas; food allergies; insect
    bites
slipped discs. *See* disc disorders
slippery elm, 132
snacks, 40
sodium oxide dismutase (SOD), 95,
  96
sodium pentobarbital, 10
spaying/neutering, 112, 185, 208
Spectra Probiotic, 192–93
spider bites, 161
spinal massage, 70–71
spinal misalignments, 64–68
spinal myelopathy, 101, 102–3
stabilized oxygen. *See* oxygen
Staphysagria, 246
steroids, 102, 203, 223–24

stool
  constipation, 129
  dehydration signs, 40
  diarrhea, 130–34, 212, 217
  digestive enzyme deficiency and,
    134
  enlarged prostate glands and, 222
  healthy diet and, 20
  vitamin C supplements and, 89,
    183
stool eating, causes and remedies,
  140–41
stress, 9, 240–44
  cancer and, 111
  common signs, 242
  ear infections and, 142
  kennel boarding and, 188
  vitamin C depletion and, 182
  See also anxiety
sulfur, 231
supplements. *See* nutritional
  supplements
surgery, 63, 110, 244–48
Sweet Chestnut (flower remedy),
  106
Symphytum, 236
skin disorders and allergies,
  vaccinations and, 74

table scraps, 29–30, 204
Tang kuei, 215
tapeworms, 217–19
taurine, 150
teabags
  for skin irritations, 237
  for teething discomfort, 220
tea tree oil, 239
teeth
  brushing, 124–25

diet appraisal and, 21
fractured, 126
pain remedy, 126
teething relief, 220
temperature. *See* body temperature
Theratox, 199–200
Thuja, for vaccinosis, 76–77
thyroid gland disorders, 203, 208
Tiao-he, 199–200
ticks, 161–62
tofu, 26, 36
toxicity and drug side effects,
     156–57, 248–51
  antibiotic complications, 130
  chemotherapy precautions, 122,
     197, 198
  liver susceptibility, 197
toxins, in commercial pet food,
     10–13
trace mineral deficiency, 141
tranquilizers, 223
trauma, Arnica for, 154
triphala, 138–39, 163, 230
trypsin deficiency, 135–36
turmeric, 116

uña de gato (cat's claw), 120
urinary tract conditions, 193–96
  incontinence, 185–87
urine, diet appraisal and, 21
Urtica urens, 236

vaccinations, 9, 72–78
  adverse reaction remedy, 76–77
  Lyme disease symptoms from,
     161–62
  overvaccination problems, 9, 226,
     228
  yeast infections from, 252

valerian root, 149
vegetables
  adding to diet, 24, 26–27, 29, 30,
     31, 34–37
  green bean weight-loss diet, 206–7
  for older dogs, 212
  raw carrot snack, 40
  as remedies, 104, 178–79, 200
vegetarian diets, 39, 170–71
vinegar, 146, 252
viruses. *See* infectious illnesses
vitamin and mineral supplements. *See*
     nutritional supplements
vitamin C, 45, 139
  arthritis, 94–95
  back problems, 103
  bowel tolerance, 89, 183
  cancer, 113–14, 115, 116, 118
  eye problems, 153
  gum disease, 126–27
  hip dysplasia, 181–83
  hyperactivity, 109
  post-surgery, 246–47
  skin disorders and allergies,
     232–34
vitamin E, 43, 45
  arthritis, 95–96
  cancer, 113–14, 115, 116
  heart problems, 173, 174–76
  hyperactivity, 109
  mange, 163
  old age, 210–11
  post-surgery, 247–48
vomiting, 130–34, 156, 187, 242

Walnut (flower remedy), 106, 188
water
  fast, 37
  importance of, 40

weight loss, recipes for, 204–7
wet eczema. *See* "hot spots"
whelping. *See* pregnancy and nursing
whole–food supplements, 92, 93,
    116–17, 211, 238
whole grains, in diet, 26, 34, 35, 37
worms, 213–19
Wormwood Combination, 215,
    216–17
wounds, 157, 161, 162

Xiao Zhong Liu Pian, 118–19

yeast infections, 251–53
    Ayurvedic remedy for, 230
    chronic, 117
    ear infections and, 141–42,
        144–45
yellow dock, 145–46, 238, 249
yogurt, 26, 29, 188
Yorkshire Terriers, 124

zinc, 44, 153, 234
Zinnia (flower remedy), 107
Zymex II, 216